Hebrews

Partners with Christ

Craig
To My New Friend
In Jesus!!
Bob Lynott

Hebrews

Partners with Christ

Kenneth W. Yates

Grace Evangelical Society
Denton, Texas 76202

To Yates and Kelly

Contents

Preface

THE BOOK OF HEBREWS has played a major role in my life. At the beginning of my Christian life, it was a book I avoided. I often heard people interpret certain verses in Hebrews to say that even if you claim to be a Christian, if you live in open and continuous sin, you will go to hell. Since I was well aware that I sinned on a daily basis, these verses presented a problem for me.

Even though I knew that a Christian could not lose his salvation, these teachings scared me. I was not sure how to respond to these passages.

All of that changed in the spring of 1986.

I was in seminary and had the opportunity to take a course by Zane Hodges on the Book of Hebrews.

Hodges was the first teacher I ever had who taught a class from what is called a Free Grace perspective. That class changed my life. I would later become a chaplain in the Army and then a pastor. What I learned in that class would impact my entire ministry. It would forever change how I taught the NT and understood many Biblical passages.

During my ministry, many have had the same questions that I had prior to sitting under the teachings of Hodges. They found the Book of Hebrews hard to understand. Over the years, I had the opportunity to teach the book in various classes, including once in a Bible college. This book is a result of my class with Hodges, thirty years of teaching Hebrews, and continued studies.

It is ironic that the book I once dreaded and avoided has become a source of comfort and motivation. Hebrews does not threaten the Christian with the loss of salvation. Instead, it greatly encourages

believers to remain faithful to the Lord in the midst of this fallen world
in which we live. Grace will do that.

    If you are a believer in Jesus Christ, at the moment of faith you knew
you had eternal life because Jesus promises this. If you are now looking
for the strength and motivation to serve the Lord and please Him,
the Book of Hebrews is for you. We will be His partners forever, if we
persevere.

Introduction

I HAVE BEEN INVOLVED in Christian ministry for thirty years. During that time I have preached that salvation is by faith apart from works and that believers are eternally secure at the moment of faith. Believers cannot lose eternal life and go to hell. Consequently, the question that I have been asked more than any other is: "How do you explain the warning passages in the Book of Hebrews?"

There are several warnings in Hebrews, but two in particular come to mind: Hebrews 6 and 10.

Even a quick glance at these verses raises critical issues.

In Heb 6:4-8 the author says that it is impossible "to renew again to repentance" those who fall away. And in 10:26-29, he says that if we sin willfully after knowing the truth, there does not remain a sacrifice for sins for us. In both cases, the results of such actions involve some type of fiery judgment—a punishment worse than death.

What do these warnings mean?

Is the author of Hebrews warning believers or unbelievers?

What does it mean to "fall away"?

What does it mean to "sin willfully"? After all, don't we all willfully sin on occasion?

If a Christian or unbeliever falls away, what does it mean that he or she cannot be renewed to "repentance"?

Does the judgment that is worse than death refer to going to hell?

You will not be surprised to find out there have been different ways to understand these warnings. Allow me to summarize three.

View #1: Christians Who Lose Salvation

According to the first view, the author is speaking to Christians. Hebrews 6 is warning that a Christian "falls away" when he commits and continues in serious sin. Such a Christian winds up being "burned" in hell.

Usually, this view does not address what it means to say that the Christian cannot "repent" again. Does that mean once a person "loses" his salvation, he can never be saved again? That would seem to be the case if we interpret the verses this way.

Likewise, Hebrews 10 is also taken as addressing Christians. To "sin willfully" means to commit serious sins over a long period of time. There is no sacrifice for that, because they have insulted God's grace. As Christians, they know that such sin is wrong, but they rebel against God anyway. Such a Christian loses his salvation and is cast into hell which is worse than death.

View #2: False Professors

According to the second view, these warnings are addressed to people who *claim* to be Christians but, in fact, are not. A person who only claims to be a Christian eventually "falls away" into sin. In the end, he winds up being "burned" in hell, but he doesn't lose salvation because he never had it in the first place.

Such a person "sins willfully" when he falls away. He has insulted God's grace by claiming to be a Christian. He has been exposed to Christian teaching but rejects it. The sin here may be rejecting the faith that he claimed to believe, and thus he becomes an apostate from Christianity. Others say the sin is not living according to the holy demands of God's commands. In any case, hell is a punishment worse than death for such an individual.

This view often explains that these people cannot repent again or that there is no sacrifice for such sin, in the sense that such a person does not *want* to repent. A false professor is one that is not convicted by the Holy Spirit and does not look at the sacrifice of Christ for the forgiveness of sins.

View #3: Christians in Danger of Missing Christ's Approval

The third view agrees with the first that "true" Christians are being addressed. However, it denies that these Christians are being warned about going to hell. That is not the punishment. True Christians can willfully sin and fall away. If they do, they can experience a punishment worse than death and still be in the Kingdom of God.

Which View is Correct?

Clearly, these issues are very important. Every student of the Bible must deal with them. Moreover, since the warning passages in Hebrews play such a vital role in the book, we cannot hope to understand it if we don't answer them.

Fortunately, even though these passages are hotly debated, their meaning is clear. Some details may be uncertain, but the overall thrust of the warnings is easy to determine.

Refuting View #1

We can reject the first view immediately. Why? The Bible never contradicts itself, and in many NT passages teach us that a believer in Jesus Christ cannot lose his eternal salvation.

First, Jesus told the woman at the well that whoever received eternal life from Him would *never* thirst for it again (John 4:14). He said the same thing in John 6:35. If believers could lose eternal life, they could thirst for it.

Second, Jesus told Martha that if someone believes in Him, that person will *never* die (John 11:26). *Never* means *never*. If a believer could lose their salvation, they would experience the second death. Jesus told Martha that is impossible.

Third, the NT is crystal clear that salvation is all by God's grace, and works have nothing to do with it (Rom 3:28; Eph 2:8-9). If we could lose our salvation by sinning, then salvation would depend upon our works.

Fourth, the very fact that the life God gives us is *eternal* (John 3:16) means we can't lose it. If we lost eternal life then it was not eternal! Related to this is the fact that the believer in Jesus Christ *already* has eternal life (John 5:24). Eternal life is not something a believer gets when he goes to heaven. It is a present possession.

One of the greatest tragedies in Christendom is the teaching that one can lose his eternal salvation. Unfortunately, countless millions of people have been exposed to this destructive teaching that denies the gospel of grace. It is both sad and ironic that the Book of Hebrews is used to promote this false view of the gospel. In Heb 10:10, just a few verses before the most severe warning in the book, the author tells us that the believer cannot lose his salvation: "By that will we have been sanctified through the offering of the body of Jesus Christ *once for all*" (emphasis added). According to the will of God, which was accomplished in the sacrifice of Christ, the believer has been sanctified *once for all*. The word *sanctified* means "made holy." Just a few verses later, the author says that those who are sanctified have been made perfect *forever* (Heb 10:14). The blood of Christ has taken care of the sins of the believer forever—all of them. Before God, every believer is holy forever. There is no sin the believer can commit that the death of Christ did not cover, not even a willful one.

Also, it needs to be said that those who teach that these warning passages refer to the loss of salvation almost never deal with the issue of such people not being able to repent (Heb 6:6). Almost all such teaching says that if a person loses his salvation, he can get it back if he only returns to the Lord. However, if the author is indeed talking about the loss of salvation, then a person cannot be saved from hell again.

Refuting View #2

The second view, namely, that the warning passages are addressed to false Christians is clearly wrong. There is abundant evidence to prove the warning passages are addressed to genuine believers.

There are five warning passages in the Book of Hebrews. All five are addressed to Christians. We should not conclude that the three "minor" warnings are addressed to Christians, while the other two harsh ones are not. They are all addressed to the same people: true Christians.

For example, in Heb 3:1 they are called *holy brethren*. Are unbelievers holy brethren? Of course not.

In Heb 10:29 they are described as those who have been made holy by the blood of Christ. Is that true of false professors, of people who have never believed in Christ? Again, no.

In Heb 10:30 they are referred to as the people of God. Is that a description of believers or unbelievers?

Not only does the author call his readers *brethren* and describe them as Christians, the examples he gives in his warning passages involve the people of God in the OT. For example, he refers to the Jews whom God had redeemed out of Egypt but who later fell away and died in the wilderness. He does not want the readers to do the same thing. That assumes they, too, are the people of God with a relationship of faith in God from which they could fall away.

In the chapters that follow, it will be shown that the whole book is addressed to believers, not to false professors, proving that view #2 is false.

The reason many have concluded the warning passages must be directed to non-Christians is because they think God would never say such harsh things to His children. They believe these warnings describe the punishment of hell. Since believers will not go to hell, they conclude the warnings must be directed to non-believers.

Another important issue is that, according to many who hold to view #2, true Christians simply cannot do the things the author of Hebrews warns against. They say a true Christian cannot "willfully sin," at least not for a long period of time, especially if that means to reject the Christian faith (i.e., apostatize).

The problem is, those are examples of letting one's theology determine what a passage of Scripture says.

As Biblicists, the teaching of Scripture should always come before your theological traditions. If a passage is clearly speaking about true Christians, and the passage says that such people can indeed willfully sin, then true Christians can willfully sin (whatever that means)! If Scripture contradicts your theology, go with Scripture.

It also needs to be said that the author of Hebrews admits that he himself could "sin willfully." Practically everyone would say that the author is a believer. He includes himself in the possibility of experiencing the things warned about when he says if "*we*" sin willfully, that is exactly what will happen.

If we are honest with the text, we simply must conclude that the author is warning *believers* about something. If we recognize that a believer cannot go to hell, and we cannot understand what a punishment worse than death is, or what it means to experience some kind of fiery punishment from the Lord, then we must simply admit that we do not know.

Fortunately, that is not the only option.

Defending View #3

The third view—that the warnings are addressed to Christians, but involve punishment short of hell—is true to the text and makes perfect sense. Believers can experience severe discipline from God. In the Bible, God's punishment of His people is often described as a fire. One can experience the "fire" of God's wrath without going to hell.

Probably the most important thing to realize is that there are certainly some punishments worse than death which do not involve going to hell. How many of us have said, "I would rather die than go through that"? We can think, for example, of contracting certain diseases. How many people have willingly died in an attempt to escape certain conditions? For example, they have lived under tyranny or a dictator but risked their lives, and in many cases lost their lives, in order to escape from such a life because it was "better to die" than continue to live like that.

But one of the keys to understanding a punishment worse than death is that Hebrews deals with heavenly and eternal rewards. These rewards include more than simply "going to heaven." In the kingdom of God, believers will be rewarded for their faithfulness to God during this life. If such rewards do indeed exist, wouldn't the loss of such rewards be worse than death? After all, for the believer, death is temporary, but rewards in the kingdom will be forever. A major part of the Book of Hebrews deals with exactly that issue.

A Preview of the Book

As the following pages will argue, the Book of Hebrews describes Jesus Christ in regard to two of the great offices in the OT: King and

High Priest. The emphasis in the first four chapters is on Jesus as the King. The emphasis in chapters 5–10 is on Jesus as our High Priest.

As King, Jesus will rule the world to come. His kingdom will be eternal. He also has supreme authority. Since He is our all-powerful and eternal King, when He speaks it is in our best interest to listen to Him.

As Christians, the readers of Hebrews are called to be faithful to this coming King. However, they are facing difficult times and persecution as the result of their faith. There was a strong temptation to abandon their faith in the midst of this persecution. This is the meaning of the "willful sin" and "falling away."

If they did that, and some already had, they could expect the discipline of God. In light of their dishonoring the all-powerful King, they could expect a punishment worse than death. This punishment would also include the loss of eternal rewards. This is the point of all the warning passages in the book.

But they need not go down that path. The other office that Jesus holds is that of High Priest. As their High Priest He is always ready and able to help His children faithfully serve Him. If they would avail themselves of the ministries of their High Priest, they would be victorious in the midst of their difficulties, avoid the discipline of God, and obtain eternal riches in His coming kingdom.

The King is coming! His kingdom is coming! While all of His children will be in that kingdom, He has called them to be *great* in that kingdom. Through the strength that He provides, all believers can obtain that calling. But failure is possible if we do not draw near to Him as our High Priest. This is what the Book of Hebrews is about.

Background

HEBREWS IS A UNIQUE book in the New Testament. In many NT books, the author states his name and identifies his audience. Hebrews does not.

One ancient writer stated that only God knows who the author of Hebrews was.

However, you do not need that kind of background information to understand the spiritual truths found in this book. You can notice details that indicate the kind of situation in which the original readers found themselves. This kind of information may shine some light on certain passages.

Of lesser importance is the question of who the author is and the date of the letter. But it might be helpful to discuss these background issues briefly.

Author

Through the centuries there have been several suggestions as to authorship: Apollos, Luke, and even the husband and wife team of Aquila and Priscilla.

The very early church, however, only mentions two options: Paul or Barnabas.

There is early testimony from the Church in the east (the area around Israel and Syria) that Paul wrote the book.

In the west (in the area around Italy), there is early witness to Barnabas as the author.

If Barnabas wrote Hebrews, that would not impact its inspiration, even though he was not one of the original Apostles. After all, Luke wrote the books of Luke and Acts, and Mark wrote the Gospel that today bears his name, and neither one of them was one of the original Apostles. Both were traveling companions of an Apostle (either Paul or Peter), and Barnabas certainly fits that description.

It is also of some interest that Barnabas is called a prophet in Acts 13:1.

While we cannot be dogmatic, perhaps it is best to agree with the ancient witnesses and suggest that either Paul or Barnabas wrote the book.

Date

It is safe to conclude that Hebrews was written before AD 95. Clement of Rome refers to it in his writings at that time.

In addition, it seems almost certain that it was written before AD 70. The book strongly indicates that the sacrifices in the Temple in Jerusalem were still going on (Heb 8:4, 13; 10:1-2; 13:10), and those sacrifices stopped when the Temple was destroyed in that year.

However, Hebrews could not have been written too early because the readers have been believers in Christ for some time (Heb 5:12*ff*) and were not part of the first generation of believers (2:3). This would suggest a date between AD 50–70.

Paul is not mentioned in the book, but his lieutenant Timothy is (13:23). This has caused some to suggest that Paul had died (unless, of course, he is the author!). If Paul died sometime around AD 65, this suggests that the book was written around AD 67-68 or a few years before the Temple was destroyed.

Original Readers

Even though some would disagree, it seems the first readers were from a Jewish background, but have become Christians. Even the title of the book, "To the Hebrews," bears this out. Though the title was not a part of the original letter, it dates from an early time, indicating that at a very early date it was held that the original readers were Jewish.

The book itself suggests this. The readers appear familiar with the OT, its stories, and its sacrificial system.

First, their "fathers" were the Jews of the OT (1:1).

Second, there is a heavy emphasis on angels and the readers evidently believed these beings would rule the coming kingdom of God (1:4, 5; 2:5).

Third, Hebrews is also the only book in the NT which discusses Melchizedek, a man we find in Genesis and Psalm 110 (5:10; chapter 7).

Fourth, the author spends a great deal of time discussing the Jews in the OT during their time in the wilderness after they were set free from Egypt. When he discusses the sacrificial system, he emphasizes the Tabernacle in the wilderness and not the temple that stood in Jerusalem.

Fifth, he perhaps makes a reference to asceticism as "strange teachings" that deal with food (13:9).

Sixth, he talks about ritual washings (6:2).

Seventh, as has already been stated, the book concentrates on the fact that Jesus is both King and High Priest.

Eighth, many have noticed similarities between the things discussed in the Book of Hebrews and the community of Jews who lived in Qumran near the Dead Sea. This community wrote the Dead Sea Scrolls. Their writings spoke much of angels, and they seemed to believe that angels would rule in the kingdom of God. They may have taught that there were two Messiahs. One would be the King, and one would be the High Priest. These writings also elevate Melchizedek.

The Qumran community idealized the time of the Jews in the wilderness. They had withdrawn from civil society to live in the wilderness near Jerusalem. They rejected the worship performed in the temple in Jerusalem and looked at the time when the tabernacle was in use as a more pure and holy period in the nation's history. They practiced asceticism, and it seems that some of them at least did not marry (13:4). It is also clear that they practiced numerous ritual washings.

Like Christendom today, no doubt there were many different strands of Judaism in the first century. The Pharisees practiced the religion in one way, the Sadducees another, and the Jews at Qumran another. The best guess seems to be that the readers were heavily influenced by a group of Jews similar to the one found at Qumran. Perhaps there were other such groups found in other parts of the Roman Empire, and the original readers lived near one.

It is also clear that the readers of Hebrews had experienced persecution for their Christian faith (10:32-34). As a result, some had

withdrawn from the church (10:25). They were tempted to go back
to Judaism, particularly the Judaism practiced by a certain sect of the
religion.

Judaism was a recognized religion in the Roman Empire.
Christianity was not. If a Christian "worshiped" God within a branch of
Judaism, the persecution would stop.

This is by far the best suggestion as to what the *willful sin* refers to
(10:26). It is something very specific. The author is warning his readers
not to publicly renounce their faith in Christ to return to the legal
religion of their parents. If they did, they would *fall away* (6:6), which is
best taken as a reference to apostasy.

These readers lived in difficult times. They saw a way out of their
difficulties by simply returning to the religion in which they were
raised. But to do so required that they renounce Jesus Christ as the
Messiah. But renouncing the coming eternal King is an action that
would certainly result in severe consequences. They needed to seriously
consider what they were contemplating.

Not only was Jesus the King, but He was also their High Priest.
They were familiar with that concept from the religion of their fathers.
He would help them in their temptation to sin against Him, as well as
with their other difficulties. If they would go to Him, they would also be
greatly rewarded for their faithfulness to the King when He set up His
kingdom.

Throughout the book, the author compares Judaism to Christianity.
In every comparison, Christianity is superior. In fact, with the coming
of Christ, the old religious system the readers were familiar with under
Judaism had been replaced. Judaism was a shadow that pointed to the
superior things that Christ brought. The shadow passed away when the
real thing appeared.

The King has spoken of these things. His words carry more weight
than those of any prophet in the past or even the angels whom the
Jews honored. The author of Hebrews sets this tone right from the very
beginning.

Christ Is the King

THE FIRST FOUR VERSES of Hebrews are often called the prologue. In it, the author introduces the readers to the two offices of Jesus Christ discussed in detail in the book: King and High Priest.

Jesus is both.

This sets the stage for the book. Because of the greatness of Christ, if His people listen to His words, they can expect great rewards. If they disobey Him, they can expect severe negative consequences.

The Prologue (1:1-4)

> [1] **God, who at various times and in various ways spoke in time past to the fathers by the prophets,** [2] **has in these last days spoken to us by *His* Son, whom He has appointed heir of all things, through whom also He made the worlds;** [3] **who being the brightness of *His* glory and the express image of His person, and upholding all things by the word of His power, when He had by Himself purged our sins, sat down at the right hand of the Majesty on high,** [4] **having become so much better than the angels, as He has by inheritance obtained a more excellent name than they.**

God has revealed Himself to His people. To the Jews, God spoke to the **fathers by the prophets** (v 1). This is a reference to the OT and strongly indicates that the original readers, though now Christians, were Jewish.

To the Jews in the OT, God spoke in **various times** and **various ways.** The words include the idea that God spoke by revealing Himself in parts. That is, the revelation of Himself in the past was in fragments and not complete. He did this in many ways—we can think about how God did this through the prophets. He spoke to them through things like dreams, visions, thunder, a burning bush, angels, and even a *still small voice* (1 Kgs 19:12).

As wonderful as these revelations were, things have changed. God has now spoken in the **last days** (v 2). This indicates that He has now given His final revelation of Himself. There won't be any more revelation.

Contrary to popular opinion, the last days did not begin in 1948 or 1967. The last days began with Jesus' ascension into heaven. The ministry of the Apostles took place during the last days (cf. Jas 5:9; 2 Pet 3:3; 1 John 2:18; Jude 18; Rev 22:12, 20).

The reason there won't be any more revelation is because now God has **spoken** to us in **His Son**. This means that God's revelation of Himself is no longer in fragments. It is complete. There will be no more because He has given the perfect revelation. In His Son, God has said His final word.

The OT was given through prophets and angels (Acts 7:53; Heb 2:2). The original readers rightfully held the OT in high esteem. If this is the case for what was only in fragments, how much more should they hold the words of Jesus Christ in high esteem? As the author will shortly say—and it is obvious—the Son is much greater than the OT prophets and angels.

Here the author introduces another idea that will be important in the book. As mentioned in the introduction, the readers were Jewish Christians who were thinking about abandoning Christianity and going back to Judaism. The author says that the revelation found in Christianity in the NT, as given by Jesus Christ, is much greater than what God has said in the past in the OT. Christianity is far superior to Judaism.

The description of Jesus Christ in the rest of the prologue shows why He is the perfect and final revelation of God. In the OT there was the office of the prophet. Jesus Christ is God's perfect prophet.

First of all, Jesus is the **heir of all things.** The idea behind these words is found in Psalm 2, from which the author of Hebrews will quote in v 5. In this Psalm, the Son is the King. What the Son will inherit are the nations of the earth. This points to a future day when Christ will own and rule the world to come. A seven-year Tribulation will follow the Rapture of the Church. After the Tribulation, Christ will return and rule upon the earth for one thousand years. Afterward, He will create a new heaven and earth and will rule forever.

It is only right that He would be the King of the world to come and that this kingdom would belong to Him. After all, He **made the worlds.** The word for *worlds* is literally "ages." This could refer to the fact that Christ made all the worlds—all the planets, the earth, the stars, etc. Or it could refer to both the seen and unseen worlds, including the spiritual world. If the Jews saw angels as being very important, they are reminded here that Christ created them, since they are a part of the spiritual world.

The idea that Christ created the *ages* could also signify that He is the One who is carrying all of history—all the ages of time—to their conclusion. He will bring in His kingdom over which He will rule. His word will bring all this about.

Whatever the meaning of the word "worlds" is, one thing is clear—Christ created all things. One day He will inherit all that He made. It will belong to Him.

The greatness of Jesus Christ is also seen in His description in v 3. He is the **brightness of His glory.** The glory of God shines forth in Jesus Christ. The idea of glory probably relates to God's power. The power of God was seen in Jesus through the miracles He performed, including raising the dead, as well as on the Mount of Transfiguration where the disciples observed His glory.

Jesus is also the **express image of His person.** The idea in the Greek is that Jesus is the exact representation of God. If we want to know what God is like in essence and character, we only have to look at the Son. Everything that God is, Jesus is. Jesus specifically taught that the one who sees Him had seen the Father (John 14:9).

This is why Jesus is the perfect and final revelation of God. He *is* God. Many have commented that this description of Jesus Christ is one of the clearest statements in the Bible that Jesus Christ is God. There could be no better revelation. The prophets and angels of the OT could not even hope to be on par with Him.

The power of Christ's words is also seen in that He upholds **all things by the word of His power.** The whole universe is held together by what He says. He is bringing all of history to its goal—His kingdom. When One like that speaks, He should be obeyed! To abandon His teaching and publicly renounce Him to return to Judaism would be the height of foolishness.

But Jesus is even more than the King who will inherit everything. The author of Hebrews introduces the idea of the other office that Jesus holds—that of High Priest. He states that **He had by Himself purged our sins.** Associated with this idea is the fact that Jesus **sat down at the right hand** of God. The author of Hebrews will spend a great deal of time discussing in chapters 5–10 that Jesus is our High Priest. Our High Priest sacrificed Himself for His people. This sacrifice paid for the sins of His people once for all.

Also, this sacrifice was perfect. It was so complete there is no need for any more sacrifices. That is why He has "sat down." His work is finished. There is no more that needs to be done for the sins of His people.

The fact that He is at the right hand of God shows that He occupies the most exalted position in the universe. He has supreme authority. Jesus said that He would occupy that position (Luke 22:69; Matt 22:43-44). It anticipates the authority He will have forever.

The amazing thing is that He had to die to bring this about. The One who is described in the prologue, the One who is the Creator and the all-powerful King of the world to come, did that for His people.

This One is **so much better than the angels**, and He has a **more excellent name** than they do. No angel is seated at the right hand of God. No angel has made purification for the sins of God's people. No angel has His name.

The **name** that Christ has inherited is **Son.** The author will discuss that name in vv 5-14. As will be seen, this name means He will be the King of the eternal kingdom to come. That is not true of any angel.

The phrase *much better* is a favorite in the Book of Hebrews. It is used thirteen times in the book. The basic argument is that Christianity is much better than Judaism. Judaism, including sects of Judaism like the one found at Qumran, placed a great deal of importance on the angels. But here the author already indicates how much greater Christianity is than Judaism, and Christ is than the angels. He is God. As such, His sacrifice is greater than any OT sacrifice. He is greater than any king or high priest found in Judaism. He is greater than any revelation found in Judaism. Listen to Him!

In the following verses, the author of Hebrews expounds on the **name** Jesus Christ has inherited—the Son. This title will drive the discussion throughout the first chapters of the book.

Jesus Christ, the Son, Is Greater than the Angels (1:5-14)

⁵ **For to which of the angels did He ever say:**
"You are My Son,
Today I have begotten You"?
And again:
"I will be to Him a Father,
And He shall be to Me a Son"?
⁶ **But when He again brings the firstborn into the world, He says:**
"Let all the angels of God worship Him."
⁷ **And of the angels He says:**
"Who makes His angels spirits
And His ministers a flame of fire."
⁸ **But to the Son He says:**
"Your throne, O God, is forever and ever;
A scepter of righteousness is the scepter of Your kingdom.
⁹ *You have loved righteousness and hated lawlessness;*
Therefore God, Your God, has anointed You
With the oil of gladness more than Your companions."
¹⁰ **And:**
"You, Lord, in the beginning laid the foundation of the earth,
And the heavens are the work of Your hands.
¹¹ *They will perish, but You remain;*
And they will all grow old like a garment;
¹² *Like a cloak You will fold them up,*
And they will be changed.
But You are the same,
And Your years will not fail."
¹³ **But to which of the angels has He ever said:**
"Sit at My right hand,
Till I make Your enemies Your footstool"?

¹⁴ **Are they not all ministering spirits sent forth to minister for those who will inherit salvation?**

To make his case that Jesus is greater than the angels, the author appeals to the OT. This would make sense if he were writing to people who had high regard for those Scriptures. The revelation found in the writings of Judaism makes a case for the supremacy of God's Son.

The Son is King (Psalm 2 and 2 Samuel 7)

In the prologue, the author stated that Jesus has a name greater than any angel. That name is here identified. In v 5 it is given. Jesus is the **Son**. But it is also obvious here that Jesus is compared to the angels. God has never called an angel by that name.

The prologue has just stated that Jesus is God. Since God is eternal, Jesus has always been God. However, we see here that Jesus inherited the name of *Son* in a special sense at a specific point in time. This special sense is understood by the way the author of Hebrews quotes from the OT. He uses two passages. One is from Psalm 2. The other is from 2 Sam 7:14.

First, he quotes from Psalm 2 which is an example of an "Enthronement Psalm." In these Psalms, a man in the OT becomes King of Israel. On the day he becomes king of the nation, he inherits the title of "son." As the King of Israel, he becomes the son of God upon earth.

The title **Son**, then, carries with it the idea of King. The idea of the King as the son of God on earth was part of the promise that God gave to David in 2 Sam 7:14, which the author of Hebrews quotes in the second part of v 5 here. The descendants of David who sat on the throne of the nation would be the "sons" of God. They were the representatives of God. God said these kings would be His sons and He would be their **Father**.

Of course, these earthly kings of Israel only foreshadowed the real King who was to come. They pointed to Him. Christ is the ultimate fulfillment of Psalm 2, just as He is the ultimate fulfillment of the promise God gave to David in 2 Samuel.

But what is the meaning of the phrase from Psalm 2, "**today I have begotten you**"? It is easy to see how this applies to the kings in the OT. On the day they were crowned king, they became a son of God in a special way. But if Jesus was always God and is eternal, how does it relate to Him? How can it be said that He was **begotten** on a certain day?

It seems highly likely that what the author has in mind is the day that Christ ascended to the right hand of the Father (1:3). On that day He had done everything necessary to be the King of the world to come. He had purged His people's sins. He had done all that was needed to ensure that men and women would reign with Him in His coming kingdom, an idea that will be discussed in detail in chapter 2. Because of His completed work, Christ entered a new relationship with His Father and His people. On the day of His exaltation to the right hand of His Father, all the prerogatives of being King were His. He was declared the Son of God in this special sense at that time. This is the same point made in Rom 1:4 in which Paul states that Christ was "declared to be the Son of God with power according to the Spirit of holiness, by the resurrection from the dead."

In the rest of the OT quotes that follow in this chapter, the author will continue to discuss the idea that Jesus is the King. A major point in this section is that no angel will rule the world to come. Jesus, since He is the King, will.

But in these OT quotes, there is also the idea that the King will defeat His enemies. This idea is present in Psalm 2 which the author uses here in v 5 (see Ps 2:1-3, 9-12). This is important because the original readers of Hebrews were being persecuted by the enemies of the King.

Jesus Is the Firstborn Son (Psalm 97)

In v 6 the author says that God will bring **His firstborn** Son **into the world**. This most likely refers to the time when Christ returns to rule over the world to come (see 2:5). In the OT the firstborn son had authority over all other sons. Christ will have that authority. Christ will inherit all things on that day (1:2).

In the second half of this verse, he quotes from Psalm 97. This Psalm also speaks of the time the Messiah sets up His kingdom, that is, when Jesus returns (see Ps 97:1-6). As with Psalm 2, Psalm 97 also states that when Christ returns, He will defeat all His enemies (Ps 97:3, 10-11).

The main point the author makes here, however, is that the Son, Jesus Christ, will be the King. The angels will not be kings. In fact, the angels will **worship Him**! If the readers were thinking about turning away from Christ and going back to a religion that emphasized the role of angels in the kingdom of God, they might want to think again! In the following verses, the author compares the role of Jesus and the role of angels in that kingdom.

The Role of Angels (Psalm 104)

Here in v 7 the author quotes from Psalm 104 in which we see that God's **angels** are **spirits**. The word for *spirit* can also be translated "wind." That may be preferable here. The reason this is the case is that angels are also called **a flame of fire**.

The point here is that angels are a part of God's creation, just as wind and fire are. Jesus Christ is God, and therefore He created everything, including angels. That is why they worship Him.

As part of creation, they can be changed. In the following verses, we will see that Jesus the Son is not part of creation. He does not change.

Another aspect here is that God can change the works of His hands to do His will. God **makes** the angels do His bidding.

Taking all these things together, we see that angels will serve the King. The King creates them. The King, who is the Son, is infinitely greater.

The Son Is God and Has Companions (Psalm 45)

In comparing the role of Jesus Christ to the angels in the world to come, the author turns to Psalm 45 here in vv 8-9. As with Psalms 2 and 97, this Psalm also says that the King will defeat all His enemies (Ps 45:3-5). Since all of His enemies will be defeated, His **throne** will be established **forever and ever**. He will have no opposition.

In this Psalm Jesus the Messiah is specifically called **God**. He is the One who created the angels. The Son in Psalm 2, the Son of the promise made to David in 2 Samuel 7, and the King of Psalm 45 all point to the same Person. As King, since He is the eternal God, He will reign forever.

His **kingdom** will be one of **righteousness**. The Son is worthy to rule that kingdom because He **loved righteousness and hated lawlessness**.

It needs to be noted that unlike Psalm 2, Psalm 45 is not an Enthronement Psalm. It does not speak about when the King is crowned. Instead, it is a Marriage Psalm. It talks about the wedding of the King. At that wedding, in particular, at the wedding feast, the King is **anointed** with the **oil of gladness**.

The feast will be a time of gladness. The King will be glad because as a righteous King, He has inherited a righteous kingdom. But the Psalm states that the King will not be alone in this celebration. Others will share in His joy.

Those who share this joy with the King are called **companions**. The picture here is the King who is having a feast. There are those who are at the head table with Him. The Greek word for *companion* (*metachoi*) signifies a close friend. Perhaps an equivalent in our time would be the President's cabinet. Those in his cabinet are close to the President.

An example of the meaning of this word is seen in Luke 5:7. Peter is fishing with his business "partners." This is the same word as *companions* used here in Hebrews. These were his close friends, those with whom he spent his time.

This is an important concept in the Book of Hebrews. When the King returns and sets up His kingdom, He will be particularly close to His *companions*, His close friends.

And who will these close friends be? It will be those who are like Him—those who loved righteousness and hated lawlessness. It will be those who have been faithful to Him.

The author will later use the same word in Heb 3:14 in which He says that believers will be the *companions* of Christ, "*if* we hold the beginning of our confidence steadfast to the end" (emphasis added).

One can easily see how this applies to the first readers. They were thinking of renouncing Christ and going back to Judaism. If they did that and did not hold steadfast to the end, they would not be the *companions* or partners of the King when He returned. They would be *in* the kingdom, but they would not be in those *positions of honor*.

Once again we can see how this applies to the President in our day. He has those who are particularly close to him. There are many people who are citizens of the United States and live in this country who are not his "companions." Only those who have faithfully served the President fit this description.

In the Book of Hebrews, this is the first indication of rewards. Jesus will **inherit all things** (1:2). But He will share His inheritance with His *partners*—those who have been faithful to Him. They will be great in His kingdom. They will have an inheritance in that kingdom. But unfaithfulness will result in the loss of that reward.

The Son Never Changes (Psalm 102)

In vv 10-12, the author quotes from Ps 102:25-27. Like the previous Psalms quoted in this section, Psalm 102 also mentions the enemies of the King (Ps 102:8). But the major point here is that the King will never change. Psalm 45 said that His throne will be forever. If He is to rule forever, He must be eternal and not subject to change.

It is interesting that God is speaking in this Psalm. He is speaking about the Son, and He calls the Son **Lord.** Whom would God call Lord? This is another statement that Jesus is God. The **earth and the heavens are the work** of Jesus.

The Psalm goes on to say that the present creation **will perish** (cf. Matt 5:18; 24:35; Mark 13:31; Luke 21:33; 2 Pet 3:10-12; Rev 20:1-3). But Christ will **remain**. The day will come when Christ will roll up the universe like an old coat, that is, **like a garment** that no longer has a use. It will be replaced by another one. This will happen after Jesus rules for one thousand years and He creates a new heaven and earth.

The universe itself **will be changed,** but Christ will remain **the same**. The point is that Christ's kingdom will survive even the universe. His kingdom will include the millennial kingdom and then will go on into the eternal state.

Of course, this had tremendous application to the original readers. Their present world was persecuting them. They were tempted to give up. The author is telling them that the troubles of this present world are temporary because the present world itself is temporary. They should keep their eyes on the coming eternal kingdom of Christ.

The Son Will Defeat His Enemies (Psalm 110)

In vv 13-14, the author concludes his OT quotes which compare Jesus with the angels. In all the Psalms quoted, it was implied that the King would defeat all of His **enemies**.

In v 13, the author quotes from Psalm 110. The day will come when all the **enemies** of the King are placed under His feet—they will become His **footstool**. If God's people, like the original readers, were being oppressed by the enemies of the King, they should find comfort in knowing that one day their King will defeat their persecutors.

Psalm 110 is crucial to the Book of Hebrews. It was alluded to in 1:3, is quoted here, and will be quoted again in 5:6. The Jews believed that the Psalm predicted the coming Messiah. Hebrews is written to Jewish Christians. The author is saying that Jesus is the fulfillment of this Psalm.

The main point here is that when Jesus comes and defeats His enemies, His people will share in that victory. Angels will not, as some Jews felt, rule the world to come. Instead, angels are simply those who **minister** to **those who will inherit salvation**.

This raises a couple of questions. First, what is the **salvation** here? And second, who are those who **will inherit** that salvation?

In all the Psalms quoted in 1:5-14, **salvation** means *deliverance from the enemies of the people of God*. The King will deliver His people and they will share in the benefits of that victory.

The salvation here is not salvation from hell. Notice that the author talks about a salvation in the *future*—those who *will* inherit salvation (contra present salvation, John 3:16-17; Eph 2:8-9). Throughout the book, as we will see, the author understands that his readers are believers. A believer already has eternal life and salvation from hell. Jesus made this clear in verses like John 5:24. To the woman at the well, Jesus said that if she believed in Him, she would have eternal life within her, and she would retain it forever (John 4:10-14). Here, in this verse, the author of Hebrews is talking about something the readers *do not yet have*. He cannot be talking about salvation from eternal condemnation because the believer already has that (John 3:18, 36; 5:24).

The word *salvation* has the basic meaning of "deliverance." The *salvation* here refers to the deliverance Jesus will bring His people when He returns—in the future. His people will share in His victory when He defeats His enemies.

Christ's inheritance is to rule the world to come (1:2). It will belong to Him. But He will share that inheritance with His companions. They will rule with Him. Not all believers will rule with Christ. While all believers will experience salvation from hell, not all believers will rule.

The author of Hebrews is telling his readers to hold on. The King is coming. He will deliver you—save you—from all your enemies. In that victory, He will reward those who have been faithful to Him. We might say they will share in the spoils of His victory. What a great *salvation* that will be!

Even though many believe that all Christians will be equal in the kingdom, the NT does not teach that. In His parables, the Lord taught that some believers will rule over ten cities, some five cities, and some will not rule over any. Paul taught that only those believers who are faithful to the Lord and suffer with Him will reign with Him (Rom 8:17; 2 Tim 2:11-13). These are the "companions" of the Lord. They are faithful to the Lord in the midst of persecution by His enemies. Christ promises to "save" them from that persecution. They are to hold firm to the end. They are the ones that wait for the righteous kingdom He will bring, in spite of the difficulties the enemies of the King throw at them.

All believers are offered this "salvation," but not all will obtain it. Those that obtain it are those that will experience deliverance from their troubles when the King returns. That is the point of the Book of Hebrews. Only those who remain faithful to the King will share in His rule. The warning passages in the book are directed toward those believers who are contemplating being unfaithful to Him and throwing all that away.

Angels serve those who are called to reign with Christ. Angels will not rule the world to come; faithful men and women will. Because men and women will rule the world to come, the Son had to become one of them. That is the subject of the second chapter of Hebrews.

Application

It may be difficult for the modern-day reader to put himself in the shoes of the original readers of Hebrews. Many of us have not experienced persecution for our faith. We have never been faced with the temptation to reject Christianity for our safety.

However, the message here in chapter 1 is timeless. In Christ, we see the coming eternal King. When we believe in Jesus Christ for eternal life, we receive it as a free gift. However, Christ offers His people even more. He calls every believer to be one of His intimate companions in His kingdom. Christ will own the kingdom over which He rules, and He wants to give His followers a share in that inheritance. There is a difference between being in a place and inheriting that place. There is a difference between being in the kingdom and being great in the kingdom.

Imagine if, when the King returns, He made you a partner with Him in ruling His kingdom. Imagine being in the cabinet of the King. Being faithful to Him in this life is difficult, whatever age in which we live. But He promises to come and deliver us from these things and reward faithfulness toward Him. Not all believers will receive this "salvation" from Him. All believers will be in the kingdom, but as the Book of Hebrews will spell out, including in the warning passages, some believers will experience the loss of eternal rewards.

The first warning passage occurs in the next verses.

The King Became a Man

THROUGHOUT THE BOOK OF Hebrews, the author develops a certain pattern: to teach and then follow with a warning passage. That is the case here. In chapter 1 he has just said that there is a salvation that is coming for the people of God. This salvation is not the same thing as "going to heaven." Instead, it is a reward for believers who are faithful to the Lord. It involves *inheriting* the kingdom of God, which is different from *entering* the kingdom. Those who obtain this inheritance will be the *partners* of Christ and will rule with Him.

In chapter 2, the author will continue discussing the fact that Christ will rule the world to come. However, before he does, he takes a break from this discussion with a warning for his readers.

What about those believers who do not remain faithful? That is the point of the five warning passages in the book. We find the first such warning in chapter 2.

The First Warning Passage (2:1-4)

¹ Therefore we must give the more earnest heed to the things we have heard, lest we drift away. ² For if the word spoken through angels proved steadfast, and every transgression and disobedience received a just reward, ³ how shall we escape if we neglect so great a salvation, which at the first began to be spoken by the Lord, and was confirmed to us by those who heard *Him*, ⁴ God also bearing witness both with signs and wonders, with various miracles, and gifts of the Holy Spirit, according to His own will?

There is a clear connection with this first warning passage and chapter 1. We see this in the word **therefore** (v 1) and the word **salvation** (v 3). The author spoke about this salvation with the very last word of chapter 1.

It is also clear that the author is speaking to believers. He includes himself when he says that we **must give more earnest heed to the things** we **have heard**. The Christian readers had heard about this coming salvation which Christ was going to bring to His people.

The Danger (v 1)

The danger was that they could **drift away** from what they had heard. Specifically, that Christ would rule the world to come and that believers could rule with Him. The idea that they could drift away from that paints a picture of a boat drifting away from a dock because the rope has come loose. The same thing could happen in a spiritual sense to these believers.

The dock was a place of security. The teachings that these believers had heard were their anchor and provided a place of refuge in a hostile world. They needed to hold on to these things lest they drift away from them.

Part of the reason they were in danger of drifting is that they were immature believers. The author will point that out in 5:11-12. Certainly we see an application here. Spiritual defeat is a real danger to believers who do not mature in their faith and walk with the Lord.

The original readers had an extra danger. They were being persecuted for their faith, as will be seen in the rest of the book. When faced with difficulties, it is easy to forget the things we have been taught and focus on the hard times we are going through. That will cause us to drift away from what Christ has told us.

The Reason to Watch Out (vv 2-4)

In chapter 1 the author said that Christ is greater than the angels. He now points out that the things **spoken through angels** were to be obeyed. The people of God who disobeyed what the angels said received a **just reward**, that is, a deserved punishment. Since Christ is greater than the angels, if we disobey Him we can expect punishment as well.

The word spoken by angels is a reference to the OT Law of Moses. Many Jews in the first century held that the Law of Moses was given through angels, and there are verses in the Bible that bear that out. These include the Greek translation of Deut 33:2, as well as Ps 68:17. In the NT the idea is present in Gal 3:19 and Acts 7:53.

Once again we need not suggest that the punishment here refers to going to hell. Many people in the OT were punished by God, but they were not sent to hell. The author will speak of such people in chapters 3–4. But we can think of someone like David in the OT. Clearly he was a believer, but he disobeyed God and was punished. His newborn son died; he had serious troubles within his family; and his kingdom was ripped away from him because he disobeyed God.

To **neglect so great a salvation** is not the same as neglecting the promise of everlasting life. As we saw in chapter 1, *salvation* in Hebrews is being one of Christ's partners (Greek, *metachoi*) in the life to come (Heb 1:9; 3:14). Neglecting this great salvation is the same as drifting away from what they had heard.

The word *neglect* means "to be unconcerned about something." The readers are to keep their minds focused on what Christ taught about His return. If they take their eyes off of it, they are in danger of forgetting these things. This could end up in disobedience and the resulting punishment.

Notice once again that the author includes himself in this warning. He says that **we** shall not **escape** if we neglect the salvation and reward Christ offers His people. It is interesting that the author does not tell his readers what the punishment will be. One could say that the punishment is that the Christian who neglects this coming salvation will not be one of the partners of Christ, that is, they won't rule with Him. But it may be that the author leaves the punishment vague. All he says here is that for those who ignore what Jesus has said and are disobedient to those things will certainly suffer loss. God is able to discipline His children in many different ways!

The author points out that these things were indeed **spoken by the Lord**. Jesus often taught about the opportunity for believers to be great in the kingdom of God, that is, to rule in it (Matt 5:3, 5, 7, 9-10; 25:34-35; Luke 6:20; 12:31-32; 22:29-30). **Those who** actually **heard** the Lord speak of these things **confirmed** them to others.

Those who heard (the Lord speak) refers primarily to the Apostles. They confirmed what they heard through their eyewitness accounts. They also spoke about being great in the kingdom. But **with signs and wonders** and **with various miracles**, they also demonstrated the truth of what they and the Lord said. The Book of Acts is a record of these miracles. Acts is a book that speaks of the coming kingdom of God (Acts 1:3, 6; 28:31).

In the Book of Acts the apostles performed the same types of miracles that Christ had performed. They did these things through His power. Since Christ was at the right hand of God (Heb 1:13), He was all-powerful (Acts 4:30; 14:3). These miracles demonstrated that Christ had the power to defeat His enemies and bring in His kingdom.

The references to **God** as well as the **gifts of the Holy Spirit** show that not only Christ and the Apostles taught the things the readers needed to pay attention to; all three members of the Trinity did. In view of all these things, the readers would understand the seriousness of the things said. To neglect such teaching would result in severe consequences.

This first warning passage was a short digression in the discussion about Christ's ruling the world to come. Now the author returns to that topic.

Mankind Will Rule with Christ (vv 5-18)

In chapter 1, Jesus is presented as the King who is also God. Now the author adds a new idea: the God-King became a human being. This means that mankind—men and women—will share in Christ's destiny to rule in His kingdom. Jesus has done everything that is needed in order for this to take place.

Jesus Became a Man (vv 5-9)

> [5] **For He has not put the world to come, of which we speak, in subjection to angels.** [6] **But one testified in a certain place, saying:**
> *"What is man that You are mindful of him,*
> *Or the son of man that You take care of him?*
> [7] *You have made him a little lower than the angels;*

You have crowned him with glory and honor,
And set him over the works of Your hands.
⁸ You have put all things in subjection under his feet."
For in *that* He put all in subjection under him, He left
nothing that is not put under him. ⁹ But now we do not
yet see all things put under him. But we see Jesus, who was
made a little lower than the angels, for the suffering of death
crowned with glory and honor, that He, by the grace of God,
might taste death for everyone.

The word **for** in v 5 connects this verse with what was said before.
Chapter 1 spoke of the fact that Jesus, as the Son, will rule the **world to
come**. This coming kingdom will not be ruled by **angels**. Once again we
see that Christ is greater than the angels.

All things will be **in subjection to** Christ. The author is about to
say that mankind can share in that subjection. This is the salvation the
author is talking about (1:14; 2:3). It is not simply "going to heaven," but
ruling the world to come. The warning passage that was just given (2:1-
4) is a warning that Christians can miss that privilege.

In the present time, angels have certain governmental roles (see Eph
6:12; Dan 10:12-13, 20-21). But whatever role they have now, they will
not rule in the kingdom of God; mankind will.

To prove his point, he once again quotes from the OT. To Jewish
Christians who respected the OT, the author shows that God has always
determined that men and women will rule the world to come.

In vv 6-8 he quotes from Ps 8:4-6. Many see Psalm 8 as describing
the role that mankind currently plays in God's creation. Mankind was
certainly created to rule over God's creation (Gen 1:26). David, the
author of the Psalm, looks at the greatness of God's creation and marvels
that God has placed man **over the works of** His **hands**. Today man is in
an exalted position. In this sense, God has **crowned him with glory and
honor**. The **glory and honor** here are to rule over what God has made.

However these verses can apply to mankind in general, it is clear
that the author of Hebrews sees them as referring to one particular
man—Jesus Christ. In the context, he is describing the world to come.

That the author does not have in mind primarily man's current
role in God's creation is seen in the fact that at this time we do not see
all things in subjection under his feet. Mankind still lives in a fallen

world. Certainly the original readers of Hebrews, who were experiencing persecution, understood this fact. They were not ruling over the world in which they lived!

If indeed these verses are describing Jesus Christ, it is not a surprise that Psalm 8 refers to Him as the **Son of Man**. This was Jesus' favorite title for Himself. It comes from Dan 7:13-14 in which the Messiah is called by this name and receives an eternal kingdom. The Son of Man is the one who is the Son and King of Hebrews 1; all things, including His enemies (1:13), will be put under His feet.

In v 8 the author makes it clear that by quoting Psalm 8 he has Jesus in mind. He is not talking about the role men and women have in God's creation now. Man was created to rule over God's creation, **but now we do not yet see all things put under him**. In fact, at this present time, we do not see everything in subjection to mankind in general or even to Jesus Christ Himself. As the author of Hebrews just said in chapter 1, Jesus is waiting until His enemies are placed under His feet.

In v 9 we have no doubt that the author sees Psalm 8 as pointing to Jesus Christ. He refers to Him by name. Even though all things are not subject to Him, **we** do **see Jesus**. He is the One **who was made a little lower than the angels**.

The One who is the eternal God was made a little lower than the angels He created! But why? It was that He **might taste death for everyone**. As God, He could not die. He became a man in order to experience that. He became a man in order to die.

Christ's death was an expression of the **grace of God**. Christ died for each and every person. Since mankind experiences death, He identified with mankind in His death.

As a result of His death, He was indeed **crowned with glory and honor** (v 9). This is a reference to the fact that after His death and resurrection, He was exalted to the right hand of God (Heb 1:13). In the midst of suffering, Christ was obedient to His Father. As a result, God highly exalted Him. This was very relevant to the original readers of Hebrews. The message of the whole book is that if the readers are obedient in their difficulties, God will exalt them as well.

We can summarize what the use of Psalm 8 here means. There are two themes present: the first is that Christ will have dominion over everything in the future eternal kingdom of God; the second is that Christ became a man. In Christ, man will rule over all of God's creation.

Christ is the fulfillment of Psalm 8. In Him, man reaches his destiny. He is not the only One that will inherit this salvation (1:14). Through Him, others will as well.

For all of this to occur, not only did Christ have to become a man, but He also had to die. In the remainder of chapter 2, the author will explain what Christ's death means.

Why Jesus Became a Man (vv 10-18)

> ¹⁰ **For it was fitting for Him, for whom are all things and by whom** *are* **all things, in bringing many sons to glory, to make the captain of their salvation perfect through sufferings.** ¹¹ **For both He who sanctifies and those who are being sanctified are all of one, for which reason He is not ashamed to call them brethren,** ¹² **saying:**
> *"I will declare Your name to My brethren;*
> *In the midst of the assembly I will sing praise to You."*
> ¹³ **And again:**
> *"I will put My trust in Him."*
> **And again:**
> *"Here am I and the children whom God has given Me."*
> ¹⁴ **Inasmuch then as the children have partaken of flesh and blood, He Himself likewise shared in the same, that through death He might destroy him who had the power of death, that is, the devil,** ¹⁵ **and release those who through fear of death were all their lifetime subject to bondage.** ¹⁶ **For indeed He does not give aid to angels, but He does give aid to the seed of Abraham.** ¹⁷ **Therefore, in all things He had to be made** *like* **His brethren, that He might be a merciful and faithful High Priest in things** *pertaining* **to God, to make propitiation for the sins of the people.** ¹⁸ **For in that He Himself has suffered, being tempted, He is able to aid those who are tempted.**

In v 10 the author still has Psalm 8 in mind. We see this with the repetition of the words **all things**. Psalm 8 spoke about the glory of mankind ruling over God's creation, all the things God created. This is the salvation that the author of Hebrews is speaking about (v 3).

Of course, Christ, as we have seen, will be the Supreme Ruler of that kingdom. But God is also **bringing many sons to glory**. Many other men and women will share in the glory of ruling with Christ, of having dominion over the works of God's hands. These **sons** are Christ's *partners* (1:9) who will inherit this salvation (1:14). This inheritance is available to all Christians, and even though a believer can never lose eternal life and go to hell, he can neglect and lose his inheritance in God's kingdom (2:3). As the Son, Christ will rule the world to come. But many other **sons** will rule with Him.

In v 9 it was first mentioned that Christ suffered. In v 10 it is said that it was **fitting**, or appropriate, for Him to do so. This is because the suffering of Christ made **the captain of their salvation perfect through sufferings**.

Jesus is the Captain of the **many sons**. The word *captain* had a military meaning, and includes within it the idea of a leader who goes before his men—he leads the way. The *captain* is an example for others to follow.

The picture here is that Christ leads others to the **glory** of ruling over God's works. Those He leads are the *many sons*. This is the salvation that He is leading them to.

But before Christ could be such a Captain, He had to be made **perfect** *for that role*. To put it another way, He had to be qualified to assume that position. What will be said in the following verses is that the *many sons* are faced with suffering and death. If their Captain was going to lead them, He had to experience such things Himself. Only in that way could He lead the way through these difficulties. After experiencing these things, He could lead them when they walked that path.

Christ walked the path to glory by suffering. It was through suffering that Christ was exalted to the right hand of the Father, where He is now waiting to rule (1:13; 2:9). What a message for the believers that first read the Book of Hebrews! They had a Captain who had gone before them. He knows what they are going through. Follow Him to glory! This is the salvation He offers to His children. But this salvation involves suffering.

The Captain and those He is leading will share the glory of the world to come. But they also share suffering. They have things in common. Therefore, the Captain had to become one of them. That is the meaning of v 11.

Both the *Captain*, **He who sanctifies**, and *the many sons*, **those who are sanctified** (the King James is better here) **are all of one**. The point here, as v 14 will say, is that Jesus and *the many sons* have the same origin. They all are human.

The word *sanctified* means *to be made holy in one's position* (i.e., *to be set apart*). In the Book of Hebrews, this word is equivalent to the way many Christians use the word *saved*. Christ is the One who makes His people holy in their position. He has paid the price for the forgiveness of their sins. The author will speak of this in detail in chapter 10. Those who have believed in Jesus for eternal life are sanctified. They have been made holy forever (Heb 10:10, 14). Those who are sanctified now have a Captain who can lead them to another kind of salvation if they will follow Him.

Because Christ shares humanity with His people, **He is not ashamed to call them brethren**. He shares in their human nature, their sufferings, and even their experience of death. He is one of them.

How amazing is it, however, that such a One like this would not be ashamed to be counted one of us? The God of the universe—the eternal Son—calls us His brothers! When we read in chapter 1 about His eternal power and realize that He humbled Himself to become one of us, He entered our world of sin and corruption, He made us holy, and now desires to lead us to eternal glory, how can we not love and follow Him? This is the whole point of the Book of Hebrews.

Because Christ shares all these things with His people, He can speak to them as One who has walked in their shoes. He can tell them how He, as a human being, trusted in God and how God delivered Him.

The author has already said that those whom Christ leads are His brothers. Now in v 12 he quotes from Psalm 22. In that Psalm the Messiah is One who suffers. This involves His death upon the cross (Ps 22:1-21). Beginning in v 22 of the Psalm, however, the Messiah is delivered from His suffering. In the case of Christ, He was resurrected from the dead and exalted to God's right hand. In other words, God delivered Him through His suffering.

Christ gives them this message **in the midst** of them. That is, He is one of them. He is not speaking from heaven with this message. He became one of them, lived among them, and experienced suffering and then deliverance from God.

Here in v 12 the author of Hebrews quotes from the victorious section of Psalm 22 (Ps 22:22). Because God saved (delivered) Him through His sufferings, Christ **will declare Your** (God's) **name to** His **brethren**. He **will sing praise to** God. Because God delivered Him, He can tell others what God has done for Him. The point is clear. Since God has delivered their Captain through His suffering, God will do the same for the many sons. Like their Captain, they need to continue to trust in God to experience the same kind of deliverance.

In v 13 the author quotes from Isaiah 8 in order to continue this idea of trusting in God. In Isaiah's day, he and the nation of Judah were threatened by their enemies. The king of Judah was tempted to turn to other nations for help. Isaiah says that instead of trusting in others, he will **put** his **trust in Him** (God). Isaiah would trust in God to deliver him from his enemies. This is the message that Christ gives to His followers as well; God delivered Jesus from His enemies.

The second part of v 13 has the same message but deals with the word of God. God had told Isaiah that even though the Jews would go into captivity, God would bring His people back. A remnant would return. In addition, He would quickly destroy their enemies. Isaiah names His two **children** with names that reflected what God had promised. One name meant "a remnant will return;" the other meant "hasten booty, speed spoil," which signified that God would quickly judge the enemies of His people.

Of course, all of this occurred just as God had promised. The prophecy of the names of Isaiah's children came to pass. The point is that God's word can be trusted. Jesus trusted in God's word, and God delivered Him. God promises to deliver His people from their enemies. The children of God can believe the same thing. In the context of Hebrews, we could also say that God will give glory and honor to those children who continue to trust in Him through difficult times.

The author clearly wants to say that Christians are the children of God and of Christ (v 13). These **children** are made up of **flesh and blood** (v 14). To become one of them, Christ **shared in the same**, that is, He took on flesh and blood. As we saw in v 11, Christ and His children are of the same origin in this respect.

We were told in v 9 that the reason Christ took on flesh and blood was to die. But now, in v 14, we are told why He died. It was so that

Christ **might destroy him who had the power of death**. This one is then identified as **the devil**.

Christ's death made the power that Satan had in this area a thing of the past. But what does that mean? It could mean that Satan's activities brought sin into the world. As a result, death entered into the world. But Christ's death paid for the sins of His people (the author will say that in v 17). His resurrection conquered death. His people no longer have to fear it.

Another possibility is that Satan often uses the threat of death against the people of God. The original readers of Hebrews, for example, might have been tempted to quit following Christ because they feared what His enemies might do. This could include killing them. However, Christ's death and resurrection means that believers never need to fear death again.

This is the point of v 15. There is a natural tendency for people, even Christians, to have a **fear of death**. They are in **bondage** to such fear when faced with persecution for their faith. But Christ's defeat of death provides His people with a **release** from that fear.

For some believers the path to the glory of ruling with Christ involves death. We can think of someone like Stephen in Acts 7. If Christ is going to lead such children to glory, He had to take away the fear of death. That is one of the reasons why He became a man and died. When believers are faced with death while following Christ, they can look at His example and see what God did for their Captain.

In vv 16-18 the author concludes his discussion about Christ becoming one with His children. He started this section by saying that angels will not rule the world to come (v 5). He concludes with the same idea here in v 16. Christ did not become a man **to give aid to angels**. Instead, He came to **give aid to the seed of Abraham**. In Gal 3:7, 29, all believers in Christ are called the seed of Abraham. That is also the meaning here. Christ came to help and lead believers to become rulers in the world to come.

In vv 17-18 the author gives a final reason why Christ became a man. He did it so **He might be a merciful and faithful High Priest**. This is a topic that the author will devote much attention to in the latter parts of the book.

It is said that Christ **had** to become **like His brethren** in order to do this. The point is that if Jesus was going to be the kind of High Priest His people needed, He had to become one of them. He had to become like them **in all things**. He had to be born, become tired, experience hunger and thirst, be tempted, and go through suffering and death.

Christ was a **faithful High Priest** in the **things pertaining to God**. This means He made propitiation for **the sins of the people**. He did all that was necessary to secure His people's relationship with God. In our **High Priest** we are holy (v 14), and we can approach God through Him. Since He obeyed His Father perfectly, He is also faithful because He is completely trustworthy.

He is merciful in the sense that He is sympathetic to His people and knows what they are going through. He knows because He became one of them. A high priest represents the people he intercedes for. In the OT the high priest was one of the people. Christ became one of us to fulfill that role.

The author specifically states that the reason Christ can be **a merciful High Priest** is because **He Himself has suffered** and has been **tempted**. The original readers were suffering and were tempted to give up.

The author introduces a very important idea here. Our King is at the right hand of the Father (1:13). He is all-powerful. But He is also our High Priest. When His people approach Him, they do not just find an all-powerful King. They also find One who intercedes for them and who understands everything they are going through.

And since this merciful High Priest is all-powerful, **He is able to aid those who** come to Him. Christ Himself was **tempted** to sin. He was tempted not to be faithful to God in the midst of difficulties. He was tempted to give up. We can think, for example, of His temptation by Satan in the wilderness for forty days. He knows what that is like. Since He overcame and is all-powerful, He can help His children who come to Him for help.

Application

Once again, for many modern day readers of Hebrews, it may be difficult to relate to the original readers since we often do not face persecution or the prospect of dying for our faith. But it is not difficult to see how chapter 2 applies to us.

We must realize that the author of Hebrews is not talking about simply going to heaven. He is talking about how Christ *leads* His children. The death of Christ made eternal life possible through faith in Him alone. But in these verses the author of Hebrews is primarily talking about Christ as our *example*, not our *Savior*.

Christ wants us to follow His path of obedience. He wants to lead us to a share in the glory He will have in His kingdom. Every Christian struggles against those things opposed to God—the world, the flesh, and Satan. Christ wants to bring us to victory over all these things.

Our King has done everything to bring this about. He humbled Himself and became a man. He gave us the example of faithfulness in the midst of suffering. He knows what we go through and will aid us in overcoming whatever is before us. He did all this to save us from our (and His) enemies. Christ is calling us to follow Him.

We simply have to get rid of the idea that Christianity is only about "going to heaven." Christians are called to not only go there, but to go there *victoriously*—walking in the footsteps of our Captain.

We can expect a great loss if we do not follow in His footsteps. We can expect to be disciplined by Him if we neglect so great a deliverance.

Unlike salvation from eternal condemnation, which occurs at a moment in time when one believes in Jesus Christ for eternal life (John 3:16-18, 36), following Christ's example involves faithfulness over a lifetime. We will only succeed in this endeavor if we *continue* looking to our Captain. That is how the author starts the next chapter.

Hold Fast or Miss Out on Ruling with Christ

The Second Warning Passage

AS WE HAVE ALREADY seen, it is the practice of the author of Hebrews to teach his readers important spiritual truths, and then to warn them about neglecting such teaching. This is the case at the beginning of chapter 3. He has just told them to follow the example of Christ. As believers we can follow in His footsteps. We can go to Him for whatever help we need. He has taught us to trust in God in the midst of any and all difficulties. If we do these things, we will not only be in His kingdom, we will be one of His partners and reign with Him as well.

But what if we don't? Chapters 3–4 are an extended warning passage addressing that possibility. The author uses an OT example of God's people who did not remain faithful to Him when confronted by their enemies. An outline of this long warning passage is as follows: 3:1-6 is the introduction; 3:7-15 gives the text of the warning from the OT and an application to the readers; 3:16–4:13 is an explanation of the text; 4:14-16 is the conclusion of the warning passage.

Introduction (3:1-6)

¹ **Therefore, holy brethren, partakers of the heavenly calling, consider the Apostle and High Priest of our confession, Christ Jesus, ² who was faithful to Him who appointed Him, as Moses also was *faithful* in all His house. ³ For this One has been counted worthy of more glory than Moses, inasmuch as He who built the house has more honor than the house.**

51

⁴ For every house is built by someone, but He who built all things *is* God. ⁵ And Moses indeed was faithful in all His house as a servant, for a testimony of those things which would be spoken *afterward*, ⁶ but Christ as a Son over His own house, whose house we are if we hold fast the confidence and the rejoicing of the hope firm to the end.

This passage is clearly connected with the end of chapter 2. We see this in a number of ways in v 1. The first is the word **therefore**, thus connecting it with what was just said. The second is that Jesus is once again called our **High Priest**, just as He was at the end of chapter 2 (2:17).

We should also notice that the readers are called **holy brethren**. The readers were called holy in 2:11 (*sanctified* is the same word). Chapter 2 also called them the brothers of Christ (2:11-14).

This very title shows that the readers were believers. The warning passage in chapters 3–4 is directed toward believers. Jesus is the High Priest of Christians only. In addition, these readers have a **heavenly calling**.

What **calling** do Christians have? In the Book of Hebrews it is clear: it is the salvation of 1:14 and 2:3. It is more than simply "going to heaven." Christ is leading many sons to glory (2:10). It is the call to be one of Christ's partners in His kingdom, that is, to reign with Him.

This **calling** is **heavenly** in the sense that Christ is seated at the right hand of the Father in heaven (1:13; 2:9). From there He calls us to obtain this reward (12:25).

That this is the **calling** is also seen in the word **partaker**. This is the same word as *companion*, or *partner*, in 1:9. This is what all Christians are called to be. However, not all Christians will obtain this reward. As this warning passage points out—indeed, all the warning passages in Hebrews point out—this reward can be lost. The Christian must remain faithful to the Lord in order to obtain it.

In order to obtain it, he must **consider Christ Jesus**. Not only is He the Christian's High Priest, He is also his **Apostle**. The word *Apostle* means one who is sent. Jesus was sent by God in order for mankind to fulfill their destiny of reigning over the works of God's hands. The readers needed to look to Him as an example of One who was faithful to the Father and follow that example.

The faithfulness of Christ is emphasized in v 2. Christ was **faithful to the One who appointed Him**. Christ did all God told Him to do. While on earth He made the sacrifice that would sanctify His people. He was faithful in the midst of difficulties. They should follow Christ's example as their Captain and Leader.

In the last part of v 2 the author mentions an OT believer who was also faithful to God—**Moses**. Moses is referenced because he was faithful in regard to a **house**. Both Moses and Jesus have proven themselves faithful over the *house* of God.

Many have assumed that the word *house* is a reference to the people of God. It is maintained that Moses was the leader of the people of God in the wilderness, and Jesus is the leader of the people of God known as the Church in the NT. Those who take this view say that the house here is the same thing as the body of Christ.

However, it is much more likely that in the case of Moses, the word *house* refers to the tabernacle that he built. Verse 2 comes from Num 12:5-8, particularly v 7. This passage in Numbers occurs at the tabernacle; Moses was faithful in building the tabernacle. The tabernacle is called the house of God in Deut 23:18 and Judg 18:31. In Moses' case, the tabernacle was a house of worship. It was where the people came to worship God.

In vv 3-6 we are told that Jesus is also faithful over a **house**. But He is over a greater house. The Book of Hebrews was written to Jewish Christians who held Moses in great esteem. However great Moses was, and however great the house he built was, Jesus is greater and **worthy of more glory**.

One reason that Jesus is greater than Moses is that the one who builds a **house has more honor than the house** (v 3). Moses was **a servant** in the tabernacle (v 5). But since Jesus is God, it was Jesus who told Moses how to build the house. Christ was the One responsible for the house Moses served in.

But Christ did not just found the house of God, the Tabernacle, in the OT. He **built all things** (v 4). The point here is that Christ made the whole universe. Christ's house is universal.

At the command of Christ, Moses built a house that was a house of worship. It had a high priest over it. The people approached and worshiped God through it.

Christ, however, is over a universal house. It is also a house of worship, and it has a High Priest.

The house that Moses was involved in was only a shadow of the house that Christ presides over. Moses' tabernacle had a Holy of Holies that represented the presence of God on earth. Christ is our High Priest in the true presence of God in the heavenly Holy of Holies (2:17; 4:14-16; 9:24).

From the heavens, Christ presides over a universal house of worship. The greatness of Jesus over Moses is also seen in that He is not a servant in His house, as Moses was, but a **Son** (v 6). Chapter 1 stated that the Son, Christ, is none other than God Himself.

We could summarize the introduction up to this point in this way: Moses was a servant in the house of the Lord in the OT. This house, the tabernacle that he faithfully built, was a place where the people of God came to worship God. It was a place of priestly activity. But Christ is also over a house. His house is greater, just as He is greater than Moses. His house is also a house of worship with priestly activity. He is High Priest over it. It is a universal house in the sense that the whole Church worships in it. Believers around the world worship Him in this house.

The house of Christ here is *not* the body of Christ, as it is made up of believers. The house here refers to the privilege believers have in their priestly functions and worship (13:10, 15-16). This is important. A believer can never remove himself from the Body of Christ, the Church. However, a believer can remove himself from the house of Christ as described here if he decides to withdraw from attending church with other believers and cease to worship God.

That is the point of the last part of v 6. Christians are part of the house of God only **if we hold fast the confidence and the rejoicing of the hope firm to the end**. Notice the author once again includes himself, by saying *we*. The word *if* tells us a Christian has an option. *If* a believer withdraws from the visible church he is no longer a part of the **house** of worship.

This is what all the warning passages are about. The author fears lest some of his Christian readers withdraw from the visible church—to quit meeting with other believers—because of the difficulties they are facing. To do that is to withdraw from the worshiping house of God. It is to withdraw from the house over which Christ as our High Priest is presiding. Unfortunately, some of the readers had already done just that (10:25).

The author wants the readers to hold onto the Christian *confession* (3:1). He wants them to hold onto their *confidence*, which has great reward (10:35). This reward is to reign with Christ, which is also the *hope* spoken of here in v 6. It is our *heavenly calling* (v 1). If we withdraw from worshiping God, we will lose this reward.

These verses are a call to faithfulness. The people of God of every generation are called to such faithfulness. But in every generation there is a danger that some will not hold fast. As a warning to his readers, the author gives an OT example of such a failure. For those in the OT, their failure resulted in the discipline of God and the loss of reward. Failure on the part of the readers of Hebrews would result in the same.

A Warning from Psalm 95 (3:7-15)

[7] **Therefore, as the Holy Spirit says:**

> *"Today, if you will hear His voice,*
> [8] *Do not harden your hearts as in the rebellion,*
> *In the day of trial in the wilderness,*
> [9] *Where your fathers tested Me, tried Me,*
> *And saw My works forty years.*
> [10] *Therefore I was angry with that generation,*
> *And said, 'They always go astray in their heart,*
> *And they have not known My ways.'*
> [11] *So I swore in My wrath,*
> *'They shall not enter My rest.' "*

[12] **Beware, brethren, lest there be in any of you an evil heart of unbelief in departing from the living God;** [13] **but exhort one another daily, while it is called "*Today*," lest any of you be hardened through the deceitfulness of sin.** [14] **For we have become partakers of Christ if we hold the beginning of our confidence steadfast to the end,** [15] **while it is said:**

> *"Today, if you will hear His voice,*
> *Do not harden your hearts as in the rebellion."*

The example the author gives deals with the failure of the Jews at Kadesh Barnea. The Jews were unfaithful toward God there, and the readers of Hebrews should not follow that example. Those Jews were a part of the house in which Moses was a servant (3:1-6). They paid a heavy price for their disobedience and unfaithfulness. Since the readers of Hebrews belong to a greater house, and Jesus is greater than Moses, what can they expect if they are disobedient to Him?

In vv 7-11 the author quotes from Psalm 95. This Psalm fits the context of what the author is talking about. The Psalm is a call to worship. In Ps 95:6, for example, it says, "Oh come, let us worship and bow down; Let us kneel before the Lord our Maker." The author of Hebrews has just said that the readers are part of a house of worship over which Jesus Christ our High Priest presides. When we attend an assembly of believers we are taking part in this *house*.

Psalm 95 was written by David centuries after the failure of the Jews at Kadesh Barnea. But David applies it to God's people of his day. They needed to **hear** the **voice** of God (v 7). They needed to hear it **today**, that is, in David's day. The author of Hebrews will say the same thing is true for his readers centuries later as well (3:15; 4:7).

In Psalm 95 David refers to the **rebellion, in the day of trial in the wilderness** (v 8). It is possible that David is referring to the whole time the Jews were in the wilderness. They rebelled against God in many ways, complaining about their water, their food, and even the leadership of Moses. But in the Psalm, it is fairly clear that David has one particular rebellion in mind.

At Kadesh Barnea (Numbers 13), God told the Jews to go in and conquer the land of Palestine. He promised to be with them and to give them victory over their enemies. The Jews sent twelve spies into the land to see what it was like. When the spies returned, ten of them said that it would not be possible to conquer the land. The enemies of the Jews were too strong. Only two of the spies, Joshua and Caleb, told the people to remain faithful to God. The nation sided with the ten spies and refused to do what God commanded. As a result, God punished the nation by declaring that all the adults, except the two faithful spies, would die in the wilderness. They would not get to defeat their enemies or possess the land God had for them. That generation of Jews did indeed die in the wilderness over the next forty years.

On that day, the Jews **hardened** their **hearts**. They rejected God's plan to enter the land and defeat their enemies.

At Kadesh Barnea they **tested** and **tried** God (v 9). These words could mean they complained about God's lack of goodness to them. Or the words could refer to testing Him to see how long it would take and how much they would have to disobey before He punished them. They complained about God's goodness to them even though He had displayed it right before their eyes. He had redeemed them out of Egypt. He had miraculously fed them and given them water. He had brought them through the wilderness to the Promised Land.

It is perhaps best to take the last part of v 9 with v 10. For **forty years** the Jews of that generation **saw** the **works** of God. That **generation** experienced the discipline of God because He **was angry with** their unfaithfulness and disobedience.

This is what it means when God says that **they always go astray in their heart, and they have not known** His **ways**. They refused to do what God told them to do. Their hearts said "no" to God's plan of defeating their enemies and possessing the land. They did not believe God could do what He said He would do.

As a result, God **swore** that they would **not enter** His **rest** (v 11). That is the price the Jews at Kadesh Barnea paid for their disobedience. But to what does this **rest** refer? This is very important because the author will soon say that the readers of Hebrews also might not enter God's rest (4:1).

As has already been stated, many think that the warning passages are admonishing people about going to hell. As a result, they see *rest* here as referring to heaven. To say that these Jews did not enter into God's rest means that they were not believers and went to hell.

But is that even a possibility? How can we say that these Jews at Kadesh Barnea represent non-believers? God had redeemed them out of Egypt. They had applied the blood of the Passover lamb to their doors. They had eaten the Passover meal. They had been brought through the Red Sea by the power of God, which Paul says was a type of Christian baptism. Paul says they ate spiritual food as well (1 Cor 10:2-3). God gave them His word at Mount Sinai. He guided them through their wanderings by a cloud during the day and a pillar of fire by night. He called them His people. He told Pharaoh they were His son (Exod 4:22). They experienced the forgiveness of God. In fact, even at Kadesh

Barnea God forgave them (Num 14:20). What a strange way to describe unbelievers!

It is simply impossible to say that the Jews whom God saved out of Egypt but who disobeyed at Kadesh Barnea are meant to be examples of unbelievers who go to hell. Instead, they are an illustration of believers who are unfaithful to God. Believers may not enter into the rest of God. Therefore, this rest must refer to something other than going to heaven.

In the context of the Jews at Kadesh Barnea, *rest* meant more than simply entering into the land. It involved *possessing and owning it* (Deut 3:18-20; 4:21; 12:8-10). In order to own the land, they had to defeat the enemies there. Their rest would involve rest from these enemies (Joshua 3–4). The Jews would not enjoy rest in the land until all their enemies were defeated *after* they entered it (Deut 25:19; Josh 1:13; 21:43-45).

As the word *rest* implies, they needed to finish the work God had given them. One rests after having completed a job. Notice that God refers to this rest as **My rest** (v 11). This probably refers to the fact that God rested from His work after He completed it in creation (Gen 2:2-3). The Jews had their work to do as well. They needed to be faithful to God, trust in Him to defeat their enemies, and go do it! They needed to go possess their land. If they did, they would be able to experience rest from their enemies. This was their destiny. This was their inheritance. But the vast majority of them lost their inheritance through unfaithfulness.

The parallel to the Christian readers of Hebrews is clear. They had their enemies. But Christ promised to defeat them (1:13). They also have an inheritance in the world to come. They could reign and possess that world with Christ (1:14; 2:3). It was their destiny to inherit all things (2:6-8).

But they had to finish their work. They must hold fast to their faith in God's promises (3:6). The Jews at Kadesh Barnea were part of the house of worship that Moses built (3:2). They simply did not believe God would be able to deliver them when faced with the giants in the Promised Land. They withdrew from the battle. They paid a heavy price and experienced the discipline of God. The readers of Hebrews could follow the same negative example. Because of that, the author of Hebrews applies Psalm 95 to them.

He tells them to **beware** (v 12); they could do the same thing as the Jews in the wilderness. But, once again, they are called **brethren** (as in

3:1). They are Christians. But they, too, could be guilty of **departing from the living God**.

The word for *depart* is sometimes translated "apostasy." That is the sin the author is concerned about for his readers. They would do that if they left Christianity and went back to Judaism. It would involve not holding on to their Christian confession (3:1). It would involve withdrawing from the worshiping house over which Christ presided as our High Priest (3:1-6).

What would cause this is **an evil heart of unbelief**. In light of what happened at Kadesh Barnea, this would be a heart that did not trust in God when there is trouble ahead. If the readers did this, neither would they enter into God's rest.

One way the readers could avoid this possibility was to **exhort one another daily**. This implies that as Christians they should meet regularly. As they meet, they should *exhort* one another. The word means to encourage. The church meeting should be a place where believers are encouraged in their Christian walk. Mutual edification in the church would prevent them from being **hardened**. In v 8 we saw that the Jews at Kadesh experienced a hardened heart.

This hardening is possible because of the **deceitfulness of sin**. The readers were being fooled by sin into believing that it was acceptable to go back to Judaism and to withdraw from the Christian Church. Perhaps they thought that in Judaism they would still be able to worship God. Sin was telling them they should seek comfort and security by leaving Christianity. Sin was telling them to fear their enemies and that God could not take care of them in the midst of their difficulties.

However, this deception usually does not happen overnight. As the author said in the first warning passage (2:1-4), it is a process that involves drifting away from the truth. The cure is for Christians to meet together to help one another in these attacks by sin.

These believers are to do this as long as **it is called "Today."** By the word *today* the author is applying Psalm 95 directly to the readers. The lesson at Kadesh applied to the Jews in the wilderness and the people of God in David's time as well. Every "day" is another "today" in which God's people need to encourage one another and heed the warning of Psalm 95. This is true for any generation of God's people.

This is important because if the readers followed the example of the Jews at Kadesh, they also would suffer great loss. What was at stake is being a **partaker of Christ** (v 14). The word for *partaker*—the very first word in the Greek text of v 14—is the same Greek word as *companion* in 1:9 (*metachoi*). These are the close, intimate partners of the King. These are the *many sons* who will share in Christ's glory and reign with Him.

But once again, the author makes it clear that not all believers will experience this. While all believers will be in the kingdom, not all will be **partakers** with Christ. It is a reward that is available **if** the readers **hold the beginning of** their **confidence steadfast to the end**. The word *confidence* can mean an "undertaking" as it does in 2 Cor 9:4 and 11:17. That certainly fits the context of the Book of Hebrews. The readers had an undertaking; their goal was to become Christ's partners in the world to come.

This is a great reward. But in order to obtain it, they needed to remain firm in their faithfulness to God. The Jews at Kadesh lost their reward, and so could the recipients of Hebrews. The **today** of Psalm 95 was their time, even though Psalm 95 was written centuries before. They must **not harden** their **hearts as in the rebellion** at Kadesh Barnea. Through the rest of this warning passage, the author drives home the lessons of what happened there.

An Explanation of Psalm 95 (3:16–4:13)

[16] **For who, having heard, rebelled? Indeed, *was it* not all who came out of Egypt, *led* by Moses?** [17] **Now with whom was He angry forty years? *Was it* not with those who sinned, whose corpses fell in the wilderness?** [18] **And to whom did He swear that they would not enter His rest, but to those who did not obey?** [19] **So we see that they could not enter in because of unbelief.**

In explaining Psalm 95, at the end of chapter 3, the author of Hebrews first addresses the issue of **who rebelled** (v 16). It was those **who came out of Egypt**, who turned away from God at Kadesh Barnea, that had been redeemed by God. They had been rescued out of Egypt. They had seen the power of God. These things are significant because the readers had been redeemed as well. They had also seen the power of God (2:3).

Even though they had seen and experienced these things, they **sinned** against God. They did not believe He could deliver them from their enemies in the Promised Land. As a result, God disciplined them with death: their **corpses fell in the wilderness** (v 17).

In addition, they lost their inheritance in the land. They lost the privilege of defeating their enemies. They did not complete their work. In the words of Psalm 95, they did not **enter** God's **rest**.

This was the case with all **those who did not obey** (v 18). When God brought them out of Egypt they had promised to obey God. God had told them to go and conquer the land and possess it. That was their "undertaking." They refused to do it. This was how they **sinned** (v 17).

Their sin and their disobedience are the same thing. The root of their sin is given in v 19—they were guilty of **unbelief**. It was not that they did not believe God existed. They knew He did. But they did not believe He would or could destroy the powerful enemies in the land of Canaan. The readers of the Book of Hebrews were in danger of not believing that God could defeat the enemies of Christ as well. This was the case even though God had already said that He would (1:13). In addition, Christ had shown them that they could trust in God in the midst of difficulties (2:12-13).

In this regard, the reader of Hebrews should not forget another important aspect of the parallels between Kadesh and the original readers. The Jews at Kadesh Barnea had a great leader in Moses. But the Christian readers had a greater One—the Son. If the people of God at Kadesh Barnea experienced punishment for their unbelief as followers of Moses, how could the followers of Christ hope to escape punishment if they did not believe Him (2:3)?

Chapter 4 spells out that punishment in more detail. It describes the loss of *rest*.

[1] **Therefore, since a promise remains of entering His rest, let us fear lest any of you seem to have come short of it.** [2] **For indeed the gospel was preached to us as well as to them; but the word which they heard did not profit them, not being mixed with faith in those who heard** *it.* [3] **For we who have believed do enter that rest, as He has said:**

> *"So I swore in My wrath,*
> *'They shall not enter My rest,' "*

although the works were finished from the foundation of the world. [4] For He has spoken in a certain place of the seventh *day* in this way: *"And God rested on the seventh day from all His works"*; [5] and again in this place: *"They shall not enter My rest."*

[6] Since therefore it remains that some *must* enter it, and those to whom it was first preached did not enter because of disobedience, [7] again He designates a certain day, saying in David, *"Today,"* after such a long time, as it has been said:

> *"Today, if you will hear His voice,*
> *Do not harden your hearts."*

[8] For if Joshua had given them rest, then He would not afterward have spoken of another day. [9] There remains therefore a rest for the people of God. [10] For he who has entered His rest has himself also ceased from his works as God *did* from His.

[11] Let us therefore be diligent to enter that rest, lest anyone fall according to the same example of disobedience. [12] For the word of God is living and powerful, and sharper than any two-edged sword, piercing even to the division of soul and spirit, and of joints and marrow, and is a discerner of the thoughts and intents of the heart. [13] And there is no creature hidden from His sight, but all things are naked and open to the eyes of Him to whom we *must give* account.

[14] Seeing then that we have a great High Priest who has passed through the heavens, Jesus the Son of God, let us hold fast *our* confession. [15] For we do not have a High Priest who cannot sympathize with our weaknesses, but was in all *points* tempted as *we are, yet* without sin. [16] Let us therefore come boldly to the throne of grace, that we may obtain mercy and find grace to help in time of need.

There is still the **promise of entering** God's **rest** for the readers of Hebrews and Christians today (4:1). This is what is at stake and what can be lost. This verse includes a warning of the possibility of such loss. The author says, **let us fear**.

Once again, we see that the author is speaking to believers. By the word *us* he includes himself in the warning. He, too, could possibly fail to enter into this rest. He might not hold firm to the end and thus not reign with Christ as one of His partners. The possibility of this occurring was something to fear.

The author then says that some of them might **seem to have come short of it**. Clearly, some of the readers thought this rest was not for them or that they had missed it. It is difficult to say exactly what they might have thought. Perhaps they thought that since Christ had delayed His Second Coming, He was not coming back to establish His kingdom. Perhaps they thought that angels would rule the world to come (2:5). Or perhaps the readers thought that the "rest" of Psalm 95 only applied to the earthly Canaan and not the kingdom of God. The author will correct this thinking here in 4:8-9.

Whatever they were thinking, the author tells them that this promise of entering into God's rest **remains**. This reward was available to them.

There was a rest available to the Jews at Kadesh and the Christian reader of Hebrews. Both groups had **the gospel preached to** them (4:2). The word *gospel* is unfortunate here. As is well known, the word means "good news," and that is the meaning here. Both groups had good news proclaimed to them. It was the *good news* that God promised them a rest if they completed the work He gave them to do. The word *gospel* here does not mean what a person must do in order to go to heaven.

The Jews at Kadesh, however, **did not profit** from this good news. This was the case because they did not have **faith** in the promise.

The readers of Hebrews had good news proclaimed to them (2:3-4). They had the promise of rest and inheritance in the world to come. They could reign with Christ! But just like at Kadesh, this rest was not automatic.

Verse 3 explains who will **enter that rest**. The first part of the verse should be translated "those who believe." The translation **do enter** (present tense) is a bad one. This makes it appear that Christians enter that *rest* now. If it is understood that way, one could say it refers to receiving eternal life; that the *rest* is the same thing as being saved from hell, and that when a person believes, he enters that rest right away.

However, it is clear that the *rest* the author refers to is something that happens in the future (see vv 9 and 11), not something a believer has now. A believer has eternal life now, so the author is not talking about that.

The word *believed* in the phrase **we who have believed** is in the past tense. Those *who have believed* will enter that *rest*. In the context of this warning in Hebrews 3–4, we understand that this belief is not a one-time thing, such as when a person believes in Jesus Christ for eternal life. Instead, it is a belief that endures (3:6, 14). It is a belief that trusts in God through difficult times and when confronted with the enemies of God.

To show that this is the kind of faith the author has in mind, he once again quotes from Psalm 95. The people of God at Kadesh did not **enter** God's **rest**. Even though they were the people of God and had been redeemed from Egypt, they did not believe in His promise concerning their enemies. They were prohibited from entering into the reward of the rest God had promised them. God **swore** they would not experience it.

The application for Christians is clear. Only those Christians who have believed in God's promises by remaining faithful to Him during times of difficulties will enter the reward of this rest.

And this is a rest that is available to the people of God in all generations. It was not just for the Jews at Kadesh. This rest was established at the very beginning of creation. It involves the **works** of God that **were finished from the foundation of the world**. When God created the world He established the domain of His people's rest. It is offered to every generation of believers. In 2:6-8 the author states that man was created to rule over the works of God's hands. This is man's inheritance. This is the rest that God offers. The unbelieving Jews at Kadesh did not enter their rest. But there is still a rest available, because it involves God's creation.

In vv 4-5 the author makes plain the connection between God creating the world and then resting on the seventh day. This is connected with what happened at Kadesh.

Verse 4 is a quote of Gen 2:2 which states God finished His creation of the universe. He **rested** when He was finished. Verse 5 quotes from Psalm 95, which said that the unbelieving Jews would not enter into God's **rest**. The Jews did not experience God's kind of rest.

But what kind of rest did God experience in Genesis 2? Clearly it was a rest **from all His works**. God finished His work and then rested from them. The Jews at Kadesh were called to finish their work and then rest. They did not finish their work; therefore they could not rest after doing so! All God's people are called to finish the work God has given them (see v 10 below).

Christians, whether the original readers of Hebrews or today, also have work to do. We must trust in God during that work.

When we take into consideration the creation of the world in Genesis 2, we get the picture of God's rest. God created the world and placed man over it to rule it (Gen 1:27-31). God rested from His work. When man rules over God's creation, he is sharing in this rest. When man does not rule over God's creation, he does not share in God's rest. To be one of Christ's partners in the world to come is to rule over God's works with Him. It is to experience the rest of God. To withdraw from Christ is to lose this experience. Since God's rest involves the creation of the world, it has been available to His people ever since He created it.

All God's people are *offered* the rest of God. **Some** will **enter it**. The Jews at Kadesh **did not enter** it **because of disobedience**. But the rest still exists. In the **day** of **David** the opportunity was there. David wrote about four hundred years after the incident at Kadesh. **Today** the offer is being made. It is always "today" for God's people.

The readers of Hebrews should not have supposed that this rest was not for them (4:1). The offer was still valid in their day. But the warning of Psalm 95 was valid as well. If they **hardened** their hearts by disobedience, neither would they enter God's rest. The author reminds them that the OT makes it clear that the rest of God is available to them (vv 8-10).

If the readers thought that this rest only involved the earthly Promised Land, the author tells them that is not the case. Joshua 22:4 and 23:1 says that **Joshua** defeated the enemies in the land and gave the Jews **rest**.

But the rest that the author of Hebrews is talking about is not the same. If it were, God **would not have spoken of another day** when the rest would be offered. His point here is that if Joshua had fulfilled the promise of God's rest, David would not have offered it to the people of his day four hundred years later.

The rest that Joshua provided was only temporary. In later years, the Jews would be driven from their land by the Assyrians and Babylonians. The rest that David speaks of in Psalm 95 is more than the temporary possession of the earthly land of Canaan. The land that faithful believers will rule over is eternal (1:8-12). All of Christ's enemies will be defeated forever (1:13), and He will rule from an eternal Jerusalem.

But this rest is future. To obtain it, a believer must hold firm to the end (3:14). No matter when a believer lives, **there remains a rest for the people of God** (v 9). Once again, this rest cannot refer to having eternal life. The believer already has that.

In this light we should add another note about the disobedient Jews at Kadesh. As already mentioned, the people of Israel at Kadesh are an illustration of believers. No doubt, many of them actually were believers, but because of their disobedience they paid a high price. Not only did they lose their inheritance in the earthly Canaan, they also lost their eternal inheritance in the eternal kingdom of God. While all believers at Kadesh Barnea will be in Christ's kingdom, they will not rule over it with Him.

In whatever time a believer lives, only those who have **ceased from his works** will **enter** God's **rest**. Believers must persevere in God-pleasing works in order to obtain this future rest. Yet again, we see that the rest here is not the same as going to heaven. Going to heaven is a free gift and does not involve works at all. But the rest offered here requires works. God's work in creation and His rest afterward are the pattern we are to follow.

Verse 11 also makes it clear that the rest described in chapters 3–4 is not the same as being saved and going to heaven.

To enter into God's rest, not only must the believer complete his work, he must **be diligent**. The idea of diligence involves concentrating on a goal. The believer is already saved from hell at the moment of faith. But there is a goal to the Christian life. That goal is to remain faithful to God and to continue in good works until the end. This will involve great reward. The goal of the Christian life is not simply going to heaven. The goal is the rest with God in the completion of our works and to reign with Christ in the world to come. It is to actually inherit a portion of that world.

But a Christian can miss that goal. Notice once again the author includes himself in this possibility of failure. He says that he, as well as his readers, needs to seek this goal—**Let us be diligent**. He or his readers may **fall**.

The word *fall* is the same word used in 3:17 to describe how the bodies of the unfaithful Jews at Kadesh fell in the wilderness. It involves the idea that God will judge His people who prove to be unfaithful. They will experience loss.

Even though a Christian cannot lose eternal life, he can experience another kind of loss if he follows the **same example of disobedience**. Christians can do the same thing the people of God did at Kadesh. God judges the disobedience of His people, regardless of the age in which they live.

The Jews at Kadesh fell under God's judgment, and since Christians can experience the same kind of judgment, the author tells us how that judgment is carried out. It is by the **word of God** (v 12).

The word **for** connects this verse with what was just said. There is a reason the readers needed to be diligent to enter into God's rest: **the word of God is living and powerful**.

God's **word is living** in the sense that it is applicable to all generations. Even though Kadesh occurred thousands of years ago, and David wrote his warning in the Psalms thousands of years ago as well, these admonitions are for Christians today since they are contained in the Word of God.

The Word of God is powerful because it produces results. It encourages, challenges, and warns people today. But it is also powerful because it pronounces judgment on God's wayward people.

God's word pronounced judgment on the Jews at Kadesh. He swore that they would not enter into the rest that was their inheritance. The Word of God says that the disobedient Christian will not enter His rest either.

The idea of judgment is certainly contained in the comment that the Word of God is **sharper than any two-edged sword**. It is sharp in the sense that it can penetrate into even **the thoughts** of a believer. The author describes the Word of God as able to penetrate into the innermost being of the child of God—into his **soul and spirit**. The **joints and marrow** of a human being are an illustration of the inner part of a man.

It may be that the author is making a distinction between the **soul** and the **spirit** of a man. Sometimes the adjectival form of the word *soul* is used to describe the flesh, as in 1 Cor 2:14. The *spirit* here could be a reference to the Spirit of God. If that is the case, the author is saying the Word of God is able to expose what is done by the flesh and what is done by the Spirit of God.

The point here is that the Word of God can, like a surgeon's knife, go into areas that cannot be seen with the eyes. It can discern the *thoughts and* **intents of the heart**. That is, the Word of God can expose the motives of a person.

Are my actions the result of the flesh, or are they motivated by the Spirit? For the original readers, perhaps they were saying to themselves that the reason they were contemplating abandoning Christianity was because they would be able to better serve God in the Jewish religion. They would be free from persecution and have more material means to serve God. They might even have argued that since the God of the OT and the God the NT was the same, it did not matter if they served Him the way they did in the OT. One could even argue that the Jewish religion was older than Christianity and was therefore better.

But the Word of God has the ability to expose the truth. It can reveal that the real motivation of such thinking was not to serve God better. It was to avoid any discomfort that might come as a result of being faithful to Christ. Christians are always susceptible to rationalizing their sins. There is always a danger of seeking the approval of the world and saying that we can better reach the world for God if we do so. We tell ourselves that if we are more acceptable to the world, the world will be more likely to listen to us. In reality, we want the approval of the world and the comfort it brings. The Word of God cuts to the chase and exposes our real motives.

In v 13 the author continues the idea that the Word of God is able to expose what cannot be seen. Before God, **no creature** is **hidden**. We cannot hide our motives and thoughts from Him. That is why we must be diligent to do what He has told us to do. We cannot hide from Him in any way.

In fact, we are **naked and open** to Him. The idea of being *naked* before somebody is that he sees everything about us. The word *open* is a little more complicated. It is sometimes translated "laid bare" or "helpless." It had a technical meaning because it was used to describe a wrestling hold in which a wrestler would grab his opponent by the neck and render him helpless. This idea finds further support in that first century wrestlers would battle one another naked.

The point here is that before God and His Word, the Christian is completely helpless and naked. He sees everything about us. This is critical, because it is God **to whom we must give account**. We must do that with the One from whom we can hide nothing—not our works, not our motives, not even our thoughts.

There is a play on words here in v 13. The word **account** in Greek is the word "word." We will one day have a "word" with God. The Word of God (v 12) leaves us naked before the One who will have His word with us (v 13).

But when will this take place? It could be that the author is referring to this life. God's Word exposes our disobedience and lack of faith. It tells us that we are open to the judgment of God as a result of these things here and now. The Word of God convicts us of these things. In addition, we see how the Jews at Kadesh experienced the judgment of the Word of God when they died in the wilderness.

However, the author may be saying that God will have His word with us at the Judgment Seat of Christ (1 Cor 3:10-15; 2 Cor 5:10). On that day Christians will either be rewarded or lose rewards based upon their works. This judgment will include the motives of one's heart (1 Cor 4:5). An unfavorable judgment would involve the loss of the rest discussed in chapter 3-4.

One could argue either position from the context of Hebrews 3-4. The Word of God judges in the present and will judge in the future. In my opinion, since the author is focusing on the loss of rest, I think the emphasis is on the future judgment of believers at the Judgment Seat of Christ.

Chapters 3-4 contain a long warning passage. The warning itself has ended with somewhat terrifying verses. We are exposed to the Judgment of God and His Word. It is impossible to hide from Him. He knows everything about us. What we can hide from others and even ourselves, we cannot hide from Him. Where can we go and what can we do to experience a favorable verdict from Him? How can I remain faithful and be a partner with Christ and reign with Him? This is the idea with which chapter 4 ends. It is the same idea with which this warning passage began (3:1). We have a High Priest to help us.

Conclusion to the Warning Passage (4:14-16)

After the terrifying words in 4:12-13, the author of Hebrews ends this warning passage with a message of **mercy**. Because of our **High Priest**, the believer does not have to experience the negative judgment of

God. In that Priest, we have all the help we could possibly need. He will help believers obtain the promised rest if they will come to Him.

As chapter 3 stated, we are part of the worshiping house of God over which Jesus Christ presides. The readers have been warned that they could fall under God's judgment. They would do that if they withdrew from that house by going back to Judaism. Here, however, is the remedy.

Our primary resource in obtaining the rest promised to believers is **Jesus the Son of God**. He is the Son of God, as chapter 1 stated. He will rule forever over God's kingdom. He is the King. The name *Jesus* reflects that He is also human, as chapter 2 stated. As a human, He can represent us before God as our High Priest.

Because our Representative is so great, the author says, **let us hold fast our confession**. This is a call for the readers to hold on to their Christian faith. A couple of details need to be pointed out. Failure is possible. This is what happened with the people of God at Kadesh. The very idea that they needed to **hold fast** states that effort is involved. In addition, the author once again includes himself in the possibility of failure.

It is also clear once again that the author is exhorting Christians. Christ is the High Priest only for Christians. And, once again, we see that the author is not talking about how a person "goes to heaven." He is talking about a reward that involves *holding on*. Eternal life, on the other hand, is a free gift.

But the One who is there to help us is not only God. He has also **passed through the heavens**. He is in the very presence of God the Father, interceding for us.

But if a believer is struggling, if he is having difficulty holding on or being diligent to enter into God's rest, what will he find if he goes to Jesus? As the King, as God, as the One who has passed through the heavens, how can He understand what an ordinary Christian goes through?

In v 15 the author tells us that in Christ **we have a High Priest** who can **sympathize with our weaknesses**. As great as He is, He knows what we are going through. He can do that because He became a man and went through everything His children go through (2:17-18). He knows what it is like to be human. He was **tempted as we are**. He knows what it is like to go through difficulties; the temptation is not to remain faithful to God during such times. He even knows what it is like to face death as the result of being faithful to God.

The difference between us and our High Priest is that He went through these things **without sin**. Because He never sinned, He felt the full power of sin's temptation. Only the One who has never sinned has felt the full force of temptation. When a person sins, he gives in to the temptation before it was fully felt. Since He is the only One to have never sinned, He is now able to understand the weaknesses we have when we are tempted to fall away.

He is sympathetic toward us. He is all-powerful. The only logical thing to do is to go **boldly** to Him (v 16). Christians have the privilege of worshiping Christ in His house and coming to Him whenever we want or need. We can come boldly to Him because we know that He knows what we are experiencing, and He has the ability to meet our needs.

And that is exactly what we find. Even though He is God, when we come to Him we find Him on a **throne of grace**. By the word *throne* we are reminded that He is the King of the world to come. He is sovereign over everything.

But this throne is characterized by grace. With the One on the throne we find **mercy and help**. Even though it is the throne of the King of the universe, He is willing to help. He will give His people the grace to endure whatever comes their way, or in mercy lessen their difficulties.

They can do that in their **time of need**. All Christians have times of need. Certainly the original readers were going through trials. All have periods of weaknesses (v 15). Our High Priest is always available to meet whatever temptation, trial, or need we have.

With this concluding message of grace we can understand this long warning passage in chapters 3–4. The readers were in danger of rejecting their faith because of the difficulties they were facing. But they belonged to a worshiping house with a Great High Priest. As long as they kept their Christian confession and remained in that house by worshiping with other believers, they could come before Him to find all the help they needed. He is there to keep us from abandoning our faith. He is there to keep us from the same mistake made by the people of God at Kadesh.

When faced with trials, enemies, persecutions, or difficulties of any type, the believer should not flee from God in an attempt to find relief from such things. Instead, he should draw near to His throne of grace and to this High Priest. Because He is gracious and all-powerful, in our times of need we find in Him all the help we need.

With this warning passage, the author has reminded us again that the King of the world to come is our High Priest. This topic will be the theme of chapters 5–10.

Christ Has Met All the Requirements for Being Our High Priest

WHEN WE COME TO Hebrews chapter 5, we begin a new section in the book. It will run from chapters 5–10. In the first part of the book, chapters 1–4, the emphasis has been on Jesus as the Son, that is, the King; He will inherit the coming kingdom of God. While all believers will be in His kingdom, only those believers who remain faithful to Him will share in that inheritance. They will reign with Him.

Now the author turns to another office that Jesus holds. He has just mentioned it at the close of chapter 4—Jesus is also our High Priest. The two offices of King and High Priest are related. If a believer wants to reign with the King, he must go to his High Priest. This High Priest will enable him to reach that goal or heavenly calling, ruling with Christ (3:1).

As the author begins his discussion of Jesus as our High Priest, the first thing he discusses is the requirements for being a high priest. If Christ is going to help us as our High Priest (4:14-16), He must be qualified to do so by meeting these requirements. Here we see that Christ has met them all.

The Requirements for Being a High Priest (5:1-4)

¹ **For every high priest taken from among men is appointed for men in things *pertaining* to God, that he may offer both gifts and sacrifices for sins. ² He can have compassion on those who are ignorant and going astray, since he himself is also subject to weakness. ³ Because of this he is required as for the people, so also for himself, to offer *sacrifices* for**

**sins. ⁴ And no man takes this honor to himself, but he who is
called by God, just as Aaron *was*.**

As we have seen, the author is writing to people who come from a
Jewish background. They know the OT, so the author turns to the OT to
discuss the requirements for a Jewish man to serve as **high priest**.

The first requirement is that the high priest had to be human.
He had to be **taken from among men** because he was to serve as a
representative for other human beings. Specifically, he represents other
men in **things pertaining to God**. In other words, the high priest acts as
man's representative before God.

In the OT, the high priest had a responsibility toward God; it was
that he must **offer both gifts and sacrifices for sins** to God. The word
gift probably refers to the OT offerings that did not include blood, such
as the meal or flour offerings. The *sacrifices* would be those that involved
the blood of an animal. The high priest performed a sacrificial role for
those he represented.

Verse 2 mentions another requirement for the high priest in the OT.
He must have **compassion** on those he represented. While he did not
condone sin, he could not let pride or disgust over the sins of the people
keep him from performing his duties as the representative of the people.

Those on whom he had to have compassion are called those who
are ignorant and going astray. In the OT there were two kinds of sin.
One was committed by a person in the nation of Israel who was in open
rebellion against God. These sins were dealt with in a different way
(Num 15:30-31). But when a person sinned because he did not know
what he was doing (**ignorant**) or because he was weak (**going astray**), he
could come to the priest to find forgiveness.

The reason the high priest was to have compassion on such people
is because **he himself is also subject to weakness**. The Greek word for
subject has the basic meaning of being surrounded. The high priest could
have compassion on the weak sinner because he was a weak sinner, too.

And because the high priest was a sinner himself, there was another
requirement he had to meet if he was going to represent other sinners
before God. He had to take care of the issue of sin for **the people** and
also for himself (v 3). He had to **offer sacrifices for** the **sins** of both.

The author of Hebrews has the Day of Atonement in mind here.
On that day, the high priest would enter into the Holy of Holies in the

tabernacle to offer a sacrifice for the sins of the people for the whole year. However, before he did, he had to offer a sacrifice for his own sins (Leviticus 16), reminding him that he, too, was a sinner in need of forgiveness. Therefore, he could have compassion on the people when they sinned.

The final requirement for a high priest is found in v 4. In v 1 the author had said the high priest must be **appointed**, and here he spells out what that means. No man **takes** the **honor** of being the high priest by his own decision. Instead, he is **called by God** to this position. God chooses who will be the high priest.

From the very beginning this was the case. **Aaron** was the first high priest. God chose him. After Aaron, only his descendants could legitimately be high priests.

These then are the requirements for being a high priest: he had to be appointed by God; be a man; have compassion on those whom he represented before God; and offer sacrifices for his own sins as well as the sins of the people. Since the author has just said that Christ is our High Priest, the natural question is: did Christ meet all these requirements?

Christ Is Fully Qualified to Be Our High Priest (5:5-10)

⁵ **So also Christ did not glorify Himself to become High Priest, but** *it was* **He who said to Him:**

> *"You are My Son,*
> *Today I have begotten You."*

⁶ **As He also says in another place:**

> *"You are a priest forever*
> *According to the order of Melchizedek";*

⁷ **who, in the days of His flesh, when He had offered up prayers and supplications, with vehement cries and tears to Him who was able to save Him from death, and was heard because of His godly fear,** ⁸ **though He was a Son,** *yet* **He learned obedience by the things which He suffered.** ⁹ **And having been perfected, He became the author of eternal salvation to all who obey Him,** ¹⁰ **called by God as High Priest** *"according to the order of Melchizedek,"*

The first requirement to be a high priest that the author takes up in reference to Christ is whether God appointed Him to that office. He says that Christ did not appoint Himself to this position. He did not **glorify Himself** by becoming **High Priest** (v 5). Even though He was the Son, greater than any angel, He did not use this position to make Himself High Priest as well. Instead, God the Father appointed Him to the office of High Priest.

To make that case, the author quotes from the OT. He reminds us of the main point of chapters 1-4, that is, that Jesus is the King of the world to come. And it is God who appointed Him to that position. He once again quotes from Ps 2:7 which says that God called Jesus "**My Son.**" As has already been seen, the word "Son" means that He is the King.

Then in v 6 the author quotes from Ps 110:4. This reference is the central verse in the whole discussion about Christ as our High Priest. In that Psalm God says of the Messiah, "**You are a priest forever.**" Not only did God appoint Christ as the King/Son, He also appointed Him to be a Priest. By the calling of God, Christ is both King and High Priest.

The fact that Christ has both offices is seen in the example of another OT person—**Melchizedek**. The author will later discuss how the mysterious person of Melchizedek was both a king and priest.

The idea that Christ holds both offices introduces an important concept for the author of Hebrews, one he will discuss at great length. Among the Jews, a man could not be both a high priest and a king. High priests came from the tribe of Levi, while since the time of David kings were to come from the tribe of Judah. If Christ was both, He was greater than any Jewish high priest.

We also see that He is greater because He was appointed a High Priest **forever**. No Jewish high priest could make that claim. All of them died and therefore had to be replaced. None of them served forever.

But there are other requirements to be a high priest. As mentioned in 5:1, the high priest had to offer sacrifices. Jesus met this requirement when He **offered** up sacrifices to God (v 7). The same word for *offered* is used here in v 7 and in v 1.

It is said that Jesus offered **up prayers and supplications**. It is interesting that for the author of Hebrews, prayers are a type of sacrifice (13:15). The Greek word for *supplication* refers to prayers from someone who humbly asks God for something. But when did Christ do that, and what did He ask for?

While we could say that Christ offered up prayers during His whole life, the remainder of v 7 suggests the author has a particular time in mind. It was when Christ offered up prayers **to Him who was able to save Him from death**. It is described as a time when Christ offered this prayer with **cries and tears**.

Obviously the One who could **save Him** is a reference to His Father. One is reminded that Christ wept tears like blood in the Garden of Gethsemane. But it would be a mistake to limit this description only to His time in the garden. It would include His time on the cross of Calvary. That was certainly a time of tears as well. On the cross Jesus was **heard**. This was the case even though Christ died on the cross. We know His Father heard Him because He raised Him from the dead. His Father saved Him from death in this way.

The sacrifices Christ offered to the Father included more than His prayers on the night and day in which He died. He also offered Himself in the midst of these cries and prayers. It was this sacrifice that purified the sins of His people (1:3; 2:11).

It is clear that His prayers were heard and His sacrifices were accepted by God. This is seen not only in the fact that He was delivered from death in the resurrection, but also in the reason why such sacrifices were accepted by God. It was because of Christ's **godly fear**. In the Greek this phrase is only one word, which indicates a reverence or piety toward God.

Jesus was heard because He was holy. His sacrifice of Himself was acceptable to God because of the same reason. Such is our High Priest. Because of His righteousness He is able to sit at the right hand of the Father (1:13).

The Father heard the Son while the Son was on earth. Now the Son in the Father's very presence is also our High Priest. He is our representative before the Father. When He intercedes to the Father for us (4:14-16), does the Father hear Him on our behalf? The answer is obvious. The believer who goes to Christ knows that God will hear Christ's intercession for that believer.

Even though it is not a major emphasis here, the author mentions in v 7 how Christ fulfilled another requirement of being a high priest. He is a man. He comes from mankind. This is indicated by the phrase **in the days of his flesh**. The author has spent a great deal of time discussing this fact in chapter 2. Christ was able to offer up Himself in death as a sacrifice because He became a man.

And as a result, He is also able to meet the final requirement of a high priest; this is mentioned in vv 1-4. He is able to have compassion on those He represents. This was also discussed in chapter 2, but here in vv 8-9 the author expands on that idea by saying two things about Christ.

First, he says that **though He was a Son, yet He learned obedience by the things which He suffered**. Even though Jesus is the Divine King—the Son—He humbled Himself and put Himself through the things that those whom He would represent experience. He became a man so that He could *learn obedience*. He had to learn what it was like to suffer. He had to learn, experientially, what it meant while a human being to obey the Father. At Calvary, Christ experientially learned as a human what remaining faithful to God could entail. Faithfulness to God can result in death. He knows what the readers of Hebrews are going through. This type of education could only be learned by suffering, so Christ became a man in order to experience it.

As a result of this educational process on the part of Christ, we see in v 9 the second reason why Christ is able to have compassion on those He represents: Christ has **been perfected**. As many have pointed out, the idea of *perfection* often carried with it the concept of reaching a goal. Christ became a man in order to reach the goal of becoming our High Priest. As a man, He **learned** what suffering for God entailed. He experienced the cost of obedience. He knows what His people go through, and that was the *goal*. He is now fully qualified to represent us before God. He has met all the requirements of being a High Priest, as listed in vv 1-4. He is now our *perfect* high priest.

Since He is that kind of High Priest, He **became the author of eternal salvation to all who obey Him** (v 9). The word *salvation* should be understood in the same way as it was used in 2:3. In the Book of Hebrews it does not mean salvation from hell, but means to remain faithful to Christ in this world and to reign with Him when He returns. Eternal life is given as a free gift through faith alone. The *salvation* here involves obedience to Christ—one must *obey* Him to obtain it, so he cannot be talking about salvation from hell. In chapter 10 we will see that the author of Hebrews uses another word to describe salvation from hell.

As the context shows, this **salvation** is possible because Christ is a person's High Priest. Christ is the High Priest only of believers. Believers already have eternal life and won't go to hell. Now they can go to Him to obtain another kind of salvation. This is a salvation that He offers as our High Priest. Just as Christ was delivered from His trials at the cross, so He can deliver His people through their trials.

He is the **author** of this salvation because He paved the way. He was obedient to the Father, and the Father exalted Him to the position of extreme and eternal authority at His right hand (1:13). As chapter 2 stated, He is our Captain who is leading His children. But they must draw near to Him (4:14-16) to find the help they need. He knows what it is like to suffer for righteousness' sake and will lead His children through it if they come to Him.

This section on the High Priesthood of Christ ends by saying that He was **called by God** to this position. This, of course, takes us back to v 6—God declared in Psalm 110 the Messiah as our High Priest. We are reminded that God made Him our High Priest and that He is perfectly acceptable to the Father in that role.

But as the author also said in v 6, Christ is a **High Priest** different from those found in the OT system. He is like **Melchizedek**. There are many things that need to be said about this topic. If the Christian readers were going to obtain the **salvation** Christ offered to them and reign in the world to come as His partners, they needed to understand and apply these things. However, the author is not sure they can. The reason is because they have a spiritual problem. This leads to another warning in the book.

Introduction to the Warning (5:11-14)

The first two warning passages in 2:1-4 and chapters 3–4 were general in nature. In this warning, however, the author tells the readers directly that they are at fault. They are in danger of losing their reward because their spiritual condition is not what it should be.

> [11] **of whom we have much to say, and hard to explain, since you have become dull of hearing.** [12] **For though by this time you ought to be teachers, you need someone to teach you again the first principles of the oracles of God; and you**

have come to need milk and not solid food. ¹³ For everyone who partakes only of milk is unskilled in the word of righteousness, for he is a babe. ¹⁴ But solid food belongs to those who are of full age, that is, those who by reason of use have their senses exercised to discern both good and evil.

The author has **much to say** about how Christ is a High Priest like Melchizedek. But there are a couple of obstacles in front of him. The first is that the things he wants to say are **hard to explain**. Melchizedek was a difficult subject because he is rarely mentioned in the Bible and so little is known of him. In fact, Hebrews is the only NT book that even mentions him. The Jews of the first century also found him hard to understand because Abraham, the father of the nation chosen by God to bless the whole world, acknowledged that Melchizedek was greater than he was. How could that be?

But the biggest obstacle in talking about Christ and Melchizedek was the readers themselves. They **have become dull of hearing**. The tense of the verb *become* tells us this condition is not something they are by nature. Instead, they have fallen into this condition and they are remaining in it. In other words, they were not always like this. We are reminded of the first warning passage (2:1-4). If believers are not careful, they can drift away from spiritual truth and health.

The fact is they were spiritually unhealthy. That is the meaning of the word *dull*. They had become ill in their hearing of sound spiritual doctrine. This has happened over a period of time, after they became believers. Therefore, a discussion of the spiritual truths of Christ's Melchizedekian priesthood would be hard to understand. It would be like explaining high school math to a five year old.

The author has indicated that Christ's High Priesthood is superior to that of the OT high priests. The readers needed to know the advantages that Christ had for them. It would keep them from drifting away and going back to Judaism and the old system of priests. It would prevent them from losing eternal rewards. However, their sick spiritual condition meant they might not be able to understand what they needed to know.

In these verses the readers are given the reason for this sick spiritual condition. They had been Christians for some time (maybe ten to twenty years), but had not progressed. They had been Christians long enough that **by this time** they **ought to** have been **teachers** (v 12). That was what was expected of them.

However, they needed somebody **to teach** them the **first principles** of God's Word. That is, they needed to be reminded of the basics. They needed to be taught these things **again**. They have neglected what they already knew (2:1-4).

Once again we see that the warning passages in Hebrews are addressed to Jewish Christians who were considering abandoning the Christian faith and going back to Judaism and animal sacrifices. They had once understood the basics. They should have progressed in their Christian living. This can only be said of Christians. This is important because this is the introduction to the warning passage that runs through the end of chapter 6, and many have felt that the author is not talking about real Christians.

The things that they needed to understand about Christ and Melchizedek involved **solid food**, spiritually speaking. These things were more than the basics of Christianity. But these readers, unfortunately, found themselves in the infant stage even though they had been Christians a long time. They were baby Christians.

In vv 13-14 the author continues his discussion of spiritual food. He gives an illustration of the Christian life. Such a life should be like the physical life of a child. The **babe** in Christ, that is, a new Christian, can only drink **milk**, just as a newborn baby drinks only milk.

The reason a new Christian can only understand the basics, or the milk, of God's Word is because he **is unskilled**. He has not put the things he knows into practice. He lacks the experience necessary to understand more complex truths, like the Melchizedekian priesthood of Christ.

This lack of experience involves the **word of righteousness**. It is difficult to determine if the author of Hebrews is talking about the moral teachings of the Bible or about doctrine. In any event, it refers to how a Christian is to live. A new Christian simply does not know how to respond and act in certain circumstances.

The knowledge of these things takes time. A babe in Christ is not expected to know them. But after a period of time, as the new Christian puts the truths he knows into practice, he is able to take in more **solid food** (v 14). He does this by making **use** of what he knows. The word *use* means "to make it a habit." He makes it a habit of putting God's Word to use in his life.

This habit is one in which the believer's **senses** are **exercised**. His spiritual ability to see and understand things is strengthened by putting into practice what he knows from the Word of God.

Through this process the believer becomes more mature, or **full age**. Such spiritual growth is just like the growth of a human baby. At first he drinks only milk; he puts this food to work and through physical exercise grows and is able to take in solid food.

The new believer can only take in the milk of God's Word. He often does not know how to act or even when he is confronted with bad doctrine. But the Christian does not have to stay in that condition. He can grow and become skilled in God's Word through time and experience.

It is clear that the problem with the original readers of Hebrews is that they have not done that, i.e., taken in God's Word and acted upon it. Just as a baby who does not eat and exercise will become sick, so have they, but in regard to spiritual growth. Since they have not progressed, they are in danger of regressing in their faith. Because of their continued spiritual immaturity, they were even in danger of renouncing Christianity and going back to Judaism. They were not able to **discern** between **good** doctrine and **evil** doctrine. Some of them were not able to understand the stark differences between Judaism and Christianity. In addition, they were faced with persecution for their faith. In times like that, spiritual immaturity is especially dangerous.

This explains why the author of Hebrews has repeatedly told them to hold on to their Christian faith (3:6, 14; 4:11). They were in danger of making the wrong decisions because the ability to make the right decisions often depends on spiritual maturity. Such maturity keeps believers from making poor decisions in regard to morality (how to live) and doctrine (what to believe). In the case of the readers of Hebrews, they were in danger of choosing wrong doctrine. One cannot expect a baby to make the right decisions. The same is true for a babe in Christ. Even if he has been a Christian for a long period of time, if he has not grown in the knowledge of God's Word and put it into practice, he cannot be expected to make the right decision. While a believer can never go to hell, the consequences of spiritual immaturity and the wrong decisions that go along with it can be serious indeed. The author drives that home in the next chapter as he continues his warning to the readers.

Application

The danger the original readers faced as a result of their spiritual immaturity was leaving the Christian faith in the face of persecution. We may not ever be faced with such a situation, but spiritual immaturity can have drastic consequences for us as well.

It is just as likely that we can make the wrong decision in the area of morality. An immature believer often does this and does not understand why such decisions are important. In light of the Book of Hebrews, if a Christian remains in the state of spiritual immaturity and makes such decisions, he, too, will suffer the loss of rewards and will experience the discipline of God in his life.

This is especially important because the Word of God is vital to our spiritual growth. It keeps us from experiencing negative consequences. But we need to be honest with ourselves. What is the level of sound Biblical teaching and the grasp of that teaching among Christians today? How many understand what the High Priesthood of Christ means to us and how it relates to Melchizedek? Even though our circumstances are very different from the original readers of Hebrews, these warning passages are directly relevant. Chapter 6 is one of the strongest warning passages in the NT. Buckle up.

The Third Warning Passage

As previously mentioned, Heb 5:11-14 introduces the third warning passage in the Book of Hebrews. In those verses the author specifically says that the readers have failed in their Christian living because they have not gone on to maturity. Here in chapter 6 the author tells them to press on to such maturity (6:1-3), what will happen if they fall back (6:4-8), and then gives them another call to hold fast to their hope (6:9-12). At the end of the chapter, he concludes this warning.

Go on to Maturity (6:1-3)

¹ **Therefore, leaving the discussion of the elementary** *principles* **of Christ, let us go on to perfection, not laying again the foundation of repentance from dead works and of faith toward God,** ² **of the doctrine of baptisms, of laying on of hands, of resurrection of the dead, and of eternal judgment.** ³ **And this we will do if God permits.**

The author had just spoken of the fundamentals of the faith (5:12). Here in 6:1-3 he gives examples of such "milk" of the Word. He wants his readers to go past these and press on to maturity.

He refers to the fundamentals as the **elementary principles of Christ**. These believers had been in their state of immaturity too long. Now they needed to **go on to perfection**. Clearly this is a call to go on to solid food (5:11-14). Part of that solid food is the discussion of the Melchizedekian priesthood of Christ that the author will take up in the next chapter.

Once again the author includes himself in this exhortation when he says, **let us** do it. As with the other warning passages, we see he is talking to Christians. Only Christians can go on to maturity in their Christian walk. You cannot grow in life if you don't have life in the first place. A baby cannot grow until after he is born!

The verb *go* in v 1 literally means "to be carried along." It seems most likely that the author means that God will carry them along to maturity if they will draw near to God through their High Priest Jesus Christ (4:14-16). If they did they would be able to discern between good and evil doctrine and not forsake Christianity and go back to Judaism.

But the word *perfection* probably also means more than maturity. This perfection is the goal of the Christian life. The goal of the Christian is not only "to go to heaven." The Christian already has that guarantee! Our goal is to be found pleasing to God and rule with Christ in His kingdom. To obtain this goal, the Christian must mature and obey the Lord.

To do that the readers needed to go beyond the basics. The author lists some of these basics. The reason he gives these examples is because they showed the difference between Christianity and Judaism. The readers needed to be able to discern between what was evil (what Judaism taught about these things) and what was good (what Christianity taught about these things, 5:14).

If they rejected the fundamentals of Christianity and returned to Judaism, they would lay **again** a **foundation**. If they went back to Judaism, they would need to be instructed again in the very basics of Christianity. They would have to start from the very beginning.

The first basic principle the author lists is **repentance from dead works**. When they practiced the Jewish religion, they attempted to gain acceptance before God by works of the Law and the sacrifices that the OT required. But all of these are dead in the sense that they cannot bring life. Christianity taught them that Christ put an end to all the rituals and that the Law cannot give life. Only the Spirit can.

This life is given by the second fundamental listed here. It is **faith toward God**. To believe in God is to believe in the One He sent, Jesus Christ (John 12:44).

To forsake the fundamentals of Christianity would lead to a need to return to those fundamentals. They would need to turn from, that is, repent from the fundamentals of Judaism. They had already done that once when they became believers. If they returned to Judaism and wanted to please God, they would have to do it **again**. They would have to be taught *again* that life is given by faith, not works of any kind. All the practices of Judaism were of no benefit spiritually.

In v 2 we find other fundamentals of the faith involved in a return to Judaism. One is the issue of **baptisms**. It is interesting that the word is in the plural. In the NT there is more than one kind of baptism. There is the baptism of John the Baptist, Christian water baptism, and the baptism of the Holy Spirit for example. An understanding of these things belongs to the basic doctrines of the Church.

Judaism also had more than one baptism. When a Gentile became a Jew, there was a baptism for that. There were also many other kinds of baptisms that involved cleansings associated with serving in the Temple or if a person became defiled by doing something like touching a dead body (Num 19:13; Heb 9:10).

The same thing was true about teachings concerning the **laying on of hands** (Lev 1:4; 3:2; 4:4; 8:14, etc.; Num 27:18, 23). In the Book of Acts, at least, the Apostles did it on occasion in order for some people to receive the Holy Spirit (Acts 8:17; 9:17; 19:6). In other instances the church laid hands on people chosen by God for a certain task (Acts 13:3; 1 Tim 5:22). Judaism also laid hands on people in designating them for certain positions (Num 8:10; 27:18-23; Deut 34:9).

There was also a great deal of difference between Judaism and Christianity when it came to teachings on the **resurrection of the dead and eternal judgment**. These were among the first teachings a new Christian would receive. The NT teaches that Christians will experience a resurrection of the physical body and salvation from an eternal hell. Their resurrected bodies will be physical but glorified (1 Corinthians 15). All of this was brought about by faith in Christ alone.

Judaism, of course, taught different things, and different Jews had various views. Whatever strand of Judaism the readers were contemplating joining would have had one such view that differed from Christianity. Some, such as the Pharisees, believed in a resurrection, but not glorified bodies. They probably did not believe in an eternal hell. The Sadducees did not believe in a resurrection or hell. Some, no doubt, believed in a kind of spiritual heaven, without bodies. Some Jews, based upon Hebrews 1, evidently believed that this spiritual heaven was going to be ruled by angels.

The basic point of the first two verses of chapter 6 is that Judaism and Christianity differed when it came to the fundamentals of religious instructions. If a believer returned to the teachings of Judaism, he could not press on to maturity because these things involved the very foundations of growth.

Verse 3 tells us that the author wants his readers to mature. The words **this we will do** take us back to v 1 and the call to do just that. The author includes himself in this exhortation once again. It is obviously not a call to be saved from hell, but to leave the fundamentals behind and move forward. But this progress to maturity is only possible by the power of **God**, as He **permits** it to occur.

But there is something that is not possible. In the next few verses we are told what that is. These verses in the NT contain some of the most sobering words addressed to Christians.

The Consequences of Falling Back (6:4-8)

> [4] **For** *it is* **impossible for those who were once enlightened, and have tasted the heavenly gift, and have become partakers of the Holy Spirit,** [5] **and have tasted the good word of God and the powers of the age to come,** [6] **if they fall away, to renew them again to repentance, since they crucify again for themselves the Son of God, and put** *Him* **to an open shame.** [7] **For the earth which drinks in the rain that often comes upon it, and bears herbs useful for those by whom it is cultivated, receives blessing from God;** [8] **but if it bears thorns and briers,** *it is* **rejected and near to being cursed, whose end** *is* **to be burned.**

The author has just told his readers to press on to maturity and leave the basics behind. That is a possibility for them. But there is another possibility as well. Instead of going forward, they can **fall away** (v 6). If they did not mature, they might not be able to discern between good teaching and bad, and do just that.

These verses have been hotly debated for centuries. The two main issues involved in the discussion are: to whom is the author referring, and what is the punishment for those who fall away?

In vv 4–6 the author describes to whom he is referring. First, he says they have been **enlightened**. The passive form of the verb *enlightened* means that this enlightenment was caused by someone else. This most naturally means that God through His Spirit brought this about.

This enlightenment is also most naturally taken to refer to when a person comes to faith in Christ. The only other time the word is used in Hebrews is to describe the readers' experience of coming to faith, their salvation experience, in 10:32. In other places in Scriptures, coming to faith in Christ—becoming a believer and receiving eternal life—is described as enlightenment or coming to light (John 12:46; 9:39; 2 Cor 4:4-7; 1 Pet 2:9).

This first description of these people indicates that the author is talking to people who are Christians. He is not talking to people who only claimed to be believers. This certainly agrees with what we have seen throughout the book. In the other warning passages, the author includes himself in the warnings; he calls them *holy brothers*, he tells them that Christ is their High Priest and that it is possible to drift away from the truth they already have. The OT example he gives of this in chapters 3–4 involved the people of God who *fell away* at Kadesh Barnea.

The rest of the description of these people supports the fact that these are true Christians. They have also **tasted the heavenly gift**. The verb *tasted* is said by some to simply mean "to be exposed to something," or to smell it. This view is held by those who say that the author is not taking about real Christians. They have only been exposed to the gospel of eternal life in Christ but have not really taken it in or really experienced it. They have *smelled* it but haven't really *eaten* it. They have heard the words but have not believed them.

The problem with that view is that the word occurs fifteen times in the NT, and it never has that meaning. Most of the time the word refers to eating food or drinking liquid or to the experience of death (Luke 9:27; John 8:52). When a person experiences death, he actually dies!

Other than here in vv 4–5, the only other time the word occurs in Hebrews is 2:9. It says that *Christ tasted death on the cross*. No one would say that Christ only caught the scent of death, but didn't really experience it on that occasion.

Whoever the author is describing has actually taken in or experienced the heavenly gift. In a letter written to holy brethren (3:1), these words would certainly be taken to refer to eternal life. Such life is given as a free gift by God's grace and comes down from heaven (John 4:10; Eph 2:8; Jas 1:17-18; in Jesus' conversation with Nicodemus in John 3:3, the Lord tells him the new birth comes from *above*).

These people have also **become partakers of the Holy Spirit**. The word *partaker* is the same word as used in 1:9; 3:1, 14. It describes those who are close associates with Christ. In fact, it is the partakers who are called *holy brethren* in 3:1. They are holy because they have been sanctified by the blood of Christ (2:11).

These people are not only partners with Christ, they are also partners with the Holy Spirit. Of course this makes sense if these people are believers. The Holy Spirit lives within every believer forever. At faith, a believer is sealed by the Spirit of God as God's possession (Eph 1:13).

Not only have these readers tasted of the heavenly gift, they have also **tasted the good word of God**. The Greek word *tasted* is the same word as that used in the previous verse. They have taken in the Word of God and found it to be good.

The closest phrase we find in the NT to this one is 1 Pet 2:3. There Peter is talking to Christians who are *newborn babes*. They should desire the milk of the Word of God so that they can grow. In the process they *taste* that the Lord is *gracious*. The word for *gracious* can mean "good," as it does in Rom 2:4 and 1 Cor 15:33.

First Peter 2:3 evidently comes from Ps 34:8. In Psalm 34 David exhorts the followers of the Lord to taste that the Lord is good. Both Peter and the author of Hebrews say this is done through the Word of God. In all three cases, it is the people of God, not unbelievers, who have this experience.

The third thing the readers have tasted is **the powers of the age to come**. The word for *powers* is the same word translated in 2:4 as *miracles*. Related to this, according to 2:4, is the work of the Holy Spirit. This would include the spiritual gifts of the Holy Spirit. The readers had seen and experienced, that is, tasted all of these things, and in them they had observed the powers of the coming kingdom of God.

Verses 4–5 describe the incredible benefits that believers have. Because of the enlightenment of the Holy Spirit, they have eternal life and are partners with the same Spirit. Through this they have also experienced what the world to come will be like. But what happens if a believer turns away from all these benefits? In v 6 the author deals with this possibility.

Many translations begin v 6 in the same way the New King James Version does: **if they fall away**. Many take the verb *fall away* to refer to apostasy or a rejection of Christianity by a believer. That is certainly the meaning here. In the Book of Hebrews the author is talking to Christians who are contemplating going back to Judaism. Because of the persecution they were facing, they were tempted to renounce Christ and go back to the safety of their old religion.

Many also take the view that a real Christian could never do that. That is why some take the view that the description of these people in vv 4–5 portrays people who are not really saved spiritually, that is, the author is talking about non-Christians. But that is simply reading one's theology into these verses. If one believes that a true Christian cannot fall away from the faith, and the author is talking about people who do just that, then the people who do it cannot be Christians. But we must take vv 4–5 at face value. He is talking about Christians.

There are some who recognize that vv 4–5 are indeed speaking about Christians, but they also believe that Christians cannot fall away from their faith, that is, apostatize. They make a big deal about the word *if* in v 6. It is maintained that the author is talking about a situation that is really impossible. He is saying that *if* a Christian were to deny the faith, he would be punished by God. But this is not possible. It would be like a person saying, *if* I could turn back time I would do this or that. But of course, I can't.

It is important to realize, however, that the word *if* does not occur in the original. The author is not talking about something impossible. There are those who have been enlightened, have tasted of the heavenly gift, and have become partners of the Holy Spirit, and have fallen away. In 10:25 he will plainly say that some have indeed done just that.

He is telling the readers to hold on to their faith (2:1; 3:13-14). They are not to drift away from the things they have heard (2:1-4; 3:13-14). They were not to remain in a state of spiritual immaturity (5:11-14). They were to go to Jesus as their High Priest for all the help they needed (4:14-16). If they did not take heed to what he was telling them, they could very well harden their hearts against God, as the people of God did at Kadesh Barnea (chapters 3–4), and fall away.

But what can be said about such a believer? Taking up from v 1, he says that it is **impossible to renew them again to repentance**. Once again we see that the author is talking to Christians. They have already *repented*. If they fall away they would need to do it *again*.

But the repentance here is not the same thing as believing in Jesus for eternal life. Repentance is not the same thing as faith. Repentance means to turn away from something. It is certainly best to take it in the same sense as in v 1. When the readers were Jewish unbelievers, they thought acceptance before God was based upon keeping the Jewish Law and rituals. When they believed in Jesus Christ for eternal life, they saw that acceptance before God was based upon faith. They had repented from the dead works of another system, that is, works that can never give life. They *repented* from trusting in the works of the Law and believed in Christ for eternal life. If they returned to Judaism and that system of worship, they would need to turn from it again.

But what can be said to such a person like that? What can another Christian say to him? The person who falls away from the faith already knows the truth. It would be impossible for us to get this person to see the error of his way and turn away from a system that cannot give life or is pleasing to God as a system of worship.

The author may be saying this. In which case, he is saying to other believers that there is nothing that the church can do for such an individual. Very few people would say that God Himself cannot do anything for this person. Even those who mistakenly say that these verses are describing someone who loses his salvation believe that person can *repent* and be saved again. *God* can certainly bring the person back.

The Apostle Paul in 1 Tim 1:19-20 describes a situation in which a believer has rejected the basics of the faith. He says that such believers are handed over to Satan in order to be disciplined. Certainly God is the One who brings this discipline about through Satan. There is nothing the church can do for those who know the truth but reject it.

It is also possible, however, that the author is saying something else. A Christian who has rejected the faith may not be able to go on to maturity. That is what the author started this warning passage with (5:11-14). It is possible to press on to maturity with the power of God and the strength that our High Priest provides. However, if we withdraw from the resources available to us as Christians, we have lost that opportunity. The dead works of Judaism cannot cause spiritual growth. The one who goes back to Judaism will need to turn from such empty works to please God. However, once again, such repentance cannot be done by another believer. The believer who has fallen away must go through the discipline of God as described in vv 7–8 that follow.

Related to this, it is possible that the author is saying that such a believer will not reign with Christ in the world to come. Even though such a believer will live with Christ forever (Heb 10:10, 14), He will not be one of Christ's partners in His Kingdom. The Jews at Kadesh Barnea lost their inheritance in the land. Later, the author will say that Esau also lost his inheritance as a result of sin (12:16-17).

It is difficult to determine exactly which of these the author means. It seems to be purposefully vague. This is probably the intent of the author. He simply wants to say that the believer who falls away will pay a heavy price. There is certainly nothing other believers can do to turn such a believer around. In addition, punishment or discipline is inevitable. The author said the same thing in very general terms in the first warning passage. How can such a believer escape punishment (2:3) when he has been given so much?

The Seriousness of Their Sin

The reason punishment is inevitable is because of the magnitude of their sin. They have crucified **again for themselves the Son of God** (v 6). In doing so, they have **put Him to an open shame**. The Romans and Jews crucified Christ, saying that He was a liar and blasphemer and therefore deserved to die the shameful death of crucifixion. When a person becomes a believer, in essence, he says that the world did not recognize that Jesus was God's anointed One.

However, when a Christian renounces his faith publicly, he is saying by his actions and words that the world's verdict of Christ was correct. Such actions are in effect placing Jesus on the cross **again**. The Christian who apostatizes hangs Christ up before the eyes of the world as One who deserved what He got. This involved the shame of the cross. In this case, this verdict is given by one who previously claimed to be a Christian.

Imagine a first century Jewish believer who walked with Christ for a time, then fell back into Judaism and animal sacrifices. By going back to animal sacrifices he would certainly be putting the Lord Jesus "to an open shame." He would be saying that the work of Christ on the cross was not finished!

And it must be remembered to Whom the Christian who falls away does this. It is the **Son of God**. In Hebrews this is the King of the world to come. This is the One who created the universe. This is the One who became a man and died to give eternal life to the believer. This is the believer's great High Priest.

It is only logical that such a step by one who had received the blessings of vv 4–5 would result in the discipline of God. Nature itself points this out.

An Illustration from Nature (vv 7-8)

The author uses an example from an agricultural practice with which the readers would have been familiar. It deals with a piece of land, that is, **the earth**. A piece of farmland can either be fruitful or unfruitful. It is important to see that there is only one piece of land here. It represents one person. In this case, it represents a believer. A believer can either be fruitful and pleasing to the Lord, or he can be unfruitful and not pleasing to the Lord.

The author speaks of a field that takes in the **rain** God gives it. It has been **cultivated** by a farmer. It is expected that such a field would be fruitful, that it will bear **herbs** that are **useful** for food. This is the crop that is expected. Such a field can be said to **receive blessing from God**.

The Christian has also received things from God. He has taken in these good things (vv 4–5). It is expected that such a person would produce spiritual fruit. If he does, then the blessing of God rests upon him as well. He can expect to grow in maturity and be a partner of Christ in the world to come.

But what if the *same* field in the illustration produces another kind of crop? The same field may indeed produce **thorns and briers**. Such a field is **rejected**. This word means "disapproved." It did not produce what was expected. Such a field is in the process of being **cursed**. This is the opposite of being blessed by God. In the end, such a field is **burned**.

Two options are laid out here: blessing or cursing. The author is giving the readers a choice. Continue with Christ and receive blessings from God. Abandon Christ and go back to Judaism and receive curses from God.

The readers would have understood this practice from agriculture. A field which produced thorns and such would be burned in order to clean out such things as well as the seeds of such bad things in the soil. The fire had a purging effect.

Up to this point in the Book of Hebrews, we see what the illustration is saying. The believer who renounces his faith is like a field that produces thorns and briers. After all the good things he has received, this is not the spiritual crop that is expected.

Every single believer has a choice. We must remember that there is only one field in the illustration and it represents only one person. It does not represent one person who is a believer and another person who is not. If a believer does not produce what is expected, he is taking a road that will result in the cursing of God. Such cursing is not hell. It is the opposite of receiving the blessing of God, as the illustration indicates.

In the OT God told His people that if they disobeyed Him they would receive many curses (Deuteronomy 27–30). None of these curses involve going to hell. They involve how God would discipline His people in this world.

The word for *rejected* or disapproved means "to fail the test." Paul uses it to describe what would happen to the Apostle himself if he did not finish his Christian race well (1 Cor 9:27). A believer, whether it is Paul or any other believer, whose life does not please God by producing the kind of crop that He expects, is not approved by Him. That would certainly be the case of a believer who abandons the Christian faith.

Such a Christian can also expect a *burning* experience. It is clear from the illustration that this is not a reference to hell. The fire on the rejected field did not destroy it, but purged it. It was used to "discipline" the field because of the bad crop it produced.

Often in the Bible the illustration of fire is used to describe God's discipline of His people, that is, of believers. This occurs in such OT passages as Isa 9:18-19. In the NT we see it as an illustration of how God will *burn up* the useless works of believers at the Judgment Seat of Christ, even though these believers will be in the kingdom (1 Cor 3:10-15). At the Judgment Seat of Christ every believer will be judged to determine his rewards or his loss of rewards. In short, God's people can experience the burning fire of God's discipline in their lives or the burning up of their works when they stand before the Lord.

It is interesting that in the illustration the author uses from agriculture, the field is burned in order that it may later produce a good crop. After the field is burned of all its bad plants and seeds, it was hoped that it would later produce a good crop.

It is possible that this is in the back of the author's mind here. If so, he is hinting that if a believer *falls away* and thus produces a bad spiritual crop, he can expect the discipline of God. God will do that in hopes that such a fallen believer will return to Him and walk in faith and obedience.

But this is not stated. All the author says is that the believer who falls away will experience the curses of God on his life. He can expect the discipline of God. Such discipline, based upon the context of Hebrews, could include the loss of the inheritance of reigning with Christ in His kingdom. Such a loss would be experienced at the Judgment Seat of Christ.

But this discipline could occur in this life as well. Once again, the author is vague. He does not spell out what God will do, only that it will be unpleasant. He will deal with this again in the next warning passage in chapter 10.

Each of the Christian readers of the Epistle of Hebrews was a field. Each one had a choice as to what kind of crop he would produce. In this stern warning passage, the author has told the readers that if they did not hold on to their faith, they could produce a crop of thorns. But he does not want to leave them on such a negative note. In the following verses he encourages them and reminds them that they can produce a good spiritual crop in their lives.

A Call to Hold On (6:9-12)

These verses form part of the conclusion of this strong warning passage. In the last warning (3:1–4:16), the author concluded it by encouraging the readers to go to Christ for the help they needed. He ends this warning on a positive note as well.

⁹ But, beloved, we are confident of better things concerning you, yes, things that accompany salvation, though we speak

in this manner. [10] For God *is* not unjust to forget your work and labor of love which you have shown toward His name, in that you have ministered to the saints, and do minister. [11] And we desire that each one of you show the same diligence to the full assurance of hope until the end, [12] that you do not become sluggish, but imitate those who through faith and patience inherit the promises.

In v 9 the author calls his readers **beloved**, which is another indication that in this warning passage he is addressing Christians. Even though he has had to give such a strong admonition, he is **confident** his readers will heed his warnings. He has to **speak in** the **manner** he has because the danger is real.

While the discipline of God on a believer who falls away is a possibility, the author is expecting that his readers will experience **better things**. This is not a reference to going to heaven because the word *things* is plural. It speaks of many things. In the Book of Hebrews it includes being blessed by God, rest from one's work, reigning with Christ, being one of His partners in the world to come, and rewards.

The author gives a couple of reasons why he has this confidence. The first is found in v 10. It is that **God is not unjust**. This means that God will not **forget** the **work** they have done for Him and how they **have ministered to the saints**. They have **shown love** towards God and other Christians. Once again, we see that these are believers. Not only are they believers, but in the past at least, they have been faithful believers. They have served one another.

Not only that, but when the author writes this letter, they are still doing such things. They **do minister**.

The whole point of the letter of Hebrews is that they would continue to do so. If they do, they will receive the better things and not experience God's discipline which the author has just described. In the process, they can know that God does not forget what they have done and is there to give them all the help and grace they need.

The second reason the author has confidence that they will receive these better things is because he knows that they can continue doing the **same** things **until the end** (v 11). Even though God gives them all the help they need, they have a responsibility. They need to have **diligence** in this endeavor because they have a **hope**.

The word *diligence* shows they need to continue doing the work they have been doing. Therefore, the *hope* here is not a reference to simply going to heaven. Going to heaven does not involve works. The hope here is the hope of great reward when the King returns. That is what is at stake.

If they would continue doing the works God requires, if they were diligent in doing so, they won't become **sluggish**. This is the same word used in 5:11 to describe how they had become *dull* of hearing. Being diligent in holding on to our Christian hope is the opposite of being sluggish.

It is interesting that in 5:11 he says they are already sluggish. Now he says he does not want them to become sluggish. Probably what is happening here is that the readers are continuing to do what God wants them to do, but they have begun to lose interest in hearing and applying God's Word (5:11-14). They are going through the motions. They have started walking on the path of sluggishness. If they continued to go down that path it would eventually cause them to be weak in their service to God and to others within the church.

Instead of becoming sluggish, they should **imitate those who** lived lives of **faith and patience**. In chapter 2 they have the greatest example of whom to imitate—Christ is their Captain Who leads them in a life of faith. In the next verses the writer will give them another example from the OT.

Those they should imitate are those who **inherit the promises**. Once again we see that this cannot simply mean going to heaven. The word *promises* is plural. It involves many things and includes all the blessings that go with doing what God wants of His people. It requires works, diligence, and patience. It is an inheritance that is given to those who remain faithful to God.

The Conclusion of the Warning (6:13-20)

¹³ For when God made a promise to Abraham, because He could swear by no one greater, He swore by Himself, ¹⁴ saying, *"Surely blessing I will bless you, and multiplying I will multiply you."* ¹⁵ And so, after he had patiently endured, he obtained the promise. ¹⁶ For men indeed swear by the greater, and an oath for confirmation is for them an end

of all dispute. [17] Thus God, determining to show more abundantly to the heirs of promise the immutability of His counsel, confirmed it by an oath, [18] that by two immutable things, in which it is impossible for God to lie, we might have strong consolation, who have fled for refuge to lay hold of the hope set before us. [19] This *hope* we have as an anchor of the soul, both sure and steadfast, and which enters the *Presence* behind the veil, [20] where the forerunner has entered for us, *even* Jesus, having become High Priest forever according to the order of Melchizedek.

Abraham is an example of one of God's people who inherit the promises (v 12). Here in v 13 we are told that **God made a promise to** him. In addition, God backed up that promise. **He swore** that He would do it. God stands behind the promise with the integrity of His own Person.

Verse 14 tells us what God promised to Abraham. Once again we see that what was promised to Abraham here is not the promise of "going to heaven" or being saved spiritually. The author of Hebrews quotes the promise of God from Genesis 22. Paul makes it clear in Romans 4 that Abraham was saved spiritually in Genesis 15. In other words, when God made this promise to Abraham he had already been saved from hell for many years. He only received this promise *after* he had obeyed God.

In Genesis 22 the promise made to Abraham was given after Abraham had demonstrated his willingness to sacrifice his son Isaac as an offering to God. God had tested Abraham to see if he would be obedient to God in the midst of a very trying time.

We can see why Abraham is used as an example here. The original readers of Hebrews were being encouraged to remain faithful to God in the midst of difficult times as well.

The promise of God is that Abraham will receive a **blessing**. This blessing included many things. God was going to **multiply** him in that he would have an innumerable number of descendants. From Gen 22:16-18 we also see that in Abraham all the nations of the earth would be blessed. In addition, his descendants would inherit the cities of their enemies. The fact that this promise included an inheritance and a victory over the enemies of God's people would be very relevant for the readers of Hebrews (1:13-2:4).

These blessings were given to Abraham only **after he had patiently endured**. This is what the readers are encouraged to do (v 12). They are to follow his example. If they did, they would receive blessings as well. They would receive what was promised to them.

But when did Abraham receive what was promised to him? In 11:9-13, 39 the author will say that Abraham has not yet received the things promised to him; they await the world to come. They await the time when the Messiah will set up His kingdom. But even in Genesis 22, Abraham received the promise that these things would be his. They will certainly come to pass. God has not only promised it, He has backed it up with an oath. If the Christian patiently endures, he will receive promised rewards as well.

In v 16 the author begins to discuss the oath of God. There are two main points that follow from this oath. The first is that it is a sure thing. The second is that God has also made an oath to the readers of Hebrews.

Verse 16 also gives the facts of an oath in general. **Men** use oaths. They **swear**, for example, in courts to make something legally binding. They give **confirmation** to what they say, and they swear by something **greater** than themselves. In theory they are saying that if they do not do what they swear to, if they lie, they call upon that greater power to punish them.

God also made a **promise** and **confirmed it by an oath** (v 17). This oath was given to the **heirs of promise**. In Genesis 22 the promise made to Abraham involved his *heirs*. The promise was that these heirs would inherit the cities of their enemies. They would rule over those enemies.

But this promise awaits the coming of the kingdom of God. Paul makes it clear in Rom 4:11-18 and Gal 3:29 that through faith, all Christians are the spiritual heirs of Abraham. The Christian readers of Hebrews, then, share in this oath and promise of God. As the partners of Christ in His kingdom, they, too, can reign over the world to come (1:13-14), over all the works of God's hands (2:6-8). To impress upon Abraham and his heirs the certainly of this promise, God swore to it by an oath. The oath was for the benefit of the heirs of Abraham. The oath of God makes the promise a source of profound comfort.

The reason it is a source of comfort is because it involves unchanging, that is, **immutable things**. The first is the oath itself. The second is that **it is impossible for God to lie**. We have God's word, and that word is reinforced with an oath by One who cannot lie.

The surety of these two things leads us to **have strong consolation**. The Greek word for *consolation* often includes the idea of encouraging somebody during difficult times. That is certainly the meaning here. In Genesis 22 Abraham had just experienced the most trying of times. The readers of Hebrews, as his heirs, were as well. This idea is reinforced in the need to flee somewhere **for refuge**.

During times of difficulty a person needs a place of safety and strength, which forms the basic meaning of *refuge*. The Christian has such a place. At that place, he can **lay hold of the hope set before** him (v 18). It is the hope that all of the Christian's enemies will be defeated. It is a hope that Christ will one day rule over the whole universe. It is a hope that lies in that future kingdom. It is the hope of being one of Christ's partners. It is the hope that God will fulfill His promise and reward believers for their faithfulness. The readers of Hebrews needed to hold on to that hope.

This hope is like an **anchor of the soul** for the believer (v 19). It is **sure and steadfast** because it is backed by the oath of God. An anchor is a place of refuge and gives security during times of storms, that is, difficult times. It is extremely important that the anchor of a ship be placed in a secure location.

And where is the anchor of the Christian? It is in the most secure place in all the universe. It is **behind the veil**. This is a reference to the OT Holy of Holies, which represented the **Presence** of God. Our hope as believers is in the very presence of God in the heavens, the *real* Holy of Holies. Our anchor will never budge, will never slip.

Perhaps we should once again remember the first warning passage in which the author said the readers could "drift" away from what they had heard (2:1-4). The readers need not do that. They had a secure anchor which would prevent that from occurring.

The reason our anchor is secure is not simply where it is, but also because of Who is there—**Jesus** (v 20). He is our **forerunner**. He has gone ahead of us into the presence of God. Believers will follow Him there. This, of course, reminds us that Jesus is our Captain, discussed in chapter 2.

Through this discussion, the author is telling the readers that their hope lies in the world to come. There are future realities that lie in the heavenly Holy of Holies. The author seems to be saying that not only is our hope in that place, but that *Jesus Himself* is our hope.

But not only is He our hope and forerunner, He is also our **High Priest**. As such, He is representing us in God's presence. This is the hope we cling to (vv 11, 18).

The readers of Hebrews were surrounded by their enemies. But their hope involved the defeat of their enemies and a future reign based upon the promise made to Abraham in Genesis 22. As their High Priest, Christ is seated behind the veil waiting until He reigns over His enemies (1:13-14). His victory is assured. Those who cling to Him, their Hope, will experience the same victory.

To lay hold of this hope is to enter into the heavenly Holy of Holies in time of need and to rely on this High Priest. If a believer does, he will find help (4:14-16). This is not a call to believe in Jesus for eternal life; this is a call to patiently endure through the strength He provides in times of trouble.

The author concludes this warning passage by reminding the readers that Jesus is a **High Priest according to the order of Melchizedek**. This warning passage began in 5:10 with a reference to Christ being like Melchizedek. This reference takes the readers back to the topic the author wanted to discuss. It would be hard for them to understand it (5:11), but it is imperative that they do so. They needed to understand what it means if they were going to obtain the promises and avoid the discipline of God. In the following chapters, the author will now tell them.

Application

This very strong warning passage completely refutes the notion that all true Christians will live a godly life. The author of Hebrews tells us that a believer can live the kind of life described as a thorn infested field.

However, it need not be that way. In fact, after all God has given us as believers, it shouldn't be that way. We have everything we need in the Word of God and our High Priest to produce the kind of fruit that pleases God.

But we must take these warning passages seriously. When we say that they are describing people who are not Christians, we deny the purpose for which they were given. Christians can then say that these verses have no meaning for them. However, Christians need to be warned that how they live and what they believe is of extreme importance. Even though Christians cannot lose eternal life, other kinds of loss are certainly possible. Such losses can be worse than dying in the wilderness at Kadesh and losing an inheritance in the earthly land of Canaan. Christians of every generation need to be given this warning.

Jesus and Melchizedek

IN THE PREVIOUS CHAPTER there was a very strong warning directed toward the Christian readers and a call to hold on until the end (6:11, 18). The readers were going through difficult times and were considering abandoning their Christian faith and practice.

The key to holding on to their faith and living successfully in the midst of their troubles is to know they have Jesus Christ as their High Priest. Chapter 7 begins a section that runs all the way through chapter 10. This section ends with another strong warning and another call to hold on (10:19-39).

Since the High Priesthood of Christ is the key, the author will now go into detail on this important subject. Because the readers are contemplating going back to Judaism, the author will compare Christ to the OT Jewish high priests. It has been said that Christ is a High Priest like Melchizedek (6:20). The author, by showing the greatness of Melchizedek, will prove that Christ is greater than the OT high priests.

Throughout this section, the author will show that Christianity is superior to Judaism. Christianity gives greater access to God. In Christ there is greater forgiveness. The New Covenant is better than the Old. Christ's sacrifice is greater than all the sacrifices of the Old Covenant. The message is clear: to return to Judaism would be a huge mistake.

The chapter breaks down in this way: the greatness of Melchizedek (vv 1-10); the need for a new High Priest to replace the old (vv 11-19); the greatness of Jesus Christ (vv 20-28).

The Greatness of Melchizedek (7:1-10)

¹ For this Melchizedek, king of Salem, priest of the Most High God, who met Abraham returning from the slaughter of the kings and blessed him, ² to whom also Abraham gave a tenth part of all, first being translated "king of righteousness," and then also king of Salem, meaning "king of peace," ³ without father, without mother, without genealogy, having neither beginning of days nor end of life, but made like the Son of God, remains a priest continually. ⁴ Now consider how great this man was, to whom even the patriarch Abraham gave a tenth of the spoils. ⁵ And indeed those who are of the sons of Levi, who receive the priesthood, have a commandment to receive tithes from the people according to the law, that is, from their brethren, though they have come from the loins of Abraham; ⁶ but he whose genealogy is not derived from them received tithes from Abraham and blessed him who had the promises. ⁷ Now beyond all contradiction the lesser is blessed by the better. ⁸ Here mortal men receive tithes, but there *he receives them*, of whom it is witnessed that he lives. ⁹ Even Levi, who receives tithes, paid tithes through Abraham, so to speak, ¹⁰ for he was still in the loins of his father when Melchizedek met him.

Even though Melchizedek is very important to the author's argument in Hebrews, he is a man hardly mentioned in the OT. The brief history of him is found in Genesis 14. In that chapter four foreign kings defeat the kings of the valley around the Dead Sea. They take Lot, the nephew of Abraham, as well as many others as slaves. In addition, they take many spoils of war.

When Abraham hears of what happened, he takes a band of men and pursues the kings and their armies. Abraham defeats them. He brings Lot and the others back to the valley, along with the spoils.

Upon **returning from the slaughter of the kings**, Abraham is **met** by **Melchizedek**. We are told that Melchizedek was the **king of Salem**. At this meeting Melchizedek **blessed** Abraham (v 1). In addition,

Abraham paid a tithe to this man, that is, he **gave** him **a tenth** (v 2) of the spoils he obtained when he defeated the four kings.

Genesis also tells us that Melchizedek was a **priest of the Most High God**. That he is a priest is seen in the fact that Abraham paid a tithe to him and that Abraham was blessed by him.

Melchizedek is obviously a great man. He is both a king and a priest. In the OT under the Law of Moses, nobody held both titles. In addition, Abraham was a great man, the father of the Jewish nation. Yet Abraham recognized that Melchizedek is greater than he is.

The greatness of Melchizedek is also seen by his name and where he was from. His name in Hebrew literally means **king of righteousness**. He was the **king of Salem**. In all probability Salem is a reference to the city of Jerusalem before it was called Jerusalem (Ps 76:2). The word **Salem** means **peace**. As king, Melchizedek was one who ruled his domain in righteousness and peace.

We already see how Christ is like Melchizedek. When He comes to rule, He, too, will rule from Jerusalem. His reign will be one of peace (Isa 9:6-7). The author of Hebrews has already said He will also rule in righteousness (1:9). And, of course, like Melchizedek, Christ is both a King and a High Priest.

The uniqueness of Melchizedek among people in the OT is seen in the author's description here in v 3: he did not have a **father**, a **mother**, or ancestors. In addition, he had no **beginning of days** or **end of life**. In other words, he did not have a birth or a death.

What does such a description mean? There have been three main ways of interpreting these words. It is possible that they simply mean that Melchizedek was a type of such a person. He had a mother and father and did have a birth and death but the OT does not mention any of these things. Since the Bible is silent on them, the author treats them as if they did not exist.

While this is a possibility, the same thing could be said about other people in the OT. The author of Hebrews seems to indicate that Melchizedek is unique. In addition, if Melchizedek is just a man, it is somewhat difficult to understand how he is greater than Abraham in the Genesis account.

The second option is that Melchizedek is an appearance of Jesus Christ before He became a man when He was born of Mary. Many believe that in the OT Jesus made such appearances as the "Angel of the

Lord." In Melchizedek we could possibly have another appearance of the Lord. The Son of God in His appearances in the OT did not have a mother, father, birth, or death.

This, too, is a possibility. However, the author of Hebrews says Melchizedek was **like the Son of God** (v 3). That does not appear to be the same thing as *being* the Son of God.

The third possibility is that Melchizedek was an angel. This would explain why he did not have a mother or father. While angels are not eternal, they were created before the world was created. From man's perspective they are not bound by time as we know it and are thus without beginning or ending of days.

In addition, in the context of Genesis 14 we see angels operating who appear to be men. Some visit Abraham in Genesis 18. Two angels in the form of men destroy Sodom and Gomorrah.

If Melchizedek was an angel, he is unique from a Biblical perspective in that he was in the form of a man but also remains that way for a period of time. Since he was the king of Salem, he evidently was in this form long enough to rule over this area. It could also be argued that he is unique in being an angel who also serves as a high priest. These two things perhaps argue against Melchizedek being an angel. Of course, one could say that this particular angel is unique in the OT.

Whether Melchizedek was a man and thus a type or pattern in the OT or not, the main point here is clear. Melchizedek draws a picture of a high priest who does not stop serving because he dies. He **remains a priest continually** (v 3). As the author will later say, the OT high priests died and thus stopped serving in that capacity.

The OT priests served because of their genealogy. They were descendents of Aaron, the first high priest. None of those high priests were kings. Melchizedek was a king. He also belonged to a new, better order that was not based upon a genealogy.

And Christ is like Melchizedek in all these "better" aspects. But it is important to see that Christ, not Melchizedek, is the standard of greatness. Melchizedek was **made like the Son of God**; Christ, the Son of God, was not made like Melchizedek.

In vv 4-10 the author of Hebrews continues to show how great Melchizedek was in comparison to both Abraham and the high priests of the OT. Melchizedek is said to be **great** because **Abraham gave a**

tenth of the spoils to him (v 4). Since Abraham paid a tithe to this man, Melchizedek was greater than Abraham.

The reader is to **consider** the greatness of Melchizedek. That means to meditate on it. He is greater than the **patriarch**, or father, of the Jewish nation. It is as if the author of Hebrews is saying, "Look how great this man was!"

Melchizedek was also greater than any of the high priests in the OT. All the high priests were **sons of Levi** (v 5). Levi was one of the grandsons of Abraham. In fact, all the priests were descendants of this man.

The priests **received tithes** from the Jews, that is, **their brethren**. They had the honor of doing that. One could say that in this sense they were greater than their brothers. Both the Levites and their brothers were descendants of Abraham.

But Melchizedek was not in the **genealogy** of Levi. Instead, he collected **tithes from Abraham** himself. In the OT in order to be a priest, one had to trace his genealogy back to Levi. When Abraham paid tithes to Melchizedek, Levi had not yet even been born! Melchizedek, since he was a priest, was a different kind of priest.

Not only did Melchizedek receive a tithe from Abraham, he also **blessed him**. Melchizedek represented Abraham before God, and Abraham was the one **who had the promises**. Melchizedek was greater than the one through whom God had promised to bless the whole world (Gen 22:18). As great as Abraham was, Melchizedek was greater because the **lesser** (Abraham) **is blessed by the better** (Melchizedek, v 7).

The Book of Hebrews was written in the first century, and the author reminds the readers that **here**, that is, in the Jewish priestly system that was still in operation in Jerusalem at that time, the Levites were serving as priests. But they were **mortal men** (v 8). They died. Their priesthood involved the need for descendants to carry on representing the people before God.

However, a priest like Melchizedek is not like that. **He lives**. His life does not end (v 3). He is greater than the OT priests in this regard. But he is also greater because **Levi**, the father of all OT priests, **paid tithes** to Melchizedek. This was the case because Levi was **still in the loins of his father** Abraham when Abraham paid tithes to Melchizedek (vv 9-10).

The point here is that a descendant of a man is not greater than his ancestor. Since Melchizedek was greater than Abraham, he had to be greater than Levi who was a descendant of Abraham. In addition, Levi was **in** Abraham when Abraham paid tithes to Melchizedek. Therefore, when Abraham paid tithes to this high priest of Salem, all the priestly descendants of Levi did as well. Melchizedek was greater than all the priests that came from Levi. He was greater than any of the OT high priests. If Christ is a High Priest according to the order of Melchizedek (Heb 5:10), He is greater than Levi.

Levi was the head of the system of priests of the Old Covenant. Christ, who is greater than Levi, brought in a new and better covenant.

The Need for a New High Priest to Replace the Old (vv 11-19)

The priests that were descendants of Levi were part of the Jewish system of worship under the Law of Moses. In chapters 7–10 the author of Hebrews will make it clear that the covenant based upon that Law could not bring the forgiveness of sins. If such forgiveness was to occur, the Old Covenant had to be replaced by something new and better. If a New Covenant was introduced, there would have to be a change in the old system of priests as well. The new priesthood would have to be better than the old.

It is easy to see the relevance of this discussion in the situation of the first readers. If they were contemplating leaving Christianity to return to Judaism, they were contemplating leaving the better and new for the old and inferior.

> [11] **Therefore, if perfection were through the Levitical priesthood (for under it the people received the law), what further need *was there* that another priest should rise according to the order of Melchizedek, and not be called according to the order of Aaron?** [12] **For the priesthood being changed, of necessity there is also a change of the law.** [13] **For He of whom these things are spoken belongs to another tribe, from which no man has officiated at the altar.** [14] **For it is evident that our Lord arose from Judah, of which tribe Moses spoke nothing concerning priesthood.** [15] **And it is yet far more evident if, in the likeness of Melchizedek, there arises another priest** [16] **who has come, not according to the**

law of a fleshly commandment, but according to the power of an endless life. [17] For He testifies:

> *"You are a priest forever*
> *According to the order of Melchizedek."*

[18] For on the one hand there is an annulling of the former commandment because of its weakness and unprofitableness, [19] for the law made nothing perfect; on the other hand, *there is the* bringing in of a better hope, through which we draw near to God.

In this section the first thing the author points out is that the Old Covenant, which was based upon the Law of Moses, was inadequate. The Old Covenant had a **Levitical priesthood** (v 11). That is, the priests were descendants of Levi. These priests were the ones who made sacrifices for the sins of the people and ran the tabernacle in the wilderness as well as the later Temple in Jerusalem.

But this system did not bring **perfection**. This is an important point for the author. He will repeat it in v 19. In chapter 10 he will say what this means. The old system of sacrifices did not completely deal with the issue of sins for God's people. It was inadequate. It did not do what God required. Something new and better was needed.

In the OT itself, as the author is soon to remind the readers, God spoke of a **need** for **another priest**. One that would be like **Melchizedek** and not one like **Aaron**. Aaron was a descendant of Levi and the first high priest under the Old Covenant.

The point here is if God were satisfied with the old system, why did He speak of the need for a new High Priest? The old system had a system of priests. If this **priesthood** was **changed**, then there must also be a **change of the law** itself (v 12). The whole Old Covenant would have to be replaced.

There has been a change in the priesthood. As believers, the readers had believed in Jesus Christ as the Messiah. But the Messiah was also a High Priest. **These things are spoken** (v 13) about in the OT, the Scriptures of the Old Covenant itself (Heb 5:10).

But Christ did not come from the **tribe** of Levi. Instead, He was from the tribe of **Judah**. The Law of **Moses** said **nothing** about a high priest coming from that tribe. Nobody from Judah ever **officiated at**

the altar as a priest (vv 13-14). Clearly, if Jesus is the Messiah, there has been a change in the Old Covenant.

In vv 15-17 the author says this is even **more evident** when we once again look at what the OT states. He reminds the readers what Ps 110:4 says about the Messiah. He quotes it here (v 17). This Psalm said that the Messiah would be like **Melchizedek**—He would be **another** kind of **priest**. He would be different from the priests that descended from Levi, including Aaron, the first high priest.

The priests under the Old Covenant were so **according to the law of a fleshly commandment**. This means they were men of flesh. They descended from other men, particularly Levi. That is what the Law said. But as mere men, they died. They needed descendants in order for this system of priests to continue.

But Christ's priesthood was not like that. His was based upon the **power of an endless life**. He did not need descendants, because He did not die. He did not need to be a descendant of Levi. He lives forever (4:14-16).

And this is exactly what Psalm 110 said about the Messiah. He would be a **priest forever** (v 17). He would be a priest **according to the order of Melchizedek**, not Levi. Melchizedek was greater than Levi. Christ is greater than Levi.

All this means that a change for the better has taken place. The old has been set aside or **annulled**. The new is better because the old was characterized by **its weakness and unprofitableness** (v 18). It was weak because it was not able to take away the sins of the people. Therefore, it was not useful in this regard.

The **law** and the system of priests under it were not able to make anything **perfect** (v 19). This is what God desired of sacrifices. This takes us back to v 11. The old sacrifices provided by the old system of priests did not take away sins once for all. They therefore did not give the worshipper a clear conscience before God and the ability to boldly approach God with confidence (4:14-16). In chapter 10 the author will show how Christ's sacrifice did all these things.

In Christ, however, the old has been replaced. In Him there is a **bringing in of** something **better**. Once again we see the superiority of Christianity over Judaism. If these readers went back to the old system of worship, they would be choosing what is inferior.

One thing better is the **hope** found in the New Covenant. This is not the same thing as "going to heaven." To have eternal life is a free gift by faith alone. In the Book of Hebrews **hope** is a reward given to those believers who are faithful to the Lord. It involves being a partner with Christ as one who will rule with Him (3:6; 6:11, 18; 10:23). The believer is encouraged to hold on to this hope. To obtain this hope we must draw near to **draw near to God**. Believers can do this because they have a great High Priest. He lives forever and intercedes for us. We can boldly enter into God's presence for strength and grace in our times of need. The Old Covenant did not provide that.

The New Covenant with Christ as our High Priest brings perfection. That is, it takes away the sin of the believer once and for all. It gives us the better hope of being a partner with Him in the world to come. It also gives us the ability to draw near to God, into His very presence. None of these things were available in the Old Covenant. The Old was weak. Clearly the priesthood of Christ is superior to that of Levi. Praise God the new has replaced the old.

The Greatness of Jesus Christ (vv 20-28)

The author has just stated that Melchizedek is greater than the OT high priests. Since Christ is like Melchizedek, He, too, is greater than they are. In this last section of the chapter, the author continues his discussion on the greatness of the Christian's High Priest. There are three things that make Him greater than the OT high priests: an oath, His eternal office, and His character.

20 And inasmuch as *He was* **not** *made priest* **without an oath 21 (for they have become priests without an oath, but He with an oath by Him who said to Him:**

> *"The Lord has sworn*
> *And will not relent,*
> *'You are a priest forever*
> *According to the order of Melchizedek'"),*

22 by so much more Jesus has become a surety of a better covenant.

²³ **Also there were many priests, because they were prevented by death from continuing.** ²⁴ **But He, because He continues forever, has an unchangeable priesthood.** ²⁵ **Therefore He is also able to save to the uttermost those who come to God through Him, since He always lives to make intercession for them.**
²⁶ **For such a High Priest was fitting for us,** *who* **is holy, harmless, undefiled, separate from sinners, and has become higher than the heavens;** ²⁷ **who does not need daily, as those high priests, to offer up sacrifices, first for His own sins and then for the people's, for this He did once for all when He offered up Himself.** ²⁸ **For the law appoints as high priests men who have weakness, but the word of the oath, which came after the law,** *appoints* **the Son who has been perfected forever.**

The main point of vv 20-21 is that Jesus is greater than the OT priests because He was **made priest** with **an oath**. The OT priests **became priests without an oath**. When God the Father declared that Christ, the Messiah, would be a High Priest, He swore on it.

Once again, the author quotes from Psalm 110. The **Lord has sworn** that Christ is **a priest**. As we saw in chapter 6, the oath of God adds a degree of solemnity to something. No such thing happened when any high priest assumed the office under the Old Covenant. The oath of God implies that Christ's priesthood is superior.

But it is also superior because Christ's office is eternal. As Psalm 110 says, Christ is a priest **forever**. This was something else that the priests in the OT could not claim. Because of the oath of God as well as the eternal nature of Christ's priesthood, He is the High Priest of a **better covenant** (v 22).

As our High Priest, **Jesus** is also the **surety** of this covenant. The word *surety* means "a guarantee" of something. Christ guarantees that everything promised in the New Covenant will be fulfilled. This certainly includes salvation from hell. But it includes more, and the author of Hebrews discusses all of them. In the sacrifice of Christ there is the taking away of sins once and for all. There is a clean conscience before God for the believer. There is complete access to God. There is the promise of eternal rewards for those who hold on to that hope. Jesus guarantees it all.

The fact that the author refers to Him simply as **Jesus** emphasizes His humanity. The author is well aware that Jesus is God (1:1-4). But as our High Priest He also had to be a man (2:5*ff.*). Jesus guarantees the fulfillment of the New Covenant as God, as the King of the world to come, but also as a man as our High Priest. He is our representative before His Father.

In vv 23-25 the author continues discussing the eternal nature of Christ's priesthood. In the OT there were **many priests**. Josephus, a historian in the first century, said that in the history of the Jewish nation there had been eighty-three high priests. The reason there had been so many is obvious. They were mortal men and **were prevented by death** from holding their office forever.

But Christ is different. Since **He continues forever**, death does not interrupt His duties as our High Priest. This is what God swore in Psalm 110. He does not transfer His office to one of His descendants. As a result, He has **an unchangeable priesthood**.

There are, of course, many advantages to having an eternal High Priest who represents us before God. When a person is replaced because of death, many times people wonder if the "new guy" will be as good as the old. With Christ, because He never dies, that is not an issue.

But in v 25 the author gives the greatest benefit of having an eternal priest. Because **He always lives**, He can **save to the uttermost** every believer who **comes to God through Him**.

Unfortunately, many see this verse as referring to salvation from hell. But that cannot be the case. It is not talking about unbelievers coming to Jesus. It is talking about people who **come to God** through Christ as a High Priest. Christ is the High Priest of *believers*, not unbelievers.

The word *uttermost* means "completely." Christ, as our High Priest, is able to save believers completely. This salvation is the same salvation we saw in 1:14 and 2:1-4. It is a reward for those Christians who draw near to Him and find the help and strength they need from Him. He will save them through trials and enemies and bless them. This salvation would result in the blessing of being one of Christ's partners in His kingdom.

This certainly fits the context of Hebrews. If the readers, who were believers, would draw near to God through Christ, Christ would save them completely. He would give them victory over all their circumstances and bless them in the world to come. He would also save them from any discipline they might receive in this life for disobeying God.

It is very important that we see that in v 25 the author is talking about the salvation that believers can experience through Christ. This salvation is available to those for whom Christ **makes intercession.** Jesus does not intercede for unbelievers before the Father. He intercedes for Christians who draw near to God through Him (4:14-16).

We also see that the author of Hebrews is talking about Christ's ministry to Christians in another way. When an unbeliever believes in Jesus Christ for eternal life and becomes a child of God, he exercises a faith which is once and for all. The believer can look back at the time he believed in Jesus Christ as something that happened once for all in the past.

But the salvation spoken of in v 25 is not like that. It is said that Christ **lives.** That verb is in the present tense. The phrase *those who come to God* is also in the present. This is a ministry that Jesus always does for His people. This is something Christians do *now*, not in the past. Whenever His people come to Him, Christ is able to deliver them *now* and *continually.* It is not like the salvation from hell that happens for the believer once.

Christ is clearly greater than the OT high priests. In vv 26-28 we are told the final way in which this is true. It also tells us why Christ is worthy to be our High Priest—His character.

It is **fitting** that Christ is our High Priest. This means He is completely qualified. He is **holy,** or morally perfect, by His nature. He is **harmless,** which probably refers to His actions. He did not practice evil of any kind.

Jesus is also **undefiled.** In light of v 27 here, as well as the discussion in chapter 10 of Christ's sacrifice of Himself, this probably refers to the fact that the sacrifice He made as our High Priest (on the cross) was a perfect sacrifice, completely acceptable to God.

The Christian's High Priest is also **separate from sinners.** In light of the last part of v 26, this probably refers to the fact that Christ as our High Priest has ascended to God. In representing us before the Father, He is in a position **higher than the heavens.** He is at the right hand of the Father (1:13). This position would also speak of His holiness.

Which OT high priest could boast of such things? Which OT priest ever fulfilled his duties at the right hand of God? Which was perfectly holy in nature and conduct? Why would the readers ever decide to go back to the priests of the Old Covenant when they had Christ as their representative before God?

Because Christ is perfectly holy, He is different from the OT priests in another way. It involves the sacrifice He made as our High Priest. First, He **does not need** to make **sacrifices for His own sins** (v 27). In the OT, before the high priest could make a sacrifice for the sins of the people, he had to make a sacrifice for himself. That was because the high priest himself was a sinner. Unlike Christ, he was not holy. The OT high priests needed constant sacrifices for their own sins. The author of Hebrews says this was a **daily** need. Christ did not have this need.

In addition, Christ did not need to make a number of sacrifices for the sins of the **people**. In the OT the priests made daily sacrifices for the people. Every year on the Day of Atonement, they made a sacrifice for the sins of the people for the whole year. Not so with Christ. He made a sacrifice **once for all**. Since that is the case, clearly His sacrifice was superior to the numerous sacrifices of the Old Covenant. As will be discussed in chapter 10, His one sacrifice was so great it took care of the sins of His people **once for all**.

The OT priests, under the **law**, were characterized by **weakness** (v 28). They were mortal. They were sinners themselves. But Christ did not have their weaknesses.

Instead, He was appointed by God **after the Law**, as recorded in Psalm 110. Psalm 110 was written hundreds of years after the Law of Moses was given. It spoke of the fact that God would give His people another High Priest. This High Priest **has been perfected forever**.

As we saw in chapter 2, He is our perfect High Priest because He became a man and knows what it means to suffer and therefore can sympathize with us. But He is also perfect, as the author has just said, because of the perfect sacrifice of Himself. Because of our perfect High Priest we can boldly enter into God's presence.

We should not skip over the fact that the author calls Jesus the **Son** here. As we saw in chapter 1, that title means He is God and King. This is who our High Priest is! Which OT priest could say that?

He is superior in every way. He has made a better sacrifice (v 27). He gives a better hope (v 19). He brings a better covenant (v 22). He is a better High Priest. The author will continue to discuss how superior the New Covenant, with its High Priest, is compared to the Old. The point is clear, though. Only a fool would reject this High Priest and return to the old system He replaced, and a distorted version of that system as well.

The High Priest of a New Covenant

IN DISCUSSING THE SUPERIORITY of Christianity over Judaism, in chapter 7, the author of Hebrews pointed out that Jesus Christ is superior to the high priests of the OT. In 7:22 he mentioned that Jesus is the High Priest of the New Covenant. Here in chapter 8 the author will say that the New Covenant is superior to the Old.

This is a theme that the author will advance all the way through chapter 10. Christianity not only has a superior High Priest and a superior covenant, but it also has a better sacrifice, a better ministry in regard to our High Priest, and better promises. Who would consider leaving the New Covenant as a means to worship God and return to the inferior Old Covenant? The readers were contemplating doing that very thing—returning to Judaism from Christianity.

In chapter 8 we see specifically that Christ has a ministry greater than the ministry of the high priests in the OT. In addition, this ministry has better promises. The ministry of Christ also involves a superior place to carry out that ministry.

Christ's Superior Ministry (8:1-6)

¹ Now *this* is the main point of the things we are saying: We have such a High Priest, who is seated at the right hand of the throne of the Majesty in the heavens, ² a Minister of the sanctuary and of the true tabernacle which the Lord erected, and not man. ³ For every high priest is appointed to offer both gifts and sacrifices. Therefore it is necessary that this One also have something to offer. ⁴ For if He were on earth,

He would not be a priest, since there are priests who offer the
gifts according to the law; [5] who serve the copy and shadow
of the heavenly things, as Moses was divinely instructed
when he was about to make the tabernacle. For He said, *"See
that you make all things according to the pattern shown you
on the mountain."* [6] But now He has obtained a more excellent
ministry, inasmuch as He is also Mediator of a better
covenant, which was established on better promises.

In v 1 the author summarizes what he has said about Christ so far.
We have a **High Priest** that is **seated in the heavens**. He is seated **at the
right hand of the throne of the Majesty**, which is a reference to God the
Father. This takes us back to 1:3 in which the author says that the Son is
seated there at the right hand of the Majesty on high. As Son, He is the
King. But He is also our High Priest.

The fact that He is seated is very important. As the author will later
say, He is seated because His work is done. He sacrificed Himself once
for all (7:27).

In v 2 the author introduces new concepts. He says that Christ is **a
Minister of the sanctuary**. The word *minister* means "servant." Christ is
performing a service for others.

Clearly, the author is speaking of the ministry that Christ performs
for others as their High Priest. But He performs this service in the **true
tabernacle**. It is not in a tabernacle **erected** by **man**. The OT tabernacle
was built by men. It was in that tabernacle that the old priests served
others and performed their ministry.

Christ's place of ministry is not like that. It is greater. The **Lord** built
it. Since this is the case, and Christ is seated in the heavens, we see that
the heavens are the place of His ministry.

Starting in v 3, we are told about Christ's ministry in the heavens.
First, the obvious is stated. All **high priests**, regardless of where they
serve, **offer gifts and sacrifices** (v 3). This is the ministry they perform
for those they represent before God. The sacrifices in the OT dealt with
the issue of sins among the Jewish people.

If Christ is a High Priest, then He must **also have something to
offer**. He, too, must have a sacrifice that deals with sins. The author has
already said that Christ has done that (1:3; 7:27), and he will discuss this
sacrifice in great detail in chapter 10.

The main point here, though, is not the sacrifice itself but where the sacrifice took place. It did not occur in the tabernacle. Nor did it occur in the temple in Jerusalem, which was built as a replacement for the tabernacle. Christ's place of ministry is not there, that is, **on earth**. If He were ministering there **He would not be a priest**. Christ did not meet the requirements of a priest in the Old Covenant, and the tabernacle was a part of that covenant.

The priests on earth **offer gifts according to the Law**. The priests of the Old Covenant do that (v 4). This is a strong indication that the temple in Jerusalem was still standing when the Book of Hebrews was written. The temple was destroyed in AD 70; therefore, the date of Hebrews is earlier than that. The author says that there are gifts being offered as he writes the book.

Christ, as was said in chapter 7, was not qualified to offer gifts in the temple on earth. He was not from the tribe of Levi, nor was He a descendant of Aaron. If He is a superior High Priest, we would expect Him to serve in a better tabernacle. Verse 5 speaks of the inferior nature of the Temple in Jerusalem.

The tabernacle or Temple that the OT high priests served in is nothing but a **copy and shadow** of the **heavenly** one. It is the heavenly one in which Christ serves. The very words **copy and shadow** indicate it is inferior. The real thing is always better than its shadow. In fact, a shadow cannot even exist if the real thing does not exist.

The OT itself, that is, the Old Covenant, proves the inferior nature of the earthly tabernacle where the high priests of the OT served. The author of Hebrews quotes from the Law of Moses (Exod 25:40). In that verse Moses was told to build the tabernacle **according to the pattern** that was **shown** him on Mount Sinai. God showed Moses the real thing in heaven. Moses was to build his tabernacle as a **copy** of what he saw.

The earthly tabernacle represented the presence of God on earth. Whatever Moses saw on the **mountain** was the heavenly dwelling place of God, the heavenly manifestation of the presence of God. It is there, in the real presence of God, that Christ ministers.

Since the old priests served in a copy of the real thing, and Christ serves in the real tabernacle in the heavens, **He has obtained a more excellent ministry** (v 6). The verb *obtained* is in the perfect tense which indicates He received that ministry in the past, but the ministry continues to the present day. He is still performing His ministry as a High Priest for His people today.

The priests of the OT were mediators, or go-betweens, between God and the Jews. The Jews had made a covenant with God. God would bless them if they obeyed and curse them if they disobeyed. The sacrifices the priests made on behalf of the people allowed for the people to be forgiven and receive blessings.

But Christ, as High Priest, is the **Mediator of a better covenant**. Since He is God and is holy, He can be in the very presence of the Father in the heavens (7:26). But since He is also a man and knows what man goes through (chapter 2), He can represent His people while in that presence. As their High Priest, He has made His people acceptable before the Father.

This is the New Covenant. And the New Covenant has **better promises**. The promises of the Old Covenant were mainly directed toward earthly blessings. The promises of the New Covenant are mainly directed toward heavenly and eternal blessings. As will be seen later, the New Covenant promises a relationship with God for the people of God that the Jews could not have. This relationship includes the permanent and inner dwelling of God in the believer as well as complete access to Him.

These promises of the New Covenant needed to be understood by the readers of Hebrews. They needed to take advantage of the privileges of the New Covenant if they were going to hold on firmly in the difficult times in which they lived. If they did so, the New Covenant promised them great reward in the coming kingdom.

The Superiority of the New Covenant (8:7-13)

⁷ **For if that first covenant had been faultless, then no place would have been sought for a second. ⁸ Because finding fault with them, He says: *"Behold, the days are coming, says the Lord, when I will make a new covenant with the house of Israel and with the house of Judah— ⁹ not according to the covenant that I made with their fathers in the day when I took them by the hand to lead them out of the land of Egypt; because they did not continue in My covenant, and I disregarded them, says the Lord. ¹⁰ For this is the covenant***

that I will make with the house of Israel after those days, says the Lord: I will put My laws in their mind and write them on their hearts; and I will be their God, and they shall be My people. ¹¹ None of them shall teach his neighbor, and none his brother, saying, 'Know the Lord,' for all shall know Me, from the least of them to the greatest of them. ¹² For I will be merciful to their unrighteousness, and their sins and their lawless deeds I will remember no more."

¹³ **In that He says, "A new covenant," He has made the first obsolete. Now what is becoming obsolete and growing old is ready to vanish away.**

Here in the last part of chapter 8, the author discusses how the New Covenant will be superior to the first. He carries on this idea all the way through 9:15. Hebrews 7:11 said that if the old system of priests had been acceptable to God, He never would have said there would be a new one, as He did in Psalm 110. The same thing could be said about the New Covenant. If the Old Covenant, given at Mount Sinai, had been acceptable to God, He never would have said a new one was coming. But that is exactly what God did say through the prophet Jeremiah.

The **first covenant**, given by Moses, was not **faultless**. As a result, God **sought a second** one with His people (v 7). The fact that God replaced the first one means the second one was better.

God found **fault** with the people under the Old Covenant. In v 8 we find a quote from the Book of Jeremiah. In Jer 31:31-34 we have the promise of the New Covenant. Jeremiah was a prophet among the Jews in the late seventh and early sixth centuries before Christ. During the time of this prophet, God was displeased with His people.

God had made the Old Covenant with the Jews; but they did not keep it. They had promised to serve and obey the Lord and not worship other gods. However, they sinned terribly against the Lord and fell into idolatry. As a result, following the covenant, God disciplined them. By the time Jeremiah lived, the northern part of the nation of Israel had been defeated by their enemies and taken off into captivity as slaves. Jeremiah prophesied to the southern part of the nation and warned them not to follow in the steps of their brothers to the north.

But the South did exactly as the North had done. They, too, broke the Old Covenant with God. Jeremiah told the people that they also would be defeated by their enemies, the Babylonians, and taken off into captivity as slaves.

The problem, of course, was not the Old Covenant itself. It was holy (Rom 7:12). The problem was the sinfulness of God's people. Because of the fallen nature of man, they did not keep it. That is why the covenant failed. To rectify the situation, God promised a New Covenant, a covenant that would not fail, because it would be different.

Jeremiah spoke of this future covenant. In the future, in **the days that are coming**, God **will make a new covenant**. Here is the promise of the New Covenant. This promise was made approximately eight hundred years after the old one was enacted at Sinai. The main point the author wants to make here is that if the old had been sufficient, God never would have promised a new one. But obviously, as the Book of Jeremiah points out, the old did not meet the needs of the people because of their weakness.

It needs to be pointed out that the New Covenant was promised to the Jews—**the house of Israel and house of Judah** (v 8). Israel was the northern part of the nation while Judah was the southern part. The days will come, says the Lord, when both will be reunited and serve God under this New Covenant. Those days are still in the future. There will come a day, in the coming kingdom of God when Christ rules upon the earth, when the Jewish nation will be a nation of believers under this covenant.

In the Book of Genesis (chapters 12, 15, 22), God promised Abraham and his descendants many blessings. Abraham and the Jews have never realized these blessings. The Old Covenant was not able to bring these about. All of these blessings await a future day when they will be fulfilled under the New Covenant.

While the promise of the New Covenant in Jeremiah is not made to the Church, Christ did say that the communion wine "is My blood of the new covenant" (Matt 26:28). The Church shares in many of the blessings of the New Covenant now (e.g., forgiveness of sins and knowing God). Part of the promises made to Abraham included the idea that through him the whole world would be blessed. This universal blessing of the world through the descendants of Abraham will occur in the future kingdom of God when Christ rules. But the Church is now experiencing some of these blessings. The author of Hebrews discusses some of these blessings here in vv 10-12.

First, however, he emphasizes that the New Covenant will succeed where the Old Covenant failed (v 9). Again, quoting from Jeremiah 31, the author tells us that the Jews did not keep God's **covenant**. As a result, God **disregarded them**. This is a reference to the fact that God disciplined them by using their enemies to defeat them and take them off into captivity. They had sinned against God and failed to keep their covenant with Him even though He had taken them **by the hand** and brought them **out of Egypt**. Under Moses, God had brought them out of slavery and into the Promised Land. He had revealed Himself to them, given them His Law, and declared He was their God and would be with them. They turned their back on this arrangement. In this regard, the Old Covenant was not "faultless" (v 7).

But the New Covenant will not be like that. It has better promises (v 6). It is superior. The first promise or blessing is that God **will put** His **laws in** the **mind** of His people and **write them on their hearts** (v 10). This, of course, is different from the Old Covenant. The Law of Moses was written on tablets of stone. The New Covenant will place the Law of God *in* the believer. This is a reference to the Holy Spirit who lives within every believer. The OT saint never experienced the permanent indwelling of the Spirit of God. Through the power of the Holy Spirit. While the New Covenant is yet future, as the future tenses here show, the church-age believer can choose to serve God and no longer has to be a slave to the power of sin (Rom 6:17-22; 7:22-25). Our service to God springs from the new nature the believer in Jesus Christ has, not from words written outside of us on stone.

The Apostle Paul in 2 Corinthians 3 discussed this difference between the Old and New Covenants. He said that the Old Covenant was a law of the "letter" written upon stone. But the New Covenant is one of the "Spirit." The letter kills but the Spirit gives life. Paul's point is that only the Spirit can empower a person to live in a way that brings the experience of life which comes from obeying God and being in fellowship with Him. Jesus speaks of this as the "abundant life" the believer can have when he or she obeys the Lord (John 10:10).

Under the Old Covenant, the Jews were called the people of God (Exod 6:7). However, under the New Covenant, God says He **will be their God, and they shall be My people** (v 10). This must mean that under the New Covenant the Jewish people will be His people in a different and better way. The NT certainly calls believers the people of God (Titus 2:14; 1 Pet 2:9-10).

The Christian believer can indeed say he is a child of God in ways that the Jew in the OT could not. The NT believer calls God "Father," which is something Jews did not do under the Old Covenant. In addition, the New Covenant believer has a spiritual union with Christ as a result of the baptism of the Holy Spirit.

Finally, the Jews in the OT, because of their disobedience, have been set aside for a period of time, as Paul discusses in Romans 9–11. Instead of God accomplishing His purposes on earth through the nation of Israel, He currently works through the Church. The Church will never experience such a setting aside.

Verse 11 is a little more difficult to interpret. The problem is the meaning of the phrase **"Know the Lord."** It could be said that all people under the New Covenant, **from the least to the greatest**, have a knowledge of God that the believer in the Old Covenant did not have. This knowledge involves having an intimacy with God. The New Covenant believer has the new revelation of the teachings of Christ as well as access to God that the Old Covenant did not provide (Heb 4:14-16). The NT believer is attached to the vine, which is Christ Himself, and can produce spiritual fruit because of that union (John 15:15).

But there is another way to understand v 11. The phrase "know the Lord" can be meant in a positional sense. It might be another way of saying a person has eternal life by believing in Jesus Christ for it (John 17:3). It is possible that what the author of Hebrews means here is that under the New Covenant, all those who are part of it have eternal life. In the OT, there were Jews in the nation that did not have eternal life. That will not be the case in the world to come. When the kingdom of God (i.e., the Millennium) begins, all Jews will be believers (Rom 11:26). That is certainly the case today with those who are part of the Body of Christ. A person becomes part of that Body when he has believed in Jesus for eternal life.

In v 12 the author concludes his quote from Jeremiah 31 and the promises of the New Covenant. This will be one of the "better promises" of the New Covenant that he will discuss in detail in chapter 10. Here he simply says that God will be **merciful** to those under the New Covenant, and **their sins** He **will remember no more**.

Under the Old Covenant, there was always a need to make sacrifices for sin. Whenever a person under that covenant sinned, he or she had to make another sacrifice. Sin was never taken care of once for all. Under the New Covenant, the sacrifice of Christ took away the sins of God's people forever. Such a privilege was something the Law of Moses did not provide.

In v 13 the author gives his main point in quoting from Jeremiah 31. Much more could be said about how the Church currently enjoys the benefits of the blessings of the New Covenant, even though that covenant was promised to the nation of Israel during the time of Jeremiah. Whatever could be said about these things, the author makes it clear that the New Covenant is vastly superior to the Old. With the coming of the **new covenant** the old has become **obsolete**.

Application

The Old Covenant is something that has become obsolete and replaced by something better, **ready to vanish away**. As already mentioned, the temple in Jerusalem was still standing when the Book of Hebrews was written. The sacrifices of the Old Covenant were still being made. Even though this was the case, the promised arrival of the New Covenant spelled the end of these things. The priests in the temple were only performing inferior duties related to an inferior covenant which had been replaced. Even the OT Scriptures themselves in Jeremiah 31 said this was the case. It was only a matter of time until these things passed from the scene. It happened in AD 70 when the Temple was destroyed. That probably occurred only a year or two after the Book of Hebrews was written.

Once again, the application to the original readers of Hebrews is crystal clear. If the Jewish religion was based upon a covenant that God said would be replaced, and that replacement covenant will be enacted through by Christ when He returns, how could a believer in Jesus Christ possibly think the way to worship God was through the old one? (In this interim time between the Old and New Covenants, we serve in anticipation of the New Covenant, being guided by the teachings and commands of the NT.)

Christ's Superior Service and Sacrifice

IN CHAPTER 8 WE SAW that Christ brought in a superior covenant.
Included in that covenant is the fact that Christ serves in a better
tabernacle. The author compares the earthly and heavenly sanctuaries in
9:1-15. Then he compares Christ's superior sacrifice with the temporary
and inferior sacrifices of Israel's high priests (9:16-28).

In comparing the tabernacle of the Old Covenant with the New,
the first thing the author does is to describe the old tabernacle. The old
tabernacle belonged to this world and was disappearing.

Inferior Furniture (vv 1-5)

[1] **Then indeed, even the first *covenant* had ordinances of
divine service and the earthly sanctuary. [2] For a tabernacle
was prepared: the first *part*, in which *was* the lampstand, the
table, and the showbread, which is called the sanctuary; [3] and
behind the second veil, the part of the tabernacle which is
called the Holiest of All, [4] which had the golden censer and
the ark of the covenant overlaid on all sides with gold, in
which were the golden pot that had the manna, Aaron's rod
that budded, and the tablets of the covenant; [5] and above it
were the cherubim of glory overshadowing the mercy seat.
Of these things we cannot now speak in detail.**

In these verses the emphasis is that the tabernacle Moses built in
the wilderness was an **earthly sanctuary** (v 1). It was made of earthly
material and belonged to this world. This will be compared in v 11 with

the sanctuary in which Christ serves as High Priest. That sanctuary does not belong to this world.

In the worldly sanctuary there were **ordinances of divine service**. This refers to what went on in the tabernacle, what the priests did in it. They will be discussed in detail in vv 6-10.

It is clear that the sanctuary the author is talking about was the one the Jews used in the early part of their history. The temple in Jerusalem later replaced the tabernacle. The temple was much larger but was modeled on the pattern of the tabernacle built in the wilderness.

This **tabernacle** had two parts. The **first part** was called the Holy Place, or **sanctuary**; the second part was **called the Holiest of All**, or the Holy of Holies (vv 2-3). These two parts formed a rectangle. The Holy Place was approximately 30 feet long and 15 feet wide. The Holy of Holies had the same width but was only 15 feet long.

To enter into the Holy Place, one went through a veil or curtain. To enter into the Holy of Holies, one had to go through a **second veil**. The Holy Place had furnishings that belonged to this world. On the southern side it had a **lampstand**. Since there were no windows in the Holy Place, this lampstand provided the light for it. This *lampstand* is often called the "menorah" and is the coat of arms for the modern day nation of Israel.

On the northern side of the Holy Place was a **table**. Every week the priests would place twelve loaves of **showbread** on this table. The old ones were eaten by the priests. Jesus refers to this practice in Matt 12:4.

In vv 4-5 there is a description of the earthly furniture found in the Holy of Holies. It is said that the **golden censer** was in this room. The two words refer to the altar of incense. This was the altar on which the priests burnt incense on a daily basis.

The problem here is that this altar was not located in the Holy of Holies. It was located in the Holy Place, right in front of the veil that separated the Holy Place from the Holy of Holies.

While some may say that the author of Hebrews made a mistake here, it is unlikely. He is very familiar with the OT tabernacle and would not have been ignorant of what was in the Holy of Holies, the most important room in the Jewish religion.

The most important day of the Jewish religion was the Day of Atonement, when the high priest would offer a sacrifice for the sins of the nation for the year. The author evidently has this day in mind and will discuss it here in vv 5 and 7. On that day, the veil between the two rooms of the tabernacle was open. At that time, since the altar of incense stood between the two rooms at the veil, it became part of the Holy of Holies.

The smoke from the incense burned on the altar probably represented the prayers of God's people. This smoke would symbolically ascend into the "ears" of God. Certainly the smoke of that incense would also enter into the Holy of Holies. It would on the Day of Atonement. In addition, when the high priest entered the Holy of Holies, he would take with him coals from the altar (Lev 16:12-13). Simply put, the altar of incense stood at the entrance of the Holy of Holies and played a major role in what happened there.

Inside the veil there was also the famous **ark of the covenant**. It was a box that contained the tablets of the covenant, which was the law written by God at Mount Sinai. But it also contained other objects. These were the **pot** of **manna** and **Aaron's rod that budded**. The manna was the food God fed the Jews in their wilderness wanderings (Exod 16:32). The rod that budded was a miracle that God performed to show that Aaron was His choice as high priest (Numbers 17).

Over the ark of the covenant there were two **cherubim**, or angels. They faced each other and were on opposite ends of the **mercy seat** where the high priest, on the Day of Atonement, would place the blood of the animal to cover the sins of the people for the past year.

These angels are described as being **cherubim of glory**. This probably means that they paint a picture for us. In the OT we are told that the cherubim are a class of angels in the presence of God in heaven (Ezek 1:5; 10:15, 20). Their presence represents the glory of the presence of God.

As impressive as these furnishings were, they were all temporary. That is the main point the author wants to make. He states in v 4 that these things often contained **gold**. Gold, though valuable, still belongs to this world. Whatever picture these things indicate, they are that—a picture. Christ, on the other hand, serves in the real tabernacle and presence of God.

In addition, when the Book of Hebrews was written, the temple in Jerusalem did not even have the ark of the covenant. It had been lost for centuries. The pot of manna, Aaron's rod, the mercy seat, and the angels overshadowing it had been lost to history as well. Again, Christ's sanctuary is not like that. Nothing is missing!

But it was not just the furniture of the old sanctuary that was temporary and inferior. The ministry that the priests conducted in the sanctuary was also inferior. The author discusses that in vv 6-10.

Inferior Ministry (vv 6-10)

> [6] Now when these things had been thus prepared, the priests always went into the first part of the tabernacle, performing the services. [7] But into the second part the high priest *went* alone once a year, not without blood, which he offered for himself and for the people's sins *committed* in ignorance; [8] the Holy Spirit indicating this, that the way into the Holiest of All was not yet made manifest while the first tabernacle was still standing. [9] It was symbolic for the present time in which both gifts and sacrifices are offered which cannot make him who performed the service perfect in regard to the conscience— [10] *concerned* only with foods and drinks, various washings, and fleshly ordinances imposed until the time of reformation.

The **priests** went into the Holy Place, or the **first part of the tabernacle**, on a daily basis, that is, **always** (v 6). They performed **services**, or ministry. These services included the burning of incense, placing bread on the table, and trimming the branches of the lampstand to provide light.

Into the Holy of Holies, or the **second part** of the tabernacle, only the **high priest** could go. But there were limitations even on this. He could only go in there **once a year**, and he had to bring **blood**. This refers to the Day of Atonement (Yom Kippur) when the high priest had to bring the blood of an animal for his own sins and the blood of another animal for the **people's sins** (v 7).

The sins of the people that this blood covered were sins done **in ignorance**. The Old Covenant made a distinction between those sins committed because of weakness or because the person did not realize his actions had violated the covenant and those sins that were done in open rebellion against God. Sins committed in rebellion against God were punishable by death.

The main point in the discussion here is that all of the ministries that were performed in the old tabernacle did not provide access to God. As a result, these ministries had their faults. Not all Jews could do these things. Only the priests could enter the Holy Place. Since women could not be priests, no woman could enter it. In other words, the privilege of getting closer to the presence of God was not for everybody. It was only for a few.

The Jewish Christian readers of Hebrews knew that under the Old Covenant, the privilege of entering into the room that represented the presence of God on earth, the Holy of Holies, was even more limited. Only the high priest could do that, and then, only with very strict restrictions. Even here it was not a permanent access.

In v 8 the author drives home the point that under the Old Covenant this limited access to God existed. It was all a picture. The **Holy Spirit** inspired the way worship was done under that system. It was set up that way to show that the **way into the** presence of God was **not yet made manifest**. While the **first tabernacle**, which existed under the Law of Moses, was operating, complete and final access into the presence of God was not a reality for God's people.

The words *not yet* tell us that this picture in the Old Covenant was temporary. There would come a time when access to God would indeed be shown. Something better was to come.

The author specifically says that the tabernacle in the OT was **symbolic**. The Greek word is literally "a parable." It was never meant to be God's final say on the sacrifice for our sins. It pointed to something. This was true even though the temple was still standing when the Book of Hebrews was written. In that **present time** there were **sacrifices** still being **offered** (v 9). The sad thing for the author of Hebrews is that people were still following the parable when the real thing, what the parable pointed to, had arrived in Christ.

It was also sad because the sacrifices still being performed would never make anyone **perfect in regard to the conscience**. The sacrifices of the Old Covenant needed to be done constantly, and the Day of Atonement occurred every year because these things did not take care of the worshiper's sins once for all. His sin was always before him, and his conscience condemned him. The idea of *perfection* here is the goal of the sacrifices. Under the old, nobody ever obtained the goal of having a clear conscience before God concerning his sins.

The idea of the *conscience* introduces the concept of the inner part of man and a need that the worshiper of God has. Communion with God involves a cleansing on the inside. This is something that the Old Covenant did not address. It only dealt with outward things. In v 10 the author lists these external things.

The **ordinances** of the tabernacle were concerned with **fleshly** things, that is, the things of this world. The Old Covenant had many regulations concerning **foods and drinks**. Some foods were clean and could be eaten, and some could not. We can see in the NT how the Pharisees endlessly discussed these things.

There were also **various washings**. When people were ceremonially unclean, such as after touching a dead body or when a woman completed her monthly cycle, they would wash themselves. The priests would wash themselves prior to performing their duties.

But what a person eats or however many baths he takes does not do anything for the conscience or the inner part of man. These things under the Old Covenant were never meant to give one a permanently clean conscience before God. They were only given **until the time of reformation**. The word *until*, like the words *not yet* in v 8, shows that God had something better coming. The Old Covenant was not God's final word on how He would meet the spiritual needs of His people. There would be a time when God would reform how His people worshiped Him. He would have a new tabernacle, a new sacrifice, and a new High Priest. These things would deal with the inner part of man.

The *until* and the *not yet* have arrived. The time of reformation has occurred. Christ has brought it about. The author plainly states that in the next section.

The Perfect Has Arrived in Christ (vv 11-15)

11 But Christ came *as* High Priest of the good things to come, with the greater and more perfect tabernacle not made with hands, that is, not of this creation. 12 Not with the blood of goats and calves, but with His own blood He entered the Most Holy Place once for all, having obtained eternal redemption. 13 For if the blood of bulls and goats and the

**ashes of a heifer, sprinkling the unclean, sanctifies for the
purifying of the flesh, ¹⁴ how much more shall the blood
of Christ, who through the eternal Spirit offered Himself
without spot to God, cleanse your conscience from dead
works to serve the living God? ¹⁵ And for this reason He is
the Mediator of the new covenant, by means of death, for the
redemption of the transgressions under the first covenant,
that those who are called may receive the promise of the
eternal inheritance.**

The author has already said that Christ is the new High Priest. Now
he tells us about the ministry this High Priest performs and how it
compares to the ministry done in the old tabernacle.

Christ has come as the **High Priest of the good things to come**.
The good things to come is a reference to the New Covenant that God
predicted would replace the Old Covenant. The word *things* is in the
plural because the New Covenant brings with it the promise of many
different things (8:6), including complete access to God. As discussed in
chapter 8, even though the New Covenant is for the nation of Israel, the
basis of the new covenant Christ has made with the church also includes
some of these things.

Unlike the tabernacle in the Old Covenant, under Christ His people
have a **greater and more perfect tabernacle**. This tabernacle involves
the heavenly Holy of Holies (8:2). This is where Christ is seated as our
High Priest. This is the one that the old tabernacle pointed to. It is not
like the old tabernacle that had earthly furniture and was part of **this
creation**.

This would be expected. If Christ brought in a better system of
approaching God, we would expect that He had a better tabernacle in
which His people would approach Him.

But it isn't just the tabernacle itself that is superior. The sacrifice
involved with our new High Priest is superior as well. In vv 6-7 the
author had discussed the sacrifices done in the old tabernacle. They
involved **the blood of goats and calves** (v 12). There were many
sacrifices that were done under the Old Covenant, and the reference to
these animals may refer to all of these sacrifices. It is also possible that
the author of Hebrews has in mind here the sacrifices offered on the Day

of Atonement. On that day the high priest would offer up a calf for his own sins and a goat for the sins of the people.

But just as the tabernacle in which Christ serves as High Priest is better than the old, so is His sacrifice. When the old high priest entered the Holy of Holies, he brought the blood of an animal. Christ, however, **entered with His own blood**.

When we remember who He is we understand how far superior this blood is. The author said in the first chapter that He is God, the Creator, the One who holds the universe together with His word, and the One who will rule over the kingdom of God forever. Compare His blood with the blood of a goat. Which is superior?

The greatness of this sacrifice is also seen in that Christ entered into the heavenly Holy of Holies **once for all**. This, of course, is in contrast to how, under the Old Covenant, the high priest had to enter the Holy of Holies every year.

Christ only had to do this once because His blood **obtained eternal redemption**. As is well known, the word *redemption* means "to pay a price." Christ's death paid the price for sins once for all. That is why it happened only once. Since this payment only occurs once, it has eternal consequences.

The author will discuss more of this in Chap. 10. Here the point is that animals could never do that. People in the OT were saved from eternal condemnation just as people today are—by believing in the Messiah. They believed in the One who was to come (Gen 3:15; 15:6; Hab 2:4; John 5:39-40; 8:56). We believe in the One who has already come.

Christ's death paid for the sins of all time in order that whoever believes in Him for the gift of eternal life will receive it. The animals in the OT did not take care of those sins. His death did.

The OT sacrifices did two things. First, they were done in obedience to God. If the people wanted to avoid the discipline of God upon themselves and the nation, they needed to obey God by making those sacrifices.

Secondly, the sacrifices pointed to the ultimate sacrifice that would come. When the Messiah came, He would make the sacrifice that would bring the forgiveness of sins. This forgiveness would make the gift of eternal life possible. Like the tabernacle itself, the blood of goats and calves was a "parable."

The OT sacrifices did nothing in regard to an inner cleansing. When a person sinned under the Old Covenant, he was unclean. He could not worship at the tabernacle until he became ceremonially clean. This involved the need for an animal sacrifice.

But this uncleanness was only outward. That is all the OT dealt with (v 10). But Christ's sacrifice dealt with an inner cleansing, one that impacted the conscience of the worshiper.

The author makes this point in vv 13-14, where he uses an example of an OT sacrifice. In Numbers 19 we are told about the **ashes of a** red **heifer**. This animal was sacrificed, then burned in the wilderness outside of the congregation. The ashes of the heifer were mixed with water. If a Jew touched a dead body, he became ceremonially **unclean**. He could not worship at the tabernacle. He could not have normal interactions with God or other men. He only became clean if the water and ashes of the heifer were sprinkled on him.

The water was sprinkled on his **flesh**. It only had a **purifying** impact on the worshipper in this sense. It was an outward cleansing.

The blood of Christ, on the other hand, is much greater than such sacrifices. First of all, His sacrifice is the sacrifice of **Himself**. It did not involve the blood of animals. Here is a sacrifice that was done willingly, as opposed to the animals that had no say in the matter.

Secondly, it is a sacrifice offered by means of the **eternal Spirit**. As such, it is one that cleanses the **conscience**, or the inner part of man. The Spirit can impact the inner part of man. In addition, since the Spirit is eternal, the sacrifice of Christ has an eternal significance, unlike the OT sacrifices that were offered continually year after year.

It also needs to be pointed out that Christ's sacrifice of Himself was **without spot**. This shows also how Christ was superior to the OT sacrifices. The animals needed to be without any defects, but these defects dealt with outward things. They could not be sick or lame, for example. Here the reference is to Christ's inner and moral perfection. He was without sin (4:15; 7:26).

It is interesting that the sacrifice of Christ, as discussed in v 14, involved all three Persons of the Trinity. **Christ** the Son **offered Himself**; this sacrifice was done **through the Spirit** of God and **offered to God** the Father.

In the next chapter the author will describe in detail what the cleansing of the conscience means. Here it is simply contrasted with the OT sacrifices. In Christ's sacrifice, the believer has a sacrifice that is eternal and has taken care of sins once for all. The believer has complete forgiveness. Our consciences are clear. It is not like the OT sacrifices which never did that. In order to have the communion with God that the Old Covenant provided, there was a constant need to make more sacrifices. The conscience of the worshiper was never cleansed.

That is the meaning of **dead works** in v 14. This is a reference to the sacrifices and rituals of the Old Covenant. They could never result in a clear conscience before God, even for the believer in the Old Covenant. They could never be the basis for obtaining life. In Christ there is no need for these dead rituals to continue.

This is all probably related to what the original readers were going through. They were being lured back to Judaism because of the persecution they were experiencing. Part of that allure was the teaching that they needed to go back to the OT system of sacrifices. They were being told that Christ's sacrifice was not sufficient. To worship God they needed to continue making sacrifices and deal with ceremonial and outward uncleanness. If they were going to please God, this is what they needed to do.

But the author says that it is only through the sacrifice of Christ that one is free to **serve the living God**. A person can only truly serve God when he has full confidence that his sins have been taken care of. He has a clean conscience before God. He does not need to go through some ritual exercise in order to approach Him.

Because of what Christ's death has accomplished—eternal redemption and an inner cleansing—**He** has become **the Mediator of the new covenant** (v 15). He has brought in the blessings of the New Covenant (8:8-12). In this New Covenant Christ is the Mediator in the sense that He is the "go between" between God and man. That is the function of a high priest, the subject of chapters 5–10.

Christ's death took care of all the **transgressions under the first covenant**. In the OT believers did not obtain forgiveness through the blood of animals. Ultimately, their sins were paid for by the *coming* sacrifice of Christ.

It is also very possible that the author has something additional in mind. If these readers were thinking about going back to Judaism because they worried about the forgiveness of sins and their ability to serve God, the author is telling them that even the sins they committed before coming to faith were paid for by the **death** of Christ. They did not need to have any guilt. They could have a clear conscience.

If they did indeed serve God and remained faithful to Him through their High Priest Jesus Christ, they would obtain a **promise**. They had been told that the New Covenant had greater promises (8:6). Here, one of those promises is given. It is one of **eternal inheritance**.

This inheritance is not simply "going to heaven." Eternal life is given to anyone who simply believes in Jesus Christ for eternal life and is a free gift. This inheritance is something promised to those who remain faithful to Christ and **serve God** (v 14). It involves taking advantage of Christ as our Mediator, that is, our High Priest (v 11). The reader needed to go to Him for help in obtaining this inheritance.

This inheritance is a reward for faithfulness. It is the reward of reigning with Christ as one of His partners in the world to come (1:9). Such a believer will actually inherit part of Christ's kingdom. He will actually reign over cities in that kingdom (Luke 19:17). This inheritance is eternal because it will be an eternal kingdom.

All believers **are called** to obtain such an inheritance. Unfortunately, not all will receive this reward. That is what the Book of Hebrews is about. If the readers went back to Judaism, they would not lose eternal life since that is impossible. But they would lose the reward of an eternal inheritance in the kingdom of God.

The believer in Jesus Christ, then, has the promise of inward cleansing and the possibility of an eternal inheritance. All of this was made possible by the death of Christ. In the rest of Chap. 9 the author will say why this death was necessary.

A Death Was Necessary in the Old Covenant (vv 16-22)

[16] For where there is a testament, there must also of necessity be the death of the testator. [17] For a testament *is* in force after men are dead, since it has no power at all while the testator lives. [18] Therefore not even the first *covenant* was dedicated without blood. [19] For when Moses had spoken every precept to all the people according to the law, he took the blood of calves and goats, with water, scarlet wool, and hyssop, and sprinkled both the book itself and all the people, [20] saying, *"This is the blood of the covenant which God has*

commanded you." [21] **Then likewise he sprinkled with blood both the tabernacle and all the vessels of the ministry.** [22] **And according to the law almost all things are purified with blood, and without shedding of blood there is no remission.**

Verse 16 is connected to v 15 by two words. Both verses contain the words *death* and *covenant*. In our English translations there is no problem with the word *death*. However, there is a problem with the word *covenant*.

In the New King James Version, as well as in other translations, the translators changed the word covenant to **testament**, even though the Greek words are the same in both verses. The reason they did so is because what is said in vv 16-17 is not true for all covenants. Not all covenants require someone to die in order to go into effect.

The Greek word for *covenant* had another meaning. It often meant "will," as in the last will and testament of someone. Some English translations of the Bible use the word *will* here. We could say that a will was a type of covenant.

What the author says about a will in vv 16-17 is indeed true. In order for a will, or testament, to go into effect, **there must be the death** of the person who made the will. What the author is saying is that the New Covenant is a type of covenant (such as a will) that requires a death.

Christ is the One who made the will. He is the **testator**. As the testator, He had to die in order for the things in the will to be valid, or **in force**. The same is true for a human will. The benefits of the New Covenant could not become a reality until Christ died.

To put it in very simple terms, a will promises certain things to the heirs. There is an inheritance involved. The author just spoke in v 15 of such an inheritance. If this inheritance was going to be given to those who are called, Christ had to die.

Of course, the New Covenant is different from an ordinary will. Christ is not only the testator, the One who made the will. He is also the executor or Mediator of the will (v 15)! This is impossible in normal wills because after the testator has died, he cannot mediate the will. But Christ can be both because He rose from the dead.

The Old Covenant was not exactly like a will. When God made the covenant, He did not die in order to put it into effect. Moses did not die, either. However, the blood of the animals pointed to the bloody nature of the covenant. This blood, the death of the animals, was needed to put the covenant into effect. We could say that the blood of the animals foreshadowed the death of Christ. It could be said that the Old Covenant was **dedicated** by blood (v 18).

In v 19 the author refers to the bloody nature of the Old Covenant by referring to the time when that Covenant was inaugurated in Exod 24:1-8. At Mount Sinai, Moses had received the book of the Covenant God had made with the people. The book contained what God promised them as well as what He required of the people. At the foot of the mountain, **Moses took the blood** of the sacrificial animals and **sprinkled the book and the people**.

Verse 20 is the main point the author wants to make. Blood was necessary in the Old Covenant. When Moses said, "**this is the blood of the covenant**," he instituted the covenant.

Blood was also necessary to sanctify the **tabernacle** and the things used in it as **vessels of ministry** (v 21). We are specifically told in Leviticus 8 that the altar of the tabernacle was sanctified by the blood of the animal. Exodus 29 tells us that the priests also were sprinkled with blood.

Verse 22 is a summary of the Old Covenant as a whole. In the OT, there were a few things that were **purified** by means other than **blood**. Some things were purified by fire (Num 31:22-23) and others by water (Exod 19:10). But these were exceptions to the rule. Purification by blood was the rule.

In any event, blood was necessary for sins to be forgiven. On the Day of Atonement, when the sins of the year were dealt with, the blood of animals was necessary. Of course, all animal sacrifices required the blood of an animal.

In order to find forgiveness and purification under the Old Covenant, blood was necessary. If the Old pointed to the New, blood would be necessary under the New Covenant as well. The author stated that already in v 16. He will repeat it in the next section. But since the New is better than the Old, there was the need for a better type of blood. The inferior nature of the OT sacrifices would not suffice under the New Covenant. The blood of animals just would not do.

Christ's Better Sacrifice (vv 23-28)

[23] Therefore *it was* necessary that the copies of the things in the heavens should be purified with these, but the heavenly things themselves with better sacrifices than these. [24] For Christ has not entered the holy places made with hands, *which are* copies of the true, but into heaven itself, now to appear in the presence of God for us; [25] not that He should offer Himself often, as the high priest enters the Most Holy Place every year with blood of another— [26] He then would have had to suffer often since the foundation of the world; but now, once at the end of the ages, He has appeared to put away sin by the sacrifice of Himself. [27] And as it is appointed for men to die once, but after this the judgment, [28] so Christ was offered once to bear the sins of many. To those who eagerly wait for Him He will appear a second time, apart from sin, for salvation.

In 8:5 the author of Hebrews stated that the OT tabernacle was a copy of the real presence of God in heaven. He has just stated that the tabernacle, as well as the things in it, were cleansed with blood of animals (9:21). He makes a logical conclusion: if the **copy of the things in the heavens**, that is, the tabernacle in the wilderness, was **purified** by blood, one would expect that the real thing would need to be purified as well. Since the real thing is greater than the copy, the real thing would need something **better** (v 23). It would require a superior sacrifice with superior blood.

It should be noted that the author says there was a need for better **sacrifices**. The word is in the plural. He has made it clear that Jesus only made one sacrifice of Himself (7:27; 9:12). Perhaps the author is using the word in a general sense. Christ's sacrifice took the place of all the many sacrifices in the Old Covenant. It is also possible that the author has in mind the fact that Christ's life included other sacrifices, such as His prayers for His people (5:7).

This raises a question. Were the heavens, the very presence of God, in need of cleansing? Some have suggested that they needed cleansing because the fall of Satan occurred there. However, it seems best to see the issue in another way.

The tabernacle and the things in it were cleansed in order to provide ministry. The priests in the OT interceded for the people, and the place and things involved in that ministry needed to be purified for that purpose in order for the priests to carry on their duties. Christ is our High Priest. He has entered into heaven to provide ministry for sinful men and women. This place of ministry needed to be an acceptable place for such sinful beings to enter. Christ's blood makes it possible for them to come into God's presence (4:14-16). Such a ministry, and such a cleansing, could not be accomplished through the blood of animals.

The greatness of the place of Christ's ministry for us is explicitly stated in v 24. At the right hand of God He performs this ministry in a place **not made with hands**. It is not a **copy of the true**. Clearly, the OT tabernacle was made with hands and was a copy. Instead, Christ's ministry on behalf of His people is in **heaven itself** and in the very **presence of God**.

The Greek word *presence* denotes a face-to-face meeting. How could the blood of animals that belong to this world purify such a place and make possible such a meeting between mankind and God? The blood of animals in the OT didn't even make such a meeting possible in the tabernacle made with hands.

But there is an additional reason why Christ's sacrifice had to be greater. Since the priestly ministry under the Old Covenant was made possible by the blood of animals, there was an endless supply of sacrifices. There was an endless supply of animals. Under that system the **high priest** could enter **the Most Holy Place every year** (v 25). Such a process could be repeated.

Christ's sacrifice was not like that. He did not **offer Himself often**, or many times. The reason is obvious. Unlike all the animals under the old system, there was only one of Him. He did not enter into the real Most Holy Place every year, but only once. His sacrifice had to take care of the sins of His people once for all.

If His sacrifice did not do that, He **would have to suffer often** (v 26). However, Christ has come **once**. The fact that this happened **once** shows that it is final. The author says that this sacrifice was at **the end of the ages**. Christ's life and death are the climax of religious history. There will be no other sacrifices. In Him God's will in sacrifices has been realized. That will is that sin would be **put away** once for all.

The greatness of Christ's sacrifice in comparison with the Old Covenant is also seen in that it was the **sacrifice of Himself**. He went into the very presence of God through His own blood. The OT high priest went into a copy of God's presence with the **blood of another** (v 25), that is, the blood of an animal.

The fact that Christ died once allows the author of Hebrews to compare Him with all men. All **men die** (v 27). Since Christ was a man, He died as well. He did that when He was **offered once to bear the sins** of mankind (v 28).

But Christ is different from all other men in another way. After men die, they face a **judgment**. Unbelievers face the judgment at the Great White Throne, where they will be cast into hell. Believers will be judged at the Judgment Seat of Christ to determine their rewards in the kingdom of God.

Christ, of course, faces neither judgment. Instead, He will bring **salvation**. Unfortunately, when many see the word *salvation*, they automatically think of salvation from hell. But that cannot be what is meant here. It says that Christ came the first time to bear our sins. This is what makes salvation from hell possible when a person believes in Jesus Christ for eternal life.

However, the salvation spoken of here is given when Christ comes **a second time**. This is a different kind of salvation. The author makes this clear when he says that this salvation has nothing to do with **sin** (v 28).

In addition, this salvation is not for those who simply believe in Jesus Christ for eternal life and are thus saved from hell. Instead it is for those **who eagerly wait for** His coming. In the context of the Book of Hebrews, Christians who eagerly look for Christ's return are those who hold fast their Christian confession and hope (3:14; 4:1; 5:9; 6:13-20). They receive a salvation or deliverance from their enemies (1:14). Christ will exalt them. This salvation will include the reward of an inheritance in God's kingdom (9:15).

Not all Christians eagerly long for the return of Christ. Certainly if the original readers of Hebrews went back to Judaism, they would cease to do so. But Paul says that those Christians who maintain this hope will receive the reward of a specific crown (2 Tim 4:8).

The author has just said that all men will be judged (v 27). The judgment for believers has nothing to do with whether they enter the kingdom of God or go to hell. The judgment at the Judgment Seat of

Christ has to do with rewards (1 Cor 3:10-15; 9:24-27; 2 Cor 5:9-10). The rewards there include reigning with Christ as one of His partners in His kingdom.

Those believers who obey the Lord, hold firm to the end, and eagerly wait for His appearing will experience salvation through the judgment at the Judgment Seat of Christ. They do not have to fear this judgment (1 John 2:28).

The whole context of chapter 9 points to the fact that the author is not talking about what a person has to do to be saved from hell. Instead, he is talking about the ministry of Jesus as our High Priest. This is something Jesus is doing in the present. His death in the past made our salvation from hell possible. But now He is interceding for His people. His ministry as High Priest is not what makes salvation from hell possible; it makes it possible for His people to find the grace, mercy, and strength they need to hold firm to the end and please Him. Those that take advantage of this ministry of the Lord will find that they will eagerly await His appearing.

Believers already have a salvation from hell. However, those who take advantage of the ministry of their great High Priest will also experience another kind of "deliverance" when He comes the second time and they stand before Him in judgment. But they must respond in an appropriate way. Chapter 10 will address this issue.

Application

As in chapter 8, in chapter 9 the author of Hebrews compares the Old and New Covenants. The New Covenant was promised to the nation of Israel and will be placed in effect with that nation in the millennial kingdom. All of the blessings of the New Covenant will only be possible because of the death of Christ.

But Christ has also made a covenant with NT believers. Complete and inward cleansing, as well as the possibility of an eternal inheritance, are also available to those in the Church. These things are also possible because of Christ's death.

The original readers were Jewish Christians who were part of the Church. The point is clear. Why would they think of going back to the Old?

For a believer today the application is clear for us as well. With all that Christ's death has done, why would we not remain faithful to Him, regardless of the difficulties we encounter?

Hold Fast the Confession of Your Hope

CHAPTER 10 MARKS THE conclusion of the author's discussion on the High Priesthood of Jesus Christ. In the entire discussion we see that Christ is superior to the high priests of the OT. In chapter 7 the author compared Him specifically to the OT priests. From 8:1–9:15 he says that Christ has a superior ministry which springs from a superior covenant. From 9:16-28 we saw that Christ's sacrifice of Himself is superior to the OT sacrifices. Now in 10:1-18 we see the results of His superior sacrifice. The author will close this discussion with another warning passage and the options available to his Christian readers. The warning is addressed to those who would abandon the greater covenant and ministry of Christ to return to the old system.

The Inferior Nature of the OT Sacrifices (vv 1-4)

¹For the law, having a shadow of the good things to come, *and* not the very image of the things, can never with these same sacrifices, which they offer continually year by year, make those who approach perfect. ² For then would they not have ceased to be offered? For the worshipers, once purified, would have had no more consciousness of sins. ³ But in those *sacrifices there* is a reminder of sins every year. ⁴ For it is not possible that the blood of bulls and goats could take away sins.

The **law**, that is, the Old Covenant, was only a **shadow** of something that would come later. A shadow is not the real thing it represents. The law pointed to the **good things** (v 1). Clearly in this context such things are found in the New Covenant which Christ brought. He and His sacrifice are the **very image** to which the old system pointed.

When it came to sacrifices for sin, the sacrifices found in the Law were not able to **make** the worshiper **perfect**. The verb *make perfect* means "to reach a goal." It was never God's intention that the sacrifices of the OT would do what God desired. They pointed to the real thing that God would later bring.

The goal that God desired for a sacrifice for sin is that it would take care of sin once for all. It would involve a cleansing of the inward man, or the conscience (9:9). It would allow the worshiper to go into the presence of God (9:8).

The old system of sacrifices could **never** do that. That is why they had to be repeated over and over. The author of Hebrews emphasizes that aspect of those sacrifices. They are the **same sacrifices** offered **continually** and **year** after **year**. Since they continued to be offered, it is clear that they never took care of the issue of sin once for all.

In v 2 the author makes the logical conclusion about the old sacrifices. If they had made the worshiper perfect, they would have **ceased to be offered**. The fact that they were offered every year shows that the goal of the sacrifices was not reached. This verse also suggests that the temple in Jerusalem was still standing, and the sacrifices were still being offered. That means that these sacrifices had been going on for around 1500 years when Hebrews was written.

Instead, the sacrifice for sin God desired would be done **once** and would leave the **worshipers purified**, that is, with no **consciousness of sins**. This means that God wanted a sacrifice that cleansed His people once for all. It involved an inner cleansing of the conscience that could not be repeated. It would provide permanent access to God.

Not only did the old **sacrifices** not accomplish this, they were a **reminder** to the people that their **sins** had not been dealt with once for all. **Every year** on the Day of Atonement, the high priest would offer another animal for the sins of the past year (v 3). On that day, the people of God would gather at the tabernacle. The high priest would represent them as he entered into the Holy of Holies. They were forbidden from entering themselves.

The reason that was the case is stated in v 4. The **blood** of animals cannot **take away sins**. Certainly God commanded the people to perform these sacrifices. When people of faith did so, they would be blessed by God because of their obedience. However, true forgiveness was not found in them. Forgiveness was given only in the sense that God did not judge the people for their sins in light of the coming sacrifice He would provide. It would be in this coming sacrifice that forgiveness would be found for believers under the Old and New Covenants.

Eternal life is given by faith alone. In the OT it was given to those who believed in the coming Messiah. The reason God can give eternal life is because the sins of those who believe have been dealt with once for all. The fact that these sacrifices in the old system were offered over and over again was a reminder that the blood of those animals was not the place to find that forgiveness.

And how could they? How could the blood of a dumb, unwilling animal take care of the sins of God's people once for all? How could it give such peace and allow unfettered access into the presence of God?

But that leads to another question. In Hebrews 1 Jesus is described as the eternal God, the Creator of all things. How could His blood *not* accomplish what God wanted in a sacrifice?

Christ's Sacrifice Accomplished God's Will (vv 5-10)

⁵ Therefore, when He came into the world, He said:

> *"Sacrifice and offering You did not desire,*
> *But a body You have prepared for Me.*
> *⁶ In burnt offerings and sacrifices for sin*
> *You had no pleasure.*
> *⁷ Then I said, 'Behold, I have come—*
> *In the volume of the book it is written of Me—*
> *To do Your will, O God.'"*

⁸ Previously saying, "*Sacrifice and offering, burnt offerings, and offerings for sin You did not desire, nor had pleasure in them*" (which are offered according to the law), ⁹ then He said, "*Behold, I have come to do Your will, O God.*" He takes away the first that He may establish the second. ¹⁰ By that will we have been sanctified through the offering of the body of Jesus Christ once for all.

It was God's will that His people would have their sins forgiven once for all and have complete access into His presence. These things were not available in the tabernacle of the Old Covenant and the animal sacrifices performed in it. Something else was needed. In vv 5-10 the author says that Christ's sacrifice of Himself accomplished God's will. The word *will*, either as a verb or noun, is found five times in these verses.

Christ **came into the world** to accomplish God's will or **desire** (v 5). This is a reference to Christ's incarnation when He became a man. The author quotes from Ps 40:6-8. In that Psalm David writes that his heart's desire is to do what God desires of him. Here the Psalm is applied to Christ.

The Psalm, of course, was part of the OT. Even in this Psalm David says that the **sacrifice and offerings** found in the Old Covenant were not what God wanted. God had **no pleasure** in them. This included the **burnt offerings** (vv 5-6). The whole system was inadequate.

In order to fulfill what was lacking in that sacrificial system, **a body** was **prepared for** Christ. In the original Psalm, David speaks of his body as being willing to obey what God wants him to do. The point is that if David was not obedient to God, all the sacrifices of the OT were worthless. God did not want His people to simply offer ritualistic sacrifices. He wanted their obedience.

Christ, at His incarnation, received a body in order to obey God's will. Christ came into this world to do what God wanted. God wanted Him to become the sacrifice for the sins of His people. Of course, as God, Christ could not die. In order to do that, He had to become a man.

Christ came to do the **will** of **God** (v 7). He came to take away our sins forever and make us perfect before God. This is something the author will drive home in vv 10 and 14. It was something the blood of animals could never do.

Once again we see that the OT, **the book**, spoke about this coming sacrifice. Psalm 40, after saying that God was not pleased with animal sacrifices, speaks of something that would come which would accomplish what God wanted. As we have seen throughout the Book of Hebrews, Christians who were contemplating returning to Judaism to worship God were returning to a system of worship God did not desire. He had replaced it with something infinitely better.

Verses 8-9 paraphrase vv 5-7. With the coming of Christ and His sacrifice, He **takes away the first**. This refers to the old system of sacrifices which did not accomplish God's will. He has removed it. The verb means to destroy something. Christ has completely abolished the Old Covenant and its sacrifices and has established **the second**. This is a reference to the New Covenant which did accomplish God's will.

In v 10 the author tells us what the **will** of God was when it comes to sacrifices. It is that His people would be **sanctified once for all**. The word *sanctified* means "to be made holy." The verb here is in the perfect tense. This means that it is something that happened in the past but the results carry on into the present. God wanted a sacrifice that would make the believer holy once and forever. The results would continue on.

In other words, the sanctification here is not a process. It is done once for all. When a person believes in Jesus Christ for eternal life, he is permanently holy and remains that way. What we see here is that the author uses the word *sanctified* to refer to what we often mean by "salvation." When a person believes in Jesus Christ, he is declared holy. He has been saved from hell.

As we saw earlier, the word "salvation" is used in Hebrews in another way (1:14; 2:3). It is used to describe how Christ will deliver His people from their enemies and reward those who are faithful to Him. In the Book of Hebrews, salvation involves work and faithfulness. It involves a process. Sanctification does not. It happens once, at the moment of faith.

Verse 10 is a strong statement about the eternal security of believers in Jesus Christ. They cannot lose their eternal life. God has made them holy *forever*.

This sanctification, or holiness before God, is brought about by the **offering of Jesus Christ**. Christ's death on the cross was the payment for all of our sins. Because our sins have been paid for, God can give eternal life to all who believe and can declare them holy. As a result, it provides the believer with access to God, a cleansing of the consciousness of our sins, and the freedom to serve God (9:9-10, 14).

I attended a college whose mascot was a falcon. Our biggest rival was West Point. The mascot of West Point was a donkey. During football games we would release the falcon, and it would do amazing feats of flight, including catching things tossed high in the air. After watching the falcon perform these stunts, we students would invariably yell, "Let's see your donkey do that!"

Here the author of Hebrews is comparing the Jewish sacrifices under the Old Covenant with the sacrifice of the Son of God. He does so because these readers were thinking about returning to the old system of animal sacrifices. He shows them what the sacrifice of Christ has done. It is as if he is saying, "Let's see your animals do that!"

We should also contemplate that in these verses we are told why Jesus became a man. He did so in order to be our sacrifice. From the very beginning He knew that He was headed to Calvary to accomplish the will of God for us. In vv 11-18 the author continues to describe the magnificent results of His sacrifice.

More Results of Christ's Sacrifice (vv 11-18)

[11] And every priest stands ministering daily and offering repeatedly the same sacrifices, which can never take away sins. [12] But this Man, after He had offered one sacrifice for sins forever, sat down at the right hand of God, [13] from that time waiting till His enemies are made His footstool. [14] For by one offering He has perfected forever those who are being sanctified.[15] But the Holy Spirit also witnesses to us; for after He had said before, [16] *"This is the covenant that I will make with them after those days, says the Lord: I will put My laws into their hearts, and in their minds I will write them,"* [17] then He adds, *"Their sins and their lawless deeds I will remember no more."* [18] Now where there is remission of these, *there* is no longer an offering for sin.

As a result of making His people holy or sanctified forever, Jesus' sacrifice of Himself means that He is finished with His sacrificial work. To make this point, once again the author of Hebrews compares Christ with the priests of the OT. A **priest** in the OT **stands** (v 11) as he performs his ministry. The reason he stands is because he is never finished with the need to make more sacrifices. Neither in the tabernacle nor the temple were there chairs on which the priests could sit.

As a result, they make these offerings **daily** and **repeatedly**. They are the **same sacrifices** over and over. In these words the author is painting a picture of continuous work. The work was exhausting because the sacrifices could **never take away sins.**

All of this is contrasted with Christ. He made **one sacrifice**, not a sacrifice that is repeated. As a result, He **sat down** (v 12). His work was finished.

He sat down **at the right hand of God**. In light of vv 5-10, the reader knows He is seated there because He fulfilled the will of God in the sacrifice of Himself. Christ's sacrifice was completely acceptable to the Father on behalf of the people He serves as High Priest. Their **sins** are taken care of **forever**.

But there is another result of the finished work of Christ. He is now **waiting** (v 13). For that day when all of **His enemies** are defeated. This, of course, takes us back to 1:13 which says the same thing and refers to the fact that Christ will be the King of the world to come. His seated position shows that to Him belongs the ultimate victory.

In vv 11-12 we are told that Christ is seated in the heavens as our High Priest. In v 13 He is seated as our coming King. These verses are a good summary of the Book of Hebrews. He fulfills both offices for His people.

This is a very important point in the Book of Hebrews. The readers were surrounded by the enemies of Christ. They needed to know that it was only a matter of time before Christ returns and defeats these enemies. The King will "save" His people from their enemies and give those who are faithful to Him an inheritance in His kingdom (9:15, 28). This is not what it means to "go to heaven." Instead this salvation and inheritance are rewards the King will give to those who hold on (3:14; 4:14, 16).

In order to hold on, they must draw near to Christ as their High Priest. To do that, they must have confidence to approach Him. They needed to know they were completely acceptable with Christ as their representative before God.

In v 14 the author says the believer can have that confidence. He describes believers as those **who are sanctified**. Unfortunately, some translations, including the New King James Version, translate it "those who are *being* sanctified." This makes it sound as though their sanctification is a process and has not been complete. But here in Hebrews 10 it is not a process at all. In vv 10 and 29 this sanctification is something that happened in the past. It is done once for all and **forever** (vv 12 and 14).

The phrase *those who are sanctified* is a participle (*hagiazomenous*). It simply describes what someone is. It is in the passive voice, which simply means they were declared holy, or set apart sanctified by God through Christ. The exact same participle is used this way in Heb 2:11 (*those who are sanctified = those who are set apart*). It is a way of saying a person is a believer. As discussed above, the word *sanctified* in the Book of Hebrews is equivalent to what Christians in America usually mean by the word *saved.* The believer has been **perfected** forever. This word is in the perfect, which means it has happened in the past but the results continue. It means that the believer's conscience is clear concerning his sins (9:8-9). They have been forgiven once and for all. He can thus approach God boldly.

To summarize, v 14 is saying that those who are sanctified (saved from hell) are perfected (they have complete access to God) forever. It is clear from this verse that the author of Hebrews believed in "once saved always saved." Much confusion about the Book of Hebrews would be avoided if the reader remembers this simple fact. The warning passages in Hebrews, including the one that soon follows in 10:26-31, *cannot* mean that a believer loses his salvation from hell.

The original readers of the Book of Hebrews came from a Jewish background. They had a great deal of respect for the OT. The author has already reminded them that the OT predicted that a New Covenant would replace the Old (8:7-12). In vv 15-17 he tells them that this New Covenant says the same thing about the sanctification and perfection of the believer in Jesus Christ.

When Jeremiah spoke of these things concerning the New Covenant in Jeremiah 31 (8:8-12), it was not just a man speaking. Jeremiah spoke through the **Holy Spirit** (v 15). God is the author of the New Covenant. If the New Covenant was going to involve an inner cleansing, there had to be a sacrifice that would remove the **sins and lawless deeds** of His people forever (vv 16-17).

In the sacrifices of the Old Covenant there was a reminder of sins (10:3). Under the New, God **remembers** them **no more**. This can lead to true worship, which the author will discuss in vv 19-22.

Since all of this comes about by the one sacrifice of Christ, the conclusion is obvious. For the believer, **there is no longer** any **offering** to be made (v 18). God put an end to all sacrifices. The Old has been replaced.

All of this is very appropriate to the original readers. If they were tempted to go back to some form of Judaism with a system of sacrifices, they were tempted to go back to a system that included meaningless rituals involving dead animals.

The New Covenant, then, has tremendous privileges, as well as magnificent promises. All of these things should encourage the believer to persevere in his Christian faith and walk. The author attempts to do just that in vv 19-25. He gives the readers three commands. He tells them to *draw near* to God, *hold fast*, and *consider* other believers.

These verses come at the close of his discussion on the High Priesthood of Christ (chapters 5–10). It is no accident that these exhortations come here. In light of what Christ's death has done for us, this is how we should respond.

It is also no accident that a very stern warning passage follows (vv 26-31). In light of the privileges the believer has, to reject such privileges would merit a severe punishment. As he leads up to this warning, it is once again clear that the warning is addressed to Christians.

Hold Fast the Confession of Your Hope (vv 19-25)

[19] **Therefore, brethren, having boldness to enter the Holiest by the blood of Jesus,** [20] **by a new and living way which He consecrated for us, through the veil, that is, His flesh,** [21] **and *having* a High Priest over the house of God,** [22] **let us draw near with a true heart in full assurance of faith, having our hearts sprinkled from an evil conscience and our bodies washed with pure water.** [23] **Let us hold fast the confession of *our* hope without wavering, for He who promised *is* faithful.** [24] **And let us consider one another in order to stir up love and good works,** [25] **not forsaking the assembling of ourselves together, as is the manner of some, but exhorting *one another*, and so much the more as you see the Day approaching.**

The **therefore** in v 19 indicates that these verses discuss the author's conclusion concerning what he has said in chapters 8 and 9 (cf. 8:1–9:18) what it means for the believer that Christ has brought in the

New Covenant. It is clear that all of the commands in this section are addressed to Christians. He calls them **brethren** (v 19). As believers, they have **boldness to enter** into the very presence of God. His presence is in the **Holiest**, that is, in the heavenly tabernacle not built with hands (9:11). Christians have this privilege because they are sanctified and have been made perfect forever (vv 10, 14). None of these things are true of unbelievers.

None of this is possible through our own efforts. It has been given **by the blood of Jesus**. Only the perfect sacrifice of the Son could give the worshiper such confidence.

This entrance into God's presence is a **new way** (v 20). Probably the simplest way to understand this is that when Hebrews was written, Christ had only offered Himself on Calvary about thirty-five years prior. In contrast to the Old Covenant, the New Covenant was inaugurated very recently.

But the way is also **living**. In the OT, once a year, the High Priest was allowed into the copy of the heavenly Holy of Holies, with the blood of a *dead* animal. By contrast, Christ is alive. He is seated at the right hand of the Father as the risen King and High Priest.

In the OT the high priest entered into the Holy of Holies through the veil between the Holy of Holies and the Holy Place. Under the New Covenant, we, too, enter through the **veil**. But this veil is the **flesh** of Christ. His body, through His sacrifice of that body, allows us as believers to enter into God's very presence.

Another reason believers can have boldness to enter into that presence is found in v 21. They have a **High Priest** that allows them to do so. Christ is this High Priest who presides **over the house of God**. This is not a reference to the Body of Christ. When a person believes in Jesus Christ for eternal life, he becomes a member of the mystical Body of Christ. He can never be separated from that.

Here the author is talking about what he spoke of in 3:1-6. In the heavenly tabernacle Christ serves as our High Priest. As believers we are part of a worshiping community. The author of Hebrews is exhorting his readers to remain a part of that visible community. He is warning them not to abandon it to return to Judaism. If they choose, they can withdraw from this community and not do the things the author is commanding them to do in vv 19-25.

The first command is to **draw near** to (or, let us approach) God (v 22). This command is in the present tense. It is something believers should do on an ongoing basis and not just once as the context clearly shows. We also see again that the author is giving commands to believers. He includes himself in the exhortation—*let us draw near.*

As believers draw near to God through Christ as a community of worshipers, they are to do so with **full assurance of faith**. They know they can approach God because in Christ they have been perfected forever. They know their sins have been removed once for all, and they are holy in His sight because of Him.

The believer in Jesus Christ can also boldly come before God because he has been completely **washed** (v 22). In the OT the high priests could only enter into the Holy of Holies after a bath. They washed their **bodies** with **water**. But this ritual only pointed to the cleansing that Christ's sacrifice would bring about. Such sacrifice would clean our inner **hearts and conscience** and render the believer with the sanctification needed to come before God.

Because of this cleansing and boldness that the believer has, the author gives the second command in v 23. He tells his readers to **hold fast** their **confession**. Once again, he includes himself in this admonition with the word **us**. (He will also include himself in the third commandment in v 24.) Clearly he is speaking to Christians, and clearly there is a possibility that they will *not* hold fast. The warning in vv 26-31 discusses the results if Christians do not.

This confession deals with their **hope**. This is not a hope that they will "go to heaven." It is a hope that the King will come again. The author will conclude this chapter with that idea (v 37). When Christ returns, those who have endured in their Christian profession will receive the reward of an eternal inheritance in His kingdom (3:6, 12-15; 6:11-12; 9:15). They will reign with the King. The author is telling his readers that he wants them and himself to hold fast to the hope of reward for those who are faithful to the Lord.

The readers were in danger of not doing so. They were contemplating going back to Judaism. They were **wavering** in their Christian walk and faith. What they needed was a reminder of what Christ had accomplished for them and that He was their High Priest. They could go to Him to get the help they needed to hold fast. This is what the author had just described in the previous verses.

God has **promised** to reward those who endure. He is **faithful**, that is, He will do what He has promised.

But it is not just going to Christ that will allow the readers to hold fast to their hope. In the third commandment of these verses, the author tells them what else they can do. They can **consider one another** (v 24). He wants them to think of other believers. We can only be strong in our faith and the hope of rewards if we do so. We should not only be concerned about how we are doing in our spiritual growth, but also how the believers around us are doing.

What they should consider is how to **stir up** other believers to **love and good works**. The verb *stir up* means to stimulate someone to do something. This needs to be done because Christians will not automatically love one another and do good works. Christians need one another to help in these areas.

This stimulation of others can occur only if they meet **together** (v 25). If Christians love one another, they will be concerned about one another's spiritual health. They will encourage each other in their Christian walk—to do good deeds.

This gathering together in v 25 is a reference to when Christians come together to worship and for mutual edification. Each believer has a spiritual gift to help others. In this process, believers draw near to God (v 22), not just as individuals, but as a group. The author is worried that his Christian readers will not do that and will **forsake** such opportunities. If they did that, they would *not* be considering one another (v 24).

If they stopped meeting together, or if they went back to Judaism, that is what they would be doing. They would be withdrawing from the house of worship over which Christ presides as our High Priest (Heb 3:6).

It is also clear that **some** believers have already done that. Because of the persecution they have faced, some have quit drawing near to God with other believers. They are no longer holding on to the hope of rewards God has given them. They have stopped considering how to help other believers hold fast.

As in the warning passage in Hebrews 6, the author is talking about those who fall away from the Christian faith. It refers to those who publicly withdraw from worshiping with other Christians.

Many say that true Christians cannot possibly do that. However, as we have seen throughout the Book of Hebrews, the author is talking to Christians. In addition, we need to talk about the psychology of apostasy. A person can publicly renounce his faith for a number of reasons. Perhaps he has suffered a tragedy and does not believe God would allow such a thing to occur and therefore no longer believes He exists. But a person can also still believe in Christian doctrine yet publicly renounce it because he is afraid for the safety and well-being of his family. That is what is happening to the original readers of Hebrews. It is also possible among these readers that they still believed in the doctrines of Christianity but did not feel such doctrines needed to be adhered to strictly. As long as they worshiped God, what difference did it make if it was in a Christian church or a Jewish synagogue?

All of these things can happen to a Christian. To avoid these possibilities, the author is encouraging them to meet together to encourage and strengthen one another. He wants them to be in the business of **exhorting one another**. What a great source of comfort it is for Christians going through persecution to be in the company of others who are experiencing the same things.

Those who quit meeting with others and drop out are like the Jews at Kadesh Barnea who gave up (Hebrews 3–4). Those Jews gave up in the face of difficulties. They quit trusting in God to do what He promised. The readers are commanded not to do the same.

But these verses don't just command them to do the right thing. They also give them something to look forward to. **The Day** is **approaching**. The Lord is about to come (vv 36-37), and it is soon. When He comes, all their enemies will be defeated (10:13). Christ will "save" them from all their difficulties and fulfill His promise to reward them for their faithfulness (10:23).

All of these things are powerful motivations to obey the commands to *draw near, hold fast,* and *consider one another* (vv 22-24). But the author of Hebrews is a realist. He knows that just as at Kadesh, some may not do so. He warns them of the consequences if they do not.

The Fourth Warning Passage (vv 26-31)

26 For if we sin willfully after we have received the knowledge of the truth, there no longer remains a sacrifice for sins,

**27 but a certain fearful expectation of judgment, and fiery
indignation which will devour the adversaries. 28 Anyone
who has rejected Moses' law dies without mercy *on the
testimony* of two or three witnesses. 29 Of how much worse
punishment, do you suppose, will he be thought worthy who
has trampled the Son of God underfoot, counted the blood
of the covenant by which he was sanctified a common thing,
and insulted the Spirit of grace? 30 For we know Him who
said, *"Vengeance is Mine, I will repay,"* says the Lord. And
again, *"The Lord will judge His people."* 31 It is a fearful thing
to fall into the hands of the living God.**

These verses contain the strongest warning passage in the book.
In fact, they probably contain the strongest words towards believers in
the entire NT. These words are so strong they have led some to say that
they simply cannot be addressed to believers. However, as we have seen,
the author is indeed addressing Christians and even includes himself
in all the warnings. These verses themselves confirm that the author
is speaking to those who have eternal life. Even though a Christian
cannot ever lose eternal life, the point the author makes is that if he or
other Christians disobey God by publicly renouncing their faith, severe
consequences will result.

Verse 26 is connected by the word **for** to what was just said. The
author has a particular situation in mind, which he just discussed. It
is a situation in which Christians do not draw near to God and do not
encourage one another in the faith because they have withdrawn from
Christian fellowship and worship. He is dealing with public apostasy
from the faith. It is the same sin discussed in 6:6 in the previous warning
passage.

This is what the author means by **if we sin willfully**. He is not
talking about sin in general, such as stealing, murder, or adultery. The
Christian who falls away from the Christian faith, even in the face of
persecution, is conscious of what he is doing. He is *sinning willfully* in
the most egregious way. He does this after having **the knowledge of the
truth**. Once again he includes himself in that possibility by using the
word "we" twice.

The knowledge spoken of here involves the truth that Christ has
paid for the sins of His people (10:5-18). The phrase *the knowledge of*

the truth only occurs in the Pastoral Epistles (1 Tim 2:4; 2 Tim 2:25; 3:7; Titus 1:1), and in each case it refers to the knowledge that believers have.

Those who have this knowledge, yet willfully fall away, find themselves in a situation where there is **no sacrifice for sins** (see 10:18, where the same idea is found). It should be clear that the author is not saying that such a believer will go to hell. He has already said that the believer has been made holy forever by the sacrifice of Christ (10:10, 14).

If the readers went back to Judaism as a system to worship God, they were going back to a system in which they sacrificed animals whenever they sinned. Such sacrifices would prevent the sinner from experiencing the discipline of God on the life of the worshiper as a result of that sin.

However, Christ put an end to such sacrifices (10:18). The sacrifice of Christ not only allows a person to receive eternal life, but it also provides the means by which the Christian can avoid the discipline of God. To avoid such discipline, the Christian needs to go to God and confess those sins. Because of Christ's sacrifice, God can also forgive the Christian on a daily basis. Such cleansing allows the believer to have communion with God and avoid the negative consequences that sin brings (1 John 1:9).

But the believer who renounces Christ has rejected the sacrifice that provides such daily forgiveness. There is no way for such a Christian to avoid the discipline of God in his life on such sin. And such a believer has committed a very serious sin.

If no sacrifice **remains** for such a Christian, what does remain? What awaits him? Since there is nothing he can turn to by which he can avoid the discipline of God, he lives with a **certain expectation of judgment**. The translation **certain** is a little confusing. In English, it can be taken in a couple of ways. One way is that the judgment is guaranteed to happen, that the person will *certainly* be punished. The other way the word can be taken is to describe something in a general way. An example of this is when a person says that he prefers to drive a *certain* type of car.

It is the latter meaning used here. The author says that those believers who renounce their faith can expect a "certain" type of judgment. What kind of judgment that will be is left vague. This is because one such believer may experience one kind of punishment. Another such believer will experience something else.

But what is clear is that the punishment will be **fearful**. The word has the basic meaning of "terrifying." It is terrifying because of the One who will do the punishing. God will carry it out (v 31). God is all-powerful and has an infinite number of ways to discipline His wayward children.

In addition, it is terrifying because the disobedient believer lives in constant **expectation** that the judgment is coming. There is no place to go to escape it (v 26).

It is also terrifying because of the punishment itself. It is described as a **fiery indignation**, or a "zealous fire." Perhaps this describes the fact that God is zealous toward His people and demands their obedience. When they disobey Him, they invite the fire of His anger toward them.

This anger is one which **devours** those who oppose Him. This is probably an allusion to Isa 26:11. In that passage Isaiah speaks of God destroying His enemies. The verb itself means "to eat." The Christian who apostatizes has left the worshiping house of God and aligned himself with the world. The world is the enemy of God (Jas 4:4). If a Christian aligns himself with the enemy of God, he can expect the wrath of God to be directed at him (Rom 1:18).

The fact that the word *fiery* is used does not mean the punishment is hell. Even in the Isaiah 26 passage, the reference is not to hell. Instead, God is going to physically destroy His enemies. The word describes God's anger at sin. God is angry at the rebellion of His children.

Whatever God does to the apostate Christian is deserved. The author is writing to people who revered the OT. He points to the OT Law to show that a similar punishment was given to rebellious Jews, even Jews who believed in Him. Those who **rejected** that **law** experienced death (v 28). That punishment was given **without mercy**, which includes the fact that the penalty was to be meted out quickly.

In the OT there were certain sins that resulted in such judgment. These included blasphemy, murder, false prophecy, and idolatry (Lev 24:11-17; Deut 17:2-6; 18:20). Perhaps the author has idolatry specifically in mind. The reference to **two or three witnesses** is found in the discussion of idolatry in Leviticus 17. There is a parallel between idolatry and the apostate Christian. Both sins involve leaving the worship of God and engaging in false worship. In the case of the original readers of Hebrews, it would involve worshiping in a system that only pointed to the real thing to come and did not provide for the forgiveness of sins.

It is very important to see that the punishment in the OT for these sins is not being sent to hell. It was a physical death. A believer in the OT could commit the sin of murder, be guilty of blaspheming God, or slide into idolatry. In fact, David was a believer and committed murder. Solomon was a believer and committed idolatry.

And the readers of Hebrews, as we have seen, were believers. But if they rejected Christianity, they could expect a **much worse punishment** than those who committed comparable sins in the OT (v 29). The author had already argued in 2:1-4 that rebellious Jews in the OT were punished, and the Christian who drifts away from Christianity will not escape punishment either.

In fact, the Christian is held even more responsible for such sin. He is even more **worthy** of God's anger and discipline. The reason is because the NT believer has much greater privileges than the believer in the OT. The author had described all these privileges. The New Covenant is far superior to the Old. To whom much is given, much is expected.

The sin of the apostate Christian is serious indeed. He has **trampled the Son of God underfoot**. The word *trampled* carries with it the idea of treating someone with disdain. The apostate has done this to the Son of God! The Son is the King of the world to come, the creator of the universe, and the One who holds all of history in His hands (chapter 1). The apostate has treated Him with contempt.

But He is also the One whose sacrifice made that believer **sanctified** forever (10:10, 14). His **blood** gave the believer all the benefits of the new **covenant**. The apostate has treated this blood as if it were a **common thing**, as if it had no special value.

Once again, we see that the author is describing a Christian. The blood of Christ has made the apostate holy, that is, **sanctified**. Just as in our English translations, the verb is in the past tense. This person was made holy in the past by the blood of Jesus Christ. In no way could this describe an unbeliever. This is why the sin of this person is so great. He has been forgiven forever for his sins and has been given all the benefits of the New Covenant (8:7-11).

The apostate has also **insulted**, or treated with disdain, **the Spirit of grace**. Of course the believer is saved by God's grace (Eph 2:8-9). The believer has become a partner with the Spirit of God (6:4). It was the

Spirit that revealed to this person the truths of the gospel when he was an unbeliever. Through the Spirit, he has come to the "knowledge of the truth" (10:26). The apostate has rejected all such benefits given by the Spirit.

The author closes this stern warning passage by once again appealing to the OT to make his case. Deuteronomy 32:25-26 instructs us that the apostate Christian does indeed have an **expectation of judgment**. These verses from Deuteronomy are very applicable to the situation the author is warning about.

In Deuteronomy 32 Moses speaks of the future of the nation of Israel. Speaking of that future day, he says that Israel has rebelled against God. This is the case even though God has been very gracious to them. Just as in the case of the Jews at Kadesh Barnea (Hebrews 3–4), this is directed against the people of God. In Deuteronomy 32 God calls the Jews *His people, His special possession,* and *His children*. He gave them birth, is their Father, and is the Rock that delivered them. It would be a gross error to say that Moses is talking to people who are examples of unbelievers.

But these same people committed the sin of idolatry, have forsaken God, and turned to false worship.

This is exactly the potential sin the readers of Hebrews were in danger of committing even though God had been infinitely gracious toward them in His Son.

In the case of the Jews, Deuteronomy 32 says that God will send forth the fire of His wrath against them (Deut 32:22), which reminds us of the fiery indignation the author just spoke about in v 27.

And what will this fire bring? In Deuteronomy 32 it is not hell, but famine, plagues, wild beasts, the bite of poisonous crawling things, and destruction. Both children and the elderly will be killed by the sword. Many will be torn to pieces.

If that is what happened to God's people under the Old Covenant, and the apostate believer under the New Covenant is worthy of a worse punishment (v 28), what can he expect? What can possibly be worse than the things described in Deuteronomy 32, or the quick death the author spoke of in 10:28-29?

Since the author is speaking to believers, it cannot refer to hell. But there are certainly things worse than a quick death. In the OT when King Saul rebelled against God, he experienced a punishment worse than death, including mental torment. He eventually lost his kingdom and committed suicide. David committed murder, one of the sins that deserved the death penalty under the Law. He did not die, but his punishment was worse. He lost the child Bathsheba had. His daughter was raped by one of his sons. He lost his older son Absalom, and his kingdom was ripped apart.

There is punishment on this earth worse than death. In addition, the Book of Hebrews is a book that deals with eternal rewards in the coming kingdom of God. The apostate Christian loses them. The author will soon refer to this in 10:35-36 and will discuss them also in the next chapter. The loss of eternal rewards would certainly be a fate worse than death. Even if the readers of Hebrews lost their lives because of the enemies they faced, that would be better than forfeiting the privilege of ruling with Christ as one of His partners in the world to come.

For the apostate, a certain kind of judgment is coming (v 27). This is purposely vague. All that needs to be said is that it results from a sin deserving a punishment worse than death. And the One that will bring it is the One that said to His apostate people in the OT, "**Vengeance is Mine, I will repay**" (v 30; Deut 32:35). The apostate has treated God the Father, God the Son, and God the Spirit (10:29) with contempt. The payment will be in kind.

In concluding this warning, the author leaves no doubt that in this passage he is warning Christians. Quoting Deut 32:36, he reminds them that, "**The Lord will judge His people**." It is not the world that is the subject of this severe punishment, but those whom God calls **His people**.

And whatever else can be said about this judgment, just as it was said at the beginning of this warning passage, it is terrifying, or **fearful** (v 27, 31). The punishment that the apostate Jews experienced is a great illustration of it.

Such punishment is given out by the **hands of the living God**. He is all-powerful to discipline His wayward children. Unlike the dead idols the Jews worshiped when they rebelled against God, God is alive and is thus able to punish. The apostate Christian has placed himself in those living and all-powerful hands, awaiting His discipline.

With the close of this extremely severe warning passage, something should be noted. It is often said that a Christian should obey God because he loves Him. That is certainly the highest motivation for serving the Lord. However, this passage, as well as others in the NT, gives other reasons as well. One is that we should fear the discipline of God in our lives. The believer can never lose his eternal salvation from hell, but sin in our lives invites the discipline of our heavenly Father. Because of His character, He takes sin seriously. It is spiritually healthy to have a reverent fear of that.

Closing Words of Encouragement and Exhortation (vv 32-39)

³² But recall the former days in which, after you were illuminated, you endured a great struggle with sufferings: ³³ partly while you were made a spectacle both by reproaches and tribulations, and partly while you became companions of those who were so treated; ³⁴ for you had compassion on me in my chains, and joyfully accepted the plundering of your goods, knowing that you have a better and an enduring possession for yourselves in heaven. ³⁵ Therefore do not cast away your confidence, which has great reward. ³⁶ For you have need of endurance, so that after you have done the will of God, you may receive the promise:

> *³⁷ "For yet a little while,*
> *And He who is coming will come and will not tarry.*
> *³⁸ Now the just shall live by faith;*
> *But if anyone draws back,*
> *My soul has no pleasure in him."*

³⁹ But we are not of those who draw back to perdition, but of those who believe to the saving of the soul.

After the stern warning of 10:26-31, the author wants to encourage his readers. This is what he did after the last warning (6:9-20). Here he exhorts them by reminding them of their faithfulness to God in the past as well as reassuring them of a glorious future.

Their past (vv 32-34)

As throughout the Book of Hebrews, these verses remind us the author is writing to Christians and the strong warning passage of vv 26-31 deals with believers. They have been faithful to the Lord in the past. They can continue to be so. That is the whole point of the Book of Hebrews!

The author describes the time **after** they **were illuminated**. The word *illuminated* is the same word used in 6:4 to describe when they were enlightened by the Holy Spirit and believed. It was their **former days**, which refers to when they first became Christians (v 32). We do not know how long that has been, but it has been a sufficient amount of time (5:12).

When they first became believers they patiently **endured sufferings** for their faith. These sufferings are described as a **struggle**, a word used to refer to an athletic contest. Their Christian walk was like a race that involved a **great** amount of suffering. Here is another indication that these readers were suffering persecution and were facing the temptation to give up. Their difficult race was wearing them down. That is why they needed to go to Christ for help and to meet with other believers for encouragement (4:14-16; 10:24-25).

Verses 33-34 describe how they suffered in the past. They **were made a spectacle**. The word *spectacle* carries with it the idea of a public display. It is related to the English word "theater." They publicly experienced **reproaches**, or insults, for their faith and **tribulations**, or various kinds of troubles, because they were Christians. All the while, it was as if they were on stage for the world's amusement.

They experienced these things as a group. They were **companions** of those who went through the same difficulties. In other words, they shared in the sufferings of other believers in this hostile environment.

Some of those who suffered were imprisoned for their faith. They were placed **in chains**. The majority of Greek manuscripts indicate that the author himself was one such believer. They were **my** chains. If that is the case, the readers of Hebrews had ministered to him in the past in his times of difficulties.

As the world enjoyed this theater, some of the readers also had lost their property, or **goods**. Their faithfulness to the cause of Christ had cost them dearly.

In the context of Hebrews we can see how all of this suffering occurred. The readers had been Jewish but had converted to Christianity. Their rejection of the religion of their families would have incurred the ridicule of the community in which they lived. They evidently lived in an area where Christianity was not considered a legal religion and thus incurred the penalties of certain laws. How tempting in light of these things to go back to worshiping God in the legal religion of Judaism!

But what had enabled them to suffer these things in the past? They had not only suffered all these things, they had done it **joyfully**. The reason they suffered the loss of so many material things is because they knew they had a **better possession** which was **in heaven**. They were losing earthly treasures, but they were laying up treasures in the coming kingdom (Matt 6:19-20). These treasures in heaven were **enduring**, or eternal. Works done like this bring a reward from the Father. The author speaks of these rewards in the next verses.

The Glorious Future (vv 35-39)

As the author has just said, in the past they exhibited great **confidence** (v 35), or boldness, in their Christian faith. They had suffered for Christ. They should continue with that same attitude. In 3:6 it was said that they should hold on to it until the end. They can do so through the strength that their great High Priest provides.

If they did so, they would receive a **great reward**. The word for *reward* means "wages paid for work." This is one of the many instances in the Book of Hebrews that shows that the author is not concerned with telling his readers how "to go to heaven." He is talking about something that takes work. Salvation from hell is free, but God will reward His children who are faithful to Him. To be rewarded they must retain their boldness.

Verse 36 makes it clear he is not talking about salvation from hell. The author is talking about something that takes **endurance** (v 36), which means holding up under difficult circumstances. They are in the midst of such circumstances (10:32-34). They must also do the **will of God**. Clearly this involves obedience to what God requires. The free gift of eternal life does not require these things.

If the readers would continue to be bold in their faith, endure difficult times, and obey the Lord, they will receive what God has promised. This **promise** involves something in the future. Once again we see he is not talking about salvation from hell. When a person believes in Jesus Christ for eternal life, he receives that gift immediately. The author is speaking of something faithful believers will receive later—

in the future. In the Book of Hebrews it is the promise of an eternal inheritance in the coming kingdom of God, which involves being a partner with Christ in His reign (3:14; 6:12; 9:15). If the readers sinned willfully (v 26) by publicly rejecting Christianity and going back to Judaism, they would not receive this great reward.

Their past conduct in the midst of difficulties would be an encouragement for them to hold on. But there is another encouragement as well. The One who has promised to reward His children for faithfulness is coming soon. Once again the author turns to the OT. He alludes to two verses. One is Isa 26:21; the other is Hab 2:3. The Isaiah passage speaks of the Lord's **coming** during the Great Tribulation. At that time, the Lord will defeat His enemies, which is very appropriate because the readers of Hebrews were oppressed by His enemies (also 1:13).

The Habakkuk passage deals with God's judgment upon the nation of Babylon. It was a judgment that would soon fall. It would **not tarry**. The author of Hebrews changes the wording and makes it **He** is coming, which obviously refers to Christ. The King is coming soon! Hold on! His reward is with Him!

In v 38 the author quotes from Hab 2:4. In Rom 1:17 Paul also quotes this verse: "He who is righteous by faith will live." In the Book of Romans it refers to the fact that a person becomes righteous before God, that is, is saved from hell, by faith.

The author of Hebrews changes the verse very slightly. He adds the word **my** to it even though some translations, including the NKJV, do not include it. He says, "*My* just one shall live by faith." The *just one* is the believer. All believers are just. He is made just, or righteous, by faith. Now he is to *live* by faith.

But the believer has another option. He can **draw back**. Unfortunately, the NKJV adds the word **anyone** in v 38. But the word does not exist in the original Greek. The sentence says, "**if he** draws back." The *he* in question is the *righteous one* in the first part of the verse.

There are not two people being discussed in v 38. There is only one. He is the righteous one. He is a believer. The believer has two options. He can live by faith, or he can draw back. In the Book of Hebrews living by faith means to endure, obey, and remain bold in one's faith. To draw back means to leave the Christian assembly and return to Judaism. Many say that a true Christian could never do that. The author of Hebrews would disagree.

It says that God **has no pleasure** in the believer who apostatizes, or falls away from the faith. Once again, we are confronted with the fact that there are some believers who fail to please the Lord.

In the closing verse of chapter 10 the author repeats the two options a believer has. Once again, the Christian is faced with a decision. Those who draw back find **perdition**. The word means "destruction," and can be a reference to hell. However, it has a very wide range of meanings, such as the destruction of one's life or even of valuable things (Matt 26:8; Acts 8:20; 1 Tim 6:9; 2 Pet 2:1). Here in Hebrews 10 it means the punishment the believer who draws back experiences. It is a fate worse than death (vv 26-31). It could also include the "destruction" of one's eternal rewards.

But the believer can also be one who **believes**, resulting in the **saving of the soul**. The translation here is very unfortunate. First of all, it doesn't say "believe," but "by faith." Secondly, it does not say "saving," but "preserving." Thirdly, the word *soul* causes much misunderstanding in English. We often only think of that part of a person that either goes to heaven or goes to hell. But in Greek it often means simply the life of a person (Matt 6:25; Mark 3:4; John 13:37; Acts 27:10).

The author is saying that the believer who lives by faith will preserve his life, the opposite of experiencing destruction. He keeps himself from experiencing the judgment of God both in this life and the world to come. It could literally save his life. Such a life will also not experience the loss of rewards, including the privilege of reigning with Christ. The unfaithful believer, even though he will be in the kingdom, will experience the destruction of many things. His life's work will be wasted.

It is interesting that the author says **we** are not those who will experience such loss. In 2:5 and 5:11 he has used the word *we* to describe either himself or also those who are with him. The Christian has two options. The author is saying he himself has decided to live by faith. He is calling the readers to follow his example. He has reminded them that they have done it in the past. He has reminded them that the King is coming soon. These things should encourage them to follow in the path he has decided to walk.

But there is another encouragement for doing so. They can look to the example of other people of God—other believers—who have chosen wisely. The author will give a long list of such examples in the next chapter.

Examples of Living by Faith

UP TO THIS POINT in the Book of Hebrews, the author has, for a lack
of better words, spoken of doctrinal things. In chapter 1–4 he has
presented Jesus Christ as the Son, the King of the world to come. In
chapters 5–10 he has presented Him as the believer's High Priest. When
the reader of the Book of Hebrews arrives at chapter 11 there is a major
change.

Because of who Christ is and the privileges the believer has, the
Christian should live a life of faith. Of course, that is one of the two
options the author laid out for the believer at the end of the last chapter.
The other option is that he can fall away.

Chapter 11 is about faith. But it is very important to understand that
it is not about the faith that leads to salvation from hell or that makes
one a Christian. Instead, it is about *living* by faith (10:38). It is a life
characterized by obedience, endurance, and often suffering.

To describe such a life, the author points out many who lived like
that. All the examples he gives are those who were *already* God's people.
They did not live the way they did because they wanted to be in the
kingdom. They lived the way they did because they wanted to gain
God's approval of their lives. They lived the way they did because they
wanted to be rewarded for their faithful living in the coming kingdom of
God. They did not draw back (10:39) when faced with difficulties. If the
heroes of the faith lived like this, so could the readers of Hebrews. The
readers of Hebrews could learn a great deal from these men and women
of old.

The Introduction (vv 1-3)

¹ Now faith is the substance of things hoped for, the evidence of things not seen. ² For by it the elders obtained a *good* testimony. ³ By faith we understand that the worlds were framed by the word of God, so that the things which are seen were not made of things which are visible.

If the author wants his readers to live by faith, he must define what faith is. Living by faith involves living in a way that looks to the future. Such a **faith** (v 1) is described as a **substance**. The word for *substance* means it is guaranteed.

That which is guaranteed involves **things hoped for**. Chapter 10 ended with God's promise of rewards for faithfulness (10:35-37). He has promised that Christ is coming soon to give those rewards. Faith means believing in those promises.

Such a faith also involves **evidence**, or the assurance, that **things** which are **not seen** exist. The life of faith lives in light of a kingdom we have not seen. It takes faith to live one's life laying up and working for rewards in a kingdom we cannot see, rather than work for the comforts of this present world which we can see.

Such a life is one that results in a **good testimony** (v 2). The word *good* does not appear in the original and the word "testimony" means approved. It is an important word in chapter 11. It not only occurs at the beginning of the chapter here, but also at the end in v 39. It refers to the fact that all the people in chapter 11, those people of God who lived by faith, received God's approval. That is the main point of chapter 11. These people are called **the elders** because they lived long ago. Their lives pleased God because they believed in the rewards He had promised even though they could not see them.

It is only natural that a believer would have faith in God in this manner. We believe in other things that we have never seen simply because God says it. **By faith** we believe that the **worlds** were created by the **word of God** (v 3). The author is alluding to the creation account in Genesis 1. He starts in the very beginning of OT history. The creation includes all the worlds of the universe as well as the angelic world. We believe this even though we were not present to observe it.

But the same Word of God says there is a new world coming. Christ will inherit that world (1:2). He will share that inheritance with those who have been faithful to Him (9:15). If we believe in the creation of the world we presently live in, shouldn't we believe and live for the world God says we will dwell in forever?

The author gives us a long list of people who did. He chooses these people because they are people who lived this way in order to gain rewards. They are people who endured when faced with difficulties. They are people who wanted an inheritance in another world. They are illustrations of the things the author has spoken of in the book.

God Rewards Faithfulness (vv 4-16)

⁴ By faith Abel offered to God a more excellent sacrifice than Cain, through which he obtained witness that he was righteous, God testifying of his gifts; and through it he being dead still speaks. ⁵ By faith Enoch was taken away so that he did not see death, *"and was not found, because God had taken him"*; for before he was taken he had this testimony, that he pleased God. ⁶ But without faith it is impossible to please Him, for he who comes to God must believe that He is, and that He is a rewarder of those who diligently seek Him. ⁷ By faith Noah, being divinely warned of things not yet seen, moved with godly fear, prepared an ark for the saving of his household, by which he condemned the world and became heir of the righteousness which is according to faith. ⁸ By faith Abraham obeyed when he was called to go out to the place which he would receive as an inheritance. And he went out, not knowing where he was going. ⁹ By faith he dwelt in the land of promise as in a foreign country, dwelling in tents with Isaac and Jacob, the heirs with him of the same promise; ¹⁰ for he waited for the city which has foundations, whose builder and maker is God.

¹¹ By faith Sarah herself also received strength to conceive seed, and she bore a child when she was past the age, because she judged Him faithful who had promised. ¹² Therefore from one man, and him as good as dead, were born *as many*

as the stars of the sky in multitude—innumerable as the sand
which is by the seashore.
[13] These all died in faith, not having received the promises,
but having seen them afar off were assured of them,
embraced *them* and confessed that they were strangers
and pilgrims on the earth. [14] For those who say such things
declare plainly that they seek a homeland. [15] And truly if they
had called to mind that *country* from which they had come
out, they would have had opportunity to return. [16] But now
they desire a better, that is, a heavenly *country*. Therefore
God is not ashamed to be called their God, for He has
prepared a city for them.

In this section the people of God who gained His approval fall into
two time periods. The first discusses those who lived during the days of
Noah before the flood (vv 4-7). Then the author deals with those who
lived during the time of the patriarchs, beginning with Abraham.

The first one discussed is **Abel**. The author has moved from Genesis
1 to Genesis 4. **Abel's sacrifice** was **more excellent** than that of his
brother. We are not told in Genesis why his sacrifice was better (v 4).
However, we are told that "the Lord respected Abel and his offering,
but He did not respect Cain and his offering" (Gen 4:4-5). Both Abel's
offering and Abel's attitude were pleasing to God. Perhaps Abel's
sacrifice was better because it was an animal sacrifice (cf. Heb 9:22,
"without shedding of blood there is no remission"). If so, it looked
forward to the sacrifice Christ would make, and we could assume that
Abel had some understanding of such things.

This is relevant to the Book of Hebrews. Christ offered a more
excellent sacrifice than the sacrifices of the Old Covenant. Through that
sacrifice we are made righteous. Abel was declared **righteous** by God
based upon his faith in the One who was to come. That faith is what
makes a person one of God's "righteous ones" (10:38).

But there is more to Abel's life than that. He also received God's
approval in regard to **his gifts**. His life was one of worship toward God.
He was righteous by faith and lived by faith.

What was the result of such a life? Abel was murdered. But he **still
speaks**. The point is that a life that gains God's approval has an impact
that outlasts life on this earth. To those readers facing persecution for

their faith, this would be a great source of comfort. They didn't even have to fear death.

Enoch was another man that gained God's approval (Gen 5:21-24). His life was one that **pleased God** (v 5). We know from Jude 14-15 that Enoch knew about the coming King and His kingdom. He lived his life in light of those facts.

There is a contrast between Abel and Enoch. Abel died, but Enoch **did not see death**. Whether the child of God dies or the Lord returns to take him prior to death, the results of such a life live on.

In order to **please** God, one must have the **faith** that was exhibited in the lives of Abel and Enoch (v 6). It is a faith that causes one to come to God. The verb **comes to** is used in 4:16; 7:25; and 10:22 and means to draw near to God, through Christ, in worship.

In addition, the life of faith requires that the one who worships God **believes** that **He is a rewarder**. God has promised to reward those who remain faithful to Him (10:35). Not all believers will receive these rewards, but only those who **diligently seek** to please God. If the readers withdrew from the Christian fellowship, they would be doing the exact opposite (10:35-38).

This reward is more than "going to heaven." It involves reigning with Christ when He returns to set up His kingdom. This is the inheritance of those who live a life of faith. The next two examples from the OT are examples of those looking for an inheritance.

First of all, the author deals with **Noah in Genesis 6-9** (v 7). God had told him about **things not seen**. Noah had never seen a flood and had probably never seen rain. Yet he believed what God told him was coming.

This **faith** caused him to obey by building **an ark**. That ark resulted in the **saving of his household**. This is clearly not salvation from hell. Noah was a believer long before the coming of the flood and was already saved from hell. The salvation here is from the judgment of the flood. Noah and his family were spared from dying in the flood.

The same is true for the readers of Hebrews. God is about to judge the world and His enemies. The readers were surrounded by these enemies, but Christ is coming soon to deliver them from His adversaries (1:13-14).

Noah's life of faith, which believed in things he had never seen (11:1), was a life that **condemned the world**. He had preached to them about the coming flood for 120 years. He had believed God's word. Why didn't they?

Because of his life of faith, Noah received an inheritance. He **became an heir of the righteousness** available to all who come by **faith**. All believers are righteous by faith (10:38). Those believers who draw near to God and believe in things unseen will also become an heir of the rewards God has promised.

Noah is a great example to the readers of Hebrews for another reason. He literally became an heir of a new world. He lived on the verge of God's judgment and the bringing in of that new world, a world he had never before seen. It was the same situation for the readers. They, too, should live in light of things they had never seen and believe that God would reward them for their faithfulness.

The author has now advanced to Genesis 11-12. **Abraham** is another example of one who lived **by faith**. This is a faith that **obeyed** God when He told him to leave his home in Ur. Abraham went to a place he had never seen. He had no idea **where he was going**. He did this in order to obtain an **inheritance** (v 8).

This inheritance is clearly not a reference to Abraham's going to heaven. Verses 9-10 make it clear that it is something he would receive by living a life of obedience. Like Noah, Abraham had already believed in God for eternal life (Gen 15:6) before he lived this life of taking God at His word.

God had promised to give Abraham the **land of promise** forever. But while Abraham was there, it did not seem that way. He lived in it as a foreigner, **dwelling in tents**, moving about from place to place. He surely didn't own it.

Israel will be the center of the coming kingdom of God. Abraham will have an eternal inheritance in it. The same applies to the readers of Hebrews. God has promised that faithful believers will have an inheritance in the world to come. Right now, as persecuted believers, they are like foreigners in God's creation. They, like Abraham, are called by God to believe in God's promise regardless of what they see (11:1).

Abraham could live in tents in this world because he knew that this world was passing away. A tent was a temporary dwelling place. But he knew that there was coming a **city** with firm **foundations**. This refers to the New Jerusalem which will be the capital of God's eternal kingdom. It will be an eternal city and an eternal kingdom because the eternal **God** is its **builder** (v 10). Abraham did not worry about owning land in this world. He wanted an inheritance that was eternal. The readers should be living in such a way as well.

In vv 11-12 the author of Hebrews continues to discuss the life of Abraham (Genesis 15-21). However, he includes **Sarah**, the wife of Abraham, in this discussion. She becomes the first woman mentioned in chapter 11 and shows that the promise of rewards also applies to female believers.

God had **promised** to Abraham an **innumerable** amount of descendants. Sarah, of course, played an indispensible role in the working out of that promise. It was a humanly impossible promise because Sarah was too old to have children, and Abraham was **as good as dead** because of his age.

The promises made to the readers of Hebrews also seemed impossible. But God is **faithful** to keep His word.

In vv 13-16 the author gives a summary of the men and woman he discussed in vv 4-12. All of them looked for an inheritance in a land they had never seen (v 1). They believed in the **promises** of God, that He would reward them for their faithfulness (v 13). God had promised the patriarchs that they would possess the land of Canaan forever. But they all **died** without realizing these things.

They looked to these things that were **afar off**. They saw the things of **earth** as temporary, because these men and women considered themselves **pilgrims** here and were just passing through. The message to the readers of Hebrews is clear. They should not worry about the loss of earthly possessions (10:34).

These heroes of the faith showed by their lives that they were looking for their **homeland** (v 14). The word literally means the place of their birth. Those who live by faith in God's promise of rewards live in such a way that says they are citizens of another world.

Abraham's place of birth was Ur of the Chaldees. But his life of faith was such that he did not see that land that way anymore. He had many opportunities **to return** there (v 15), but he gave no thought of doing so.

This probably has an application to the readers of Hebrews. They were contemplating returning to their "home" of Judaism, which would be a mistake.

The life of faith that Abraham lived showed that he was looking for a **better country** (v 16). It was better than Ur because it originates from heaven. It is better because it is eternal (Heb 1:8; 11:10). Rewards in that country are better than any rewards in this world.

The approval of God rests on people who take Him at His word, live their lives that way, and thus long for the coming kingdom of God (v 2). As a result, God **is not ashamed to be called their God** (v 16). This is another way of saying that He is proud of them and takes pleasure that this kind of men and women are called His people.

This cannot be said about all the people of God. God was not proud of the Jews at Kadesh Barnea (chapters 3–4). God is proud of His children who walk by faith. He is not proud of those who do not. It is simply an error to say that when Christ returns He will be full of praise and will be proud of every believer.

The application to the readers of Hebrews is evident. If they fall away by withdrawing from the worshiping community of believers and no longer live for the coming kingdom of God, God will be ashamed of them (1 John 2:28).

One of the rewards for the faithful children of God is that God has **a city for them**. Once again, this is a reference to New Jerusalem (v 10; Rev 21:10-27) from which those who rule with Christ will share in His reign.

The Acts of Faith in the Lives of the Patriarchs (vv 17-22)

Verses 13-16 were a summary statement. Now the author returns to his discussion of the patriarchs. He shows how they demonstrated their faith in the promises of God.

> [17] **By faith Abraham, when he was tested, offered up Isaac, and he who had received the promises offered up his only begotten** son, [18] **of whom it was said,** *"In Isaac your seed shall be called,"* [19] **concluding that God was able to raise him up, even from the dead, from which he also received him in a figurative sense.** [20] **By faith Isaac blessed Jacob and Esau concerning things to come.** [21] **By faith Jacob, when he was dying, blessed each of the sons of Joseph, and worshiped,** *leaning* **on the top of his staff.** [22] **By faith Joseph, when he was dying, made mention of the departure of the children of Israel, and gave instructions concerning his bones.**

In once again looking at Abraham, the author considers the most difficult time in his life. In Genesis 22 God told **Abraham** to offer **up Isaac** as a sacrifice. This was an extremely hard test, because Isaac was his **son**. In addition, Isaac was the one that God had said would be the **seed** of Abraham through whom the world would be blessed (vv 17-18). Through Isaac, Abraham would have innumerable descendants. At this time in his life, Isaac had no children. If Abraham killed him, God could not fulfill His **promises** to Abraham.

In this most difficult of tests, Abraham believed God. Once again, we see that this is not believing in God for eternal life. Abraham had been saved for decades. This is living by faith in what God has said.

Abraham knew what God had said. He knew that he would have innumerable descendants through Isaac. His faith in God's promise was such that even if Isaac were **dead**, God would accomplish these things through this boy (v 19).

Even though Abraham had never seen anyone raised from the dead, he concluded that **God was able** to do it (v 19). That was the only way God could fulfill His promises to Abraham if Isaac died. Abraham had seen God give "life" to his and Sarah's "dead" bodies (v 11) and believed God would do the same to a literally dead Isaac.

In the end, God stopped Abraham from killing his son. From this situation, then, Abraham **received** Isaac back.

But Abraham was not the only patriarch who believed that God would fulfill His promises even in the event of death. When Isaac grew up, he demonstrated a similar faith. He was well aware of the promises God had made to Abraham.

When Isaac was dying, he **blessed** his own sons. These blessings dealt with **things to come**. God had promised the patriarchs future blessings. Isaac knew that even his death would not prevent these things from coming to fruition. Through his sons these promises would be realized. It was through **Jacob** that all the promises in the covenant with Abraham would be fulfilled (v 20). This included the eternal possession of the land in the kingdom of God (Gen 27:29; 28:4).

Jacob followed the example of his father. **When he was dying**, he had the proper attitude toward God and **worshiped** Him. He did so even though death was imminent. He could do so because he knew God would keep His word.

Just as in the case of Isaac, Jacob showed his faith when he **blessed** his descendants. Genesis 48–49 says that he blessed all of his sons. But the author of Hebrews only mentions **the sons** of his son **Joseph** (v 21). The reason for this is probably because the author will discuss Joseph next.

And Joseph did the same thing his father did. **When he was dying** he also remembered the promises made to Abraham. God had said the descendants of Abraham would live in the land of Canaan forever. God had also said that the Jews would leave Egypt in the future (Gen 50:22-26). Joseph believed these promises and told the **children of Israel** not to leave his bones in Egypt when they left. On that day, they were to take **his bones** back to Canaan (v 22).

Joseph lived in the most powerful nation on earth and was a powerful man in that nation. But he knew that his future, even after death, was in another place. He knew that he had an eternal inheritance in that land. He knew that his bones would be resurrected. Even death cannot stop the promises of God.

Abraham lived by faith when severely tested. The other patriarchs lived by faith in the face of death. In the following verses the author will discuss those men and women in the past who lived by faith when faced with opposition from the world. The original readers of Hebrews were facing such opposition.

Living by Faith in a Hostile World (vv 23-31)

²³ **By faith Moses, when he was born, was hidden three months by his parents, because they saw** *he was* **a beautiful child; and they were not afraid of the king's command.** ²⁴ **By faith Moses, when he became of age, refused to be called the son of Pharaoh's daughter,** ²⁵ **choosing rather to suffer affliction with the people of God than to enjoy the passing pleasures of sin,** ²⁶ **esteeming the reproach of Christ greater riches than the treasures in Egypt; for he looked to the reward.** ²⁷ **By faith he forsook Egypt, not fearing the wrath of the king; for he endured as seeing Him who is invisible.** ²⁸ **By faith he kept the Passover and the sprinkling of blood, lest he who destroyed the firstborn should touch them.** ²⁹ **By faith they passed through the Red Sea as by** *dry land, whereas the*

Egyptians, attempting to do so, were drowned. ³⁰ By faith the walls of Jericho fell down after they were encircled for seven days. ³¹ By faith the harlot Rahab did not perish with those who did not believe, when she had received the spies with peace.

The author moves from Genesis to Exodus. He now discusses Moses, but before doing so he addresses **his parents.** When **Moses was born** the Jews lived in Egypt and were told they had to kill all their male children (Exod 1:15-22). However, these parents looked at the child and saw that he was **beautiful** (v 23). The meaning here is probably that they concluded that God would not have given them this **child** only to have him killed.

Pharaoh the king was the most powerful man on earth. Disobeying his law would have brought a severe penalty. But Moses' parents **were not afraid of the king's** orders.

Their **faith** in God was rewarded. Not only was the life of their son saved, but their son would eventually be the instrument through whom God would deliver the Jewish people from slavery.

Moses followed in the **faith** of his parents (v 24). He also did not fear **the king** of Egypt (v 27). Moses, who was raised as the **son of Pharaoh's daughter,** had a choice. When he became an adult, he could take advantage of all the benefits of his position. Or he could **suffer affliction** with the Jewish people.

Moses chose the latter. Acts 7:25 tells us that Moses understood that God was going to use him to deliver the Jews from slavery in Egypt. He knew that he was a Jew and therefore knew about the promises made to Abraham. To have taken advantage of all the **pleasures** of Egypt and forget all these things would have been a **sin** (v 25).

He left the palace and identified himself with a nation of slaves. He did that because he realized that the **treasures in Egypt** were **passing,** or temporary. In light of that, he also understood that suffering for **Christ** would result in **greater riches.**

Like Abraham, Moses knew that the Christ would come (Deut 18:15). The promise made to Abraham included the coming of the One through whom the world would be blessed. How much Moses knew cannot be determined.

But there is no doubt Moses knew that siding with the people of the Christ would result in a **reward**. He **looked to** it. While he had the opportunity to possess unbelievable but temporary wealth in Egypt, he chose eternal rewards in the coming kingdom of Christ.

The readers had also lost many things of this world because of their Christian faith (10:32-34). Some of them were thinking that perhaps that was a bad decision. The author of Hebrews is reminding them that rewards in the coming kingdom of God are greater than anything this world has to offer. They are being called to make the same decision that Moses made.

Moses led the people out of **Egypt** (Exodus 7-14), going against the **wrath** of the strongest **king** on earth. He could do so because he saw **Him who is invisible**. Moses could see the riches of Egypt and its king. But he had **faith** in the King he could not see and in a kingdom he could not see. He **endured** through the opposition he faced.

Clearly there is a direct application for the readers. They need to endure the difficulties they face, believe in what they cannot see, and look for the reward that goes with that faith (10:36; 11:1, 6).

In v 28 the author speaks about the Jewish nation as a whole during the time of Moses. They sacrificed a lamb and **kept the Passover**. They took the **blood** of that lamb and sprinkled it on their doors (Exodus 12). As a result, their **firstborn** sons were not **destroyed** by the judgment of God that fell upon Egypt.

All of this was an act of faith. They believed that if they obeyed God they would avoid that judgment. Of course, the Passover and the blood of the lamb pointed to Christ. It was the blood of Christ that had placed the readers under the New Covenant (8:10-13). The readers are reminded that if they abandoned their confession they would face the judgment of God as well. Even though they couldn't go to hell, the penalty would be severe (2:1-4; 6:7-8; 10:26, 29-31).

The Jews ate that first Passover meal in Egypt, the land of the enemy. It was a meal that involved the worship of God and all that He was doing for them. The readers were also surrounded by their enemies but were encouraged to continue worshiping God (10:19-25). God would judge their enemies, just as He judged the Egyptians (1:13; 10:27). They did not need to fear what their enemies could do to them.

In v 29, the author plainly states that God judged their enemy. The Jewish people were pursued by the army of Pharaoh. But God brought them through that time of opposition, delivering them out of Egypt **through the Red Sea**. In faith the Jews walked through the Sea as God held the water back.

But those opposed to them died. The Egyptian army **drowned**. They were completely destroyed. This is the destiny of the enemies of the readers of Hebrews as well, even though at that time their enemies appeared to be strong.

By their walk of faith, the Jews were "saved" while their enemies were destroyed. In the next two examples, in vv 30-31, these same ideas are repeated. As in the case of the Jews in the Exodus, this salvation occurred when there appeared to be no hope.

The generation that followed the death of Moses is such an example. While the Jews at Kadesh Barnea were unfaithful (chapters 3–4), the next generation under Joshua exhibited great faith. The author has now moved beyond the Pentateuch to Joshua. The nation faced a strong enemy at **Jericho**. It was a walled city, and the Jews had no way of defeating it.

God told them to simply march around it for six **days**. When they did it on the seventh day and blew the trumpets, the great wall **fell down** (Joshua 6).

Even though it made no sense, the Jews obeyed and did what God commanded. No doubt the inhabitants of Jericho, their enemies, laughed at them. But in the end, their enemies fell under the judgment of God. They, like the Egyptians, were destroyed.

The world ridicules the life of faith. The readers of Hebrews had already experienced such ridicule (10:32-33). They must believe that God would deliver them from such ridicule and opposition.

Rahab the harlot was another example in the generation under Joshua of someone who showed **faith** (Joshua 2). She lived among the enemies of God. They had heard about the God of Israel, the Exodus, and what God had done for the Jews. However, they **did not believe**.

But Rahab did believe and acted upon that faith. She **received the spies** that had come to spy out the land. She hid them and then sent them out in **peace**. This involved a great deal of risk. The people of her city would have killed her and her family for siding with the enemy if she had been discovered.

Her faith brought "salvation" to her and her family. They were spared when the enemies of God **perished** as the Jews destroyed the city. In

Rahab's example the readers would see that anyone can live a life of faith. After all, she was a Gentile and a harlot. Not only was her life spared, she would also become an ancestor of Jesus Christ, the King of Kings (Matt 1:5). God certainly rewards faith!

Conclusion on the People of Faith (vv 32-40)

³² And what more shall I say? For the time would fail me to tell of Gideon and Barak and Samson and Jephthah, also *of* David and Samuel and the prophets: ³³ who through faith subdued kingdoms, worked righteousness, obtained promises, stopped the mouths of lions, ³⁴ quenched the violence of fire, escaped the edge of the sword, out of weakness were made strong, became valiant in battle, turned to flight the armies of the aliens. ³⁵ Women received their dead raised to life again.

Others were tortured, not accepting deliverance, that they might obtain a better resurrection. ³⁶ Still others had trial of mockings and scourgings, yes, and of chains and imprisonment. ³⁷ They were stoned, they were sawn in two, were tempted, were slain with the sword. They wandered about in sheepskins and goatskins, being destitute, afflicted, tormented— ³⁸ of whom the world was not worthy. They wandered in deserts and mountains, *in* dens and caves of the earth.

³⁹ And all these, having obtained a good testimony through faith, did not receive the promise, ⁴⁰ God having provided something better for us, that they should not be made perfect apart from us.

Up to this point in chapter 11, the author of Hebrews has spoken of men and women of great faith from the creation of the world until the time of Joshua. In v 32 he says that he could give many more examples from Biblical history. He does not have the **time** to discuss them all. He simply summarizes the time after Joshua, known as the time of the Judges, by listing four of them: **Gideon, Barak, Samson, and Jephthah.**

After the time of the Judges was the time of the kings. **David** is an example of this period. During the time of the kings through the end of the OT, **prophets** ministered to the nation. **Samuel** is representative of this group.

Some of these men, like Samson and Jephthah, had moral lapses. In this sense they could be compared to someone like Rahab the harlot. One of the lessons here is that anyone can live a life of faith. Samson, for example, was faithful before his moral fall with Delilah, and was faithful to God at the end of his life.

The judges and the kings listed fought against the enemies of God. The prophets spoke the word of God, often in the midst of a disobedient people. These things all required faith.

The author of Hebrews shows how all of these people overcame the difficulties they faced while being faithful to the Lord. They experienced victory over their enemies, **fire, the sword, weakness**, and even **lions** and death (vv 33-35). God can bring "salvation" to those who are faithful to Him in many ways.

The judges and kings often **subdued kingdoms**. Gideon defeated the Midianites, Barak the Canaanites, and David defeated numerous countries. Samuel and the prophets were instruments to proclaim and turn the people to **righteousness**.

Their lives of faith meant that they **obtained promises**. David received the promise of the Davidic Covenant (2 Sam 7:8-16). In the context of Hebrews this could also mean that they believed in the promise that God would reward those who are faithful to Him in the world to come.

After moving through Judges, Samuel, Kings, and Chronicles, the author now moves to the prophets. Daniel closed the **mouths of lions** (Daniel 6). His friends Shadrach, Meshach, and Abednego survived through **fire** (Daniel 3). Many of the Judges, kings, and prophets survived the threat of death by sword. The same could be said about those who were brave **in battle**, as well as those who put to **flight the armies** of Israel's enemies. There were many who also exercised great faith when in a position of **weakness** but who **were made strong**. Samson, for example, destroyed more enemies of God when he was a blind slave than he had previously.

As we saw in the case of the patriarchs, even the enemy death is no match for God. **Women**, such as the widow in 1 Kings 17 and the woman of 2 Kings 4, saw their sons **raised** from the **dead** by the power of God through His prophets. In the NT the author of Hebrews also has in mind the widow of Nain who received her son back from the dead, the wife of Jairus whose daughter was raised from the dead by Christ, and Mary and Martha whose brother Lazarus came forth from the grave (Luke 7:11-15; 8:49-56; John 11).

In all of these instances we see people of faith who experienced great victory over their enemies. But the author of Hebrews knows that while faith is always victorious, such victory and rewards from God are sometimes not seen in this world. They often await people of faith in the world to come. The author points these things out in vv 35-38.

The readers of Hebrews needed to hear that sometimes lives of faith will experience hardships. They could look at the examples of faithful men and women in the past who experienced the same things they were going through, and even worse.

In the past some people of faith did not accept **deliverance**. They could have denied their faith and been set free from their difficulties. However, in many instances, they chose to be **tortured** instead. Perhaps the author has primarily in mind many people who lived during the period between the Old and New Testaments; these believers experienced intense suffering for their faith. This has a direct application to the readers of Hebrews. They could have a much easier time if they simply denied their Christian beliefs. They could accept deliverance at the hands of their enemies by denying the faith and going back to Judaism.

But why did these people in the past make the choice to suffer? It was so they **might obtain a** better **resurrection** (v 35, emphasis added). As believers they already knew they were going to be in the kingdom of God. They knew that they were going to be resurrected. But they wanted to have a **better** life in the life to come. It would be one that would be rewarded in that kingdom. In the words of the Book of Hebrews, this type of resurrection would include reigning with Christ the King.

The difficulties they endured for faithful living included **mockings and scourgings.** Scourging was a cruel form of punishment which involved whipping the back of the victim and tearing away the flesh. Experiences such as these were the lot of men of faith like Jeremiah (Jer 20:2), Paul, and of course the Lord Himself.

Many people of God throughout history have also endured **chains and imprisonment**. In fact, even some of the readers of Hebrews may have been so treated (10:34).

Others **were stoned**. Tradition says that Jeremiah died by stoning. We know that many prophets met their fate in this manner (Matt 23:37), as did Stephen and Zechariah (Acts 7:57-60; 2 Chron 24:21).

Others were **sawn in two**. The author probably has in mind the prophet Isaiah. Jewish tradition says he was cut in two with a wooden saw.

In all of these sufferings these men and women were **tempted** to give up (v 37). That is always the case when the children of God suffer. There is the thought that the rewards are not worth the price paid. That temptation is present. Even Jesus, our Captain in the life of faith (Hebrews 2), was tempted to take the easy way out when tested by Satan in the wilderness. It is clear that the readers of Hebrews were facing that decision.

The list of sufferings includes the fact that some were **slain with the sword** (v 37). This was the case even though other faithful people had escaped such a fate (v 34). Again, the list of such stalwarts of the faith is long.

Others were reduced to wearing **sheepskins and goatskins** and living in holes **of the earth** (vv 37-38). Their existence was such that they survived with only the bare necessities of life. Once again, the author probably has in mind the faithful Jews who lived between the Old and New Testaments. Jewish tradition has examples of their living this way.

They lived this way because the world had rejected them. The world viewed them as unworthy to live among civilized society. But God had a different opinion. He says that **the world was not worthy** of *them* (v 38)!

Throughout chapter 11 we have seen that men and women of faith live in such a way that they do not look for the things of this world. They look for a world that cannot be seen. This is the kind of people who will be greatly rewarded when God brings His kingdom. *This* world is not worthy of such people, but the world to come will be.

Verses 39-40 provide a summary statement for all of the people discussed in chapter 11. People of faith were given promises (v 33), but none of these people received **the promise** (v 39). The particular promise the author has in mind is reigning with Christ in the coming kingdom of God. They have not seen the coming city built by God (11:13-16). They have not been rewarded for being faithful to God during the difficult times in which they lived. The reason they have not received the fulfillment of this promise is because the kingdom has not yet come.

But they did obtain a **good testimony**. In the Greek **having obtained a good testimony** is only one word. It is the same word used in 11:2. It ties together the whole chapter. God was pleased with their lives. They gained God's approval because they trusted Him when He said that those who are faithful to Him will be rewarded with a **better resurrection** in a world they cannot see (11:1, 35).

The reason they have not received this reward yet is because **God** has **something better for us**. The Book of Hebrews has made a point that the New Covenant was better than the Old in many ways. It has better promises, a better sacrifice, a better High Priest, and better tabernacle. With Christ's coming, the better has arrived and made possible all the promises made to the believers in the OT.

Application

If the faithful people of OT times had already received the reward of reigning with Christ in His kingdom, it would mean that the kingdom of God had already arrived. God waited in order for NT believers to have the same opportunity. God has determined that those who reign with Christ will come from both Old and New Covenant believers. The faithful OT believers will not **be made perfect** without the faithful NT believers. The Greek word *made perfect* means "to reach a goal." The goal of faithful living is to be greatly rewarded in the kingdom of God. The readers of Hebrews can be rewarded in the same way the faithful men and women of chapter 11 will be rewarded in the glorious future that is coming.

What a great motivation to go to Christ and live a life of faith! Like the men and women in this chapter, we should endure whatever comes into our lives that we too might have a better resurrection.

A Call to Endure

IN CHAPTER 11 THE author of Hebrews gave his readers many examples of God's people who lived by faith. They persevered under difficult times. The readers of the Book of Hebrews should follow their example. This is discussed here in chapter 12.

Introduction (12:1-2)

¹ Therefore we also, since we are surrounded by so great a cloud of witnesses, let us lay aside every weight, and the sin which so easily ensnares *us*, and let us run with endurance the race that is set before us, ² looking unto Jesus, the author and finisher of *our* faith, who for the joy that was set before Him endured the cross, despising the shame, and has sat down at the right hand of the throne of God.

The word **therefore** in v 1 takes us back to chapter 11. The faithful OT saints are examples for us to follow. They remained faithful to God. They are **witnesses** for us. Their lives are a testimony, which is what the word means. Such a life of faith can be lived. If they did it, so can we. Their testimony surrounds us.

The lives of these saints were like a grueling athletic event. The life of the Christian believer is as well. It is as if we are in an arena and have a **race** to **run**. The word for *race* means a contest, and we get our English word "agony" from it. It is a race that requires **endurance**. It will take effort on the part of the Christian.

The readers knew this very well. In 10:32-34 the author had spoken of how they had suffered hardship in the past. They had gone through great struggles because of their Christian faith and the enemies who opposed them. He wants them to continue on that path.

No good athlete will carry extra **weight** when he runs such a race. He removes from his body anything that will slow him down.

The author says if we are going to run our race, if we are to finish well as the people in chapter 11 did, we must not weigh ourselves down. This seems to be a reference to letting go of things that keep us from faithfully serving the Lord, even if those things are not sinful. The Christian may give up certain hobbies if they take up too much time, for example.

In addition, the Christian who desires to serve the Lord faithfully will desire to **lay aside sin**. Sin in the life of a believer is like a long coat. No athlete would run with such a garment. It would **easily** entangle the legs of the runner. He could not run well. Sin does that in the life of the believer.

While we can certainly look at the lives of faithful believers in the past who ran their race well, in chapter 2 the author tells us that the perfect example of such faithfulness is **Jesus**. When the Christian runs his race, he should do so while **looking** at how Jesus lived (v 2).

Jesus is the Christian's **author and finisher** when it comes to living a life of **faith**. Based upon 2:10 and 5:8-9, these words mean that Jesus paved the way for us. He showed us how to live by faith. He finished His race well.

Clearly the author is not talking about the faith that saves a person from hell. In this context he is talking about a faith that trusts in God when things are difficult.

In the life of Jesus we see that He exercised endurance. He **endured the cross** and despised **the shame**. The cross was the worst way for a man to die in the first century. It was a shameful death, reserved for the lowest of criminals.

Jesus did this because He had a **joy that was before Him**. He knew that He would reign over the coming kingdom of God (1:8-9). It will be an eternal kingdom. The pain and shame of the cross were worth it. Afterwards **He sat down**. He finished His work. He is at the most exalted position in the universe.

The readers also had a joy set before them. They could reign with Christ in that kingdom. They are to finish their work. Whatever agony they go through is nothing compared to the promised rewards for those who faithfully complete their race.

The saints in chapter 11 endured. Christ endured. When we need endurance we can look to them for inspiration.

The Importance of Endurance (vv 3-11)

3 For consider Him who endured such hostility from sinners against Himself, lest you become weary and discouraged in your souls. 4 You have not yet resisted to bloodshed, striving against sin. 5 And you have forgotten the exhortation which speaks to you as to sons:

> *"My son, do not despise the chastening of the Lord,*
> *Nor be discouraged when you are rebuked by Him;*
> *6 For whom the Lord loves He chastens, And scourges*
> *every son whom He receives."*

7 If you endure chastening, God deals with you as with sons; for what son is there whom a father does not chasten? 8 But if you are without chastening, of which all have become partakers, then you are illegitimate and not sons. 9 Furthermore, we have had human fathers who corrected *us*, and we paid *them* respect. Shall we not much more readily be in subjection to the Father of spirits and live? 10 For they indeed for a few days chastened us as seemed best to them, but He for *our* profit, that we may be partakers of His holiness. 11 Now no chastening seems to be joyful for the present, but painful; nevertheless, afterward it yields the peaceable fruit of righteousness to those who have been trained by it.

Throughout the Book of Hebrews the author has exhorted his readers to stay the course and remain faithful in their Christian walk. Since they were experiencing difficult times they would need to endure those hardships. The author has emphasized the fact that if they did, they would be greatly rewarded in the kingdom of God. In these verses he gives other benefits as well.

The first thing he points out is that when a Christian faithfully endures difficulties, he is following in the steps of Jesus Christ. In difficulties the believer should **consider Him**. The word means to compare oneself with. The point of vv 3-4 is that Christ went through much harder times than the readers did. When they realize that He remained faithful to God, they could look at their trials and not become **discouraged**.

Unlike Christ, the readers had not **resisted** to the point of **bloodshed**. Even though they had experienced difficult times because they were Christians (10:32-35), none of them had experienced martyrdom.

They had **resisted** against **sin**. The word *sin* here may refer to the temptation to give up in the midst of difficulties. Or it could refer to the unbelievers who opposed them. In either case, Christ is their example, and He endured much more. In addition, they should look at their difficult circumstances from the right perspective.

The right perspective is that God has a purpose for the hard times Christians go through. In vv 5-6 the author quotes from Prov 3:11-12 to prove this point. When the readers were contemplating giving up on their public Christian confession because of the persecution they were facing, they had **forgotten** these verses from the OT.

When God allowed these difficulties to occur, He was treating them as **sons**. Therefore, they should **not despise** such things—they should not resent or complain about them. They should not become **discouraged** by them because they are all a part of the **chastening of the Lord**.

The word *chastening* has the basic meaning of raising up a child. It refers to all the discipline that a father gives to his child to teach that child the things he needs to know. It involves all that goes into educating a child.

Raising up a child involves many things. The author uses the Christian life as a comparison. God can use a variety of means to cause the Christian to grow. Certainly the Christian needs an education in the Word of God (5:11-14). But here the author primarily has in mind the persecution and difficulties the readers were facing because they were Christians. This is certainly implied by the word **scourges**. The word means to beat with a whip.

The author says God is using these things to make them what He desires them to be. One thing we could say is that He wants them to be like Christ (vv 1-3) who also went through difficult times.

In v 7 the author makes it clear that he wants the readers to **endure** such training by **God**. Our trials give us the opportunity to endure. They teach us that God will enable us to get through them, and He will accomplish His purposes in our trials.

Every good **father** educates his **son**. Sometimes such training involves learning things through difficulties. When the readers go through what they are going through, they should understand that in these things **God deals with** them as **sons**. Their persecutions are a display of God's love and care for them.

Verse 8 states that all **sons** experience this **chastening** or discipline of the Lord. If a person does not, then he is **illegitimate**. Most take the reference to an illegitimate son as referring to an unbeliever. If that is the case, the author is saying that God is in the process of training up all Christians for what they will be. This may indeed be what the author is saying.

However, if that is the case, the illustration the author uses seems a little strange. If a father had a son he wanted to leave his business or fortune to, he would spend a great deal of time training him for that future role. An illegitimate son, on the other hand, was a son that did not have that future. It could refer to a son, for example, that was born to a foreign woman. Such a son was not going to be the heir of the father. But such sons were still the children of their fathers. In what way is an unbeliever a child of God?

We see OT examples of this in the cases of Jacob and Esau, as well as Isaac and Ishmael. Later, the author will use the example of Esau. In both of these cases, Esau and Ishmael were the sons of their fathers. But in neither case were they the heirs of those fathers.

It may be, then, that the author has something else in mind. In the context of Hebrews it seems that this is the case. A *son* in v 8 is a mature child who endures the training his Heavenly Father puts him through. He learns what God wants him to learn and allows the process to turn him into what God desires. A *son* is a faithful believer who will reign with *the* Son, Jesus Christ. Christ is bringing many *sons* to that glory (2:10).

An illegitimate son would be a Christian who does not inherit that reward. He has lost his inheritance. In the context of Hebrews he is one that has denied the faith because of the persecutions he has experienced. He has rejected the discipline of his father. This is what the warning passages in the Book of Hebrews are about. God is going to judge that child, as 6:4-8 and 10:26-31 describe. But God continues to train up those Christians who remain faithful to Him.

It is interesting that the author uses the word **partakers** (*metachoi*) to describe those believers who undergo the discipline of the Lord. That is the same word used in 1:9, 3:1, and 3:14 to describe those believers who receive the reward of reigning with Christ in His kingdom.

If this is what the author has in mind, he is saying that God is training up Christians for the role they will fulfill in Christ's kingdom. Just as Christ endured hardship, so can we. God will use those hardships to mold us into those who will not only be in the kingdom, but will have an inheritance in it. Christians should look at the trials in their lives in this light. Christ went through those things and obtained the most exalted position in all the universe. One day He will be ruler over everything (1:13). We can share in that rule. No wonder the author tells the readers to look at Christ's example (vv 1-3).

In vv 9-10 the author says that the benefits of God's discipline do not deal only with rewards in His eternal kingdom. There are also benefits here and now. He points out that **we** all **have had human fathers**. These fathers disciplined us. They administered such discipline **as seemed best to them**.

The point here is that our human fathers sometimes made mistakes. They did what they thought was best for us. As a result, we gave **them respect**. Even though they made mistakes, we recognized their value.

God is not a human father. He is the **Father of spirits**. Through His Spirit we have life in Him. And He never makes mistakes. His discipline is always for **our profit**. He knows exactly what we need. Any trial, persecution, insult, or any other difficulty is used by Him to educate us. If we respected our earthly fathers, how much more should we accept and respect the discipline of our perfect Heavenly Father.

If we allow this educational process to take place, **we** experience a sharing **of His holiness**. This does not refer to being saved from hell and being declared holy by God through faith in Christ. As the author said in chapter 10, that happened once and for all when we believed. Instead, if we allow the work of God to have its purpose in our lives, we can really **live** now.

Christ did not just come so that we might have eternal life. He wants us to have abundant life (John 10:10; Rom 8:13). When we experience that life on a daily basis, we are transformed into the image of Christ (2 Cor 3:18). This involves a daily experience of God's holiness in our lives.

But submitting to the discipline of God results not only in an abundant experience of life and a sharing in the holiness of God here and now, it also results in a harvest of **the peaceable fruit of righteousness** (v 11). In the life of the believer there is a close relationship between peace and righteousness.

When we believed in Jesus Christ for eternal life we were made righteous before God and as a result have peace with God (Rom 5:1). Once again we should also understand this as a daily experience. When through the Spirit we live righteously, we *enjoy* the experience of being at peace with God.

The benefit of experiencing the peace of God on a daily basis does not come automatically. The Christian must go through the **chastening** or discipline of God. Such discipline is not fun to go through. Even the discipline given by our earthly fathers was **painful**.

But those believers who are **trained by** this discipline enjoy all of these benefits. Once again we see that this is not an easy process. The Greek word for *trained* is the word from which "gymnasium" comes. In this passage we see that the faithful Christian life is like an athletic event. It is a race that involves training. However, if believers endure what God is doing through these things, they will reign with Christ, and they will have holiness, peace, and righteousness produced in their lives.

All of this fits the context of the Book of Hebrews. These Christians were in an agonizing race (v 1). They were faced with many opponents. Instead of losing heart, they should be encouraged that all they were going through was the result of the plan of God for their benefit.

Living Together under the Discipline of God (vv 12-17)

[12] **Therefore strengthen the hands which hang down, and the feeble knees, [13] and make straight paths for your feet, so that what is lame may not be dislocated, but rather be healed.**

> ¹⁴ **Pursue peace with all *people*, and holiness, without which no one will see the Lord:** ¹⁵ **looking carefully lest anyone fall short of the grace of God; lest any root of bitterness springing up cause trouble, and by this many become defiled;** ¹⁶ **lest there *be* any fornicator or profane person like Esau, who for one morsel of food sold his birthright.** ¹⁷ **For you know that afterward, when he wanted to inherit the blessing, he was rejected, for he found no place for repentance, though he sought it diligently with tears.**

As is common teaching in the NT, the Christian life is not just about the individual. Each Christian is a part of the Body of Christ. As such we have a responsibility to other members of that Body. In 10:24-25 the author has already told them they need to meet together and encourage one another.

In this chapter the author has compared the Christian life to a long race (v 1). In any such race there is a tendency to get tired and weak. The readers were certainly in danger of that (5:11-14). Some did not want to finish the race.

In v 12 the author alludes to Isa 35:3. He describes some of the readers as having **hands** that **hang down** and as having **feeble knees.** This is a graphic picture of those tired from running. They need **strength.**

Of course, that strength comes through their High Priest, Jesus Christ. They should go to Him to find it (4:16). Christians are encouraged to **make straight paths** for their feet as well as the feet of others (v 13). In vv 14-15 we are told how.

The point here in v 13 is that if we make our paths straight we help those who are **lame.** This probably pictures the lame person as a believer who is having a difficult time. He is undergoing trials and the training of God. Other believers can encourage him by walking on a straight path and going to the Lord to strengthen themselves. When they do so, by enduring and being faithful to God, they are an encouragement for others. When Christians are going through a difficult time and are thinking of giving up, the presence of other believers who are also running the race with the strength that God provides gives those other believers an example to follow.

This is a teaching for Christians in any age. We are not simply to be faithful to the Lord for our own benefit. We have a responsibility for those around us. We can benefit them. That is why it is so important for believers to meet together on a regular basis. As we run our race, we can be an encouragement for other runners.

In vv 14-15 the author tells us how we can strengthen ourselves, make straight paths for ourselves, and help others. We are to **pursue peace with all**. The word *people* does not appear in the Greek. The question is whether this refers to all people, including unbelievers, or if it refers to all Christians.

The context here suggests it is talking about all Christians. We should desire peace with our fellow believers. It is much easier to encourage those in the congregation if we are at peace with them. It is a sad state of affairs today when we see so many churches in which Christians fight one another over irrelevant issues.

Of course peace is not to be sought at any cost. The author of Hebrews tells us that we must also pursue **holiness**. We are not to get along with others if it means we live immorally or do not speak out against sin.

This is how, at least in part, we make straight paths for ourselves—by living holy lives. Such lives are examples for others to follow.

Without holiness, **no** believer will **see the Lord**. This is not saying that if we do not live holy lives we will not be in the kingdom of God. That is contrary to what the Scriptures teach. Many Christians live ungodly lives. Even in the case of the original readers there is the possibility that they will live immorally, as the author will say in v 16.

The author may be saying that when we believe in Christ we are declared righteous—that is, we are holy before the Lord. We will see Him because of that. We should live like it.

More likely, however, it seems that what the author means is that when we live holy lives we "see" God in our actions. Others see Him as well. In v 10 the author has said that if Christians allow God to train them up, they will have a daily experience of sharing in the holiness of God. The word is very similar to the word used here in v 14. Live a holy life, and you are sharing in the character of God. As such, you will "see" Him in your life.

Verse 15 makes it clear that we should faithfully serve God because we have a responsibility toward other Christians. We are to be **looking**

carefully after others. There is a danger that we, as well as other Christians around us, will **fall short of the grace of God**.

In Hebrews, and especially here in chapter 12, the author is talking about a Christian who drops out of the race. All believers have God's grace, through Christ, available to them to run the race well (4:16). However, a believer can fail to take advantage of that grace.

Such a believer then becomes a **root of bitterness**. That is, he becomes a source of bitterness within the Body of Christ. He can cause **many** to be **defiled**. He can cause others to become discouraged in their own race. We as Christians need to look after our fellow believers by doing all we can—by our own lives and encouragement—to prevent this from happening.

In v 16 the author tells us what can lead to a believer's falling short of God's grace and becoming a root of bitterness. It is much more likely if he is a **fornicator or profane person**. The first word refers to a person who lives immorally. The second refers to a person who does not value spiritual things—the things of God.

Clearly the immoral person is not pursuing holiness or making straight paths for his feet (12:13-14). When difficulties come as a result of the Christian faith, he is much more likely to quit. The same could be said for the profane person. He does not see the value of enduring hardships because the value of these things involves spiritual realities and rewards.

Esau is certainly an example of a profane person. Whether he was also immoral is not the emphasis of the author. As the firstborn son of Isaac, he had the promise of a wonderful inheritance. The promises made to his grandfather Abraham, including the promise that all nations would be blessed through his descendant, the coming Messiah, were his.

But Esau did not value these things. Instead, he **sold** that **birthright**. These spiritual blessings were of less value than **one morsel of food** in his eyes. We know the story well. He gave up all these things because he was hungry and wanted a bowl of soup. He chose the things of earth over heavenly realities and rewards. He is the exact opposite of the men and women of faith in chapter 11.

One of the mistakes often made in studying the Book of Hebrews is that people say that Esau represents an unbeliever. That is clearly not the case. Esau was the son of Isaac. He remained his son even after he sold his birthright to his brother Jacob. We can assume that Esau believed in the coming Messiah and knew about the blessings of the inheritance that belonged to him as the firstborn son. In fact, at one point, all of this belonged to him. He simply didn't value it. It also needs to be said that even though he did not receive the firstborn inheritance, his father Isaac gave him another blessing.

The connection with the readers of Hebrews is clear. They have an inheritance in the coming kingdom of God. They can reign with Christ. It is the birthright of every Christian. However, to obtain that inheritance a believer must run the race well. He must value that heavenly reward. He must not desire earthly comforts and treasures more. It is possible to throw away our birthright. Although we cannot lose eternal life, we can lose the inheritance that is available to us.

In v 17 we are told that even though Esau was still the son of Isaac, his lack of concern for spiritual things caused him to suffer great loss. As we know from the Book of Genesis, after he sold his birthright he **wanted** it back. He wanted the **blessing** that went with it. He wanted to be the one through whom the Messiah would come and the world would be blessed. But he lost it all. Esau is not an illustration of an unbeliever. He is the illustration of a believer who loses a great blessing.

When Esau desired to receive it back, **he was rejected**. This was the case even though he **sought** to get it back. In **tears** Esau went to his father Isaac. Esau wanted Isaac to give him the blessing he had traded for a bowl of soup. But Esau **found no place for repentance**. Many have said that what this represents is that a person who renounces his faith can never repent again (Heb 6:6). But this verse says the exact opposite. Esau *did* repent. He turned from his decision to sell the birthright. He wanted it back. He deeply regretted what he had done. *Isaac* was not willing to repent. Isaac was not willing to turn from his decision to give the inheritance to Jacob after Esau sold his birthright to his brother. Esau found no repentance *from his father*. Isaac was not willing to give to Esau what he had despised and thrown away.

Once again we can see how this connects with the Book of Hebrews. If a Christian turns from the faith and devalues his inheritance right of ruling with Christ in the world to come, the day will come when he will regret it. Such a reward can be lost forever. At the Judgment Seat of Christ, Christ will not give the reward to the one who has thrown it away. Even though that believer will be in the kingdom and will still be the child of God, he will have suffered a terrible loss.

In light of vv 12-17, we could add something else on this theme. Believers should be in the business of encouraging other believers not to treat lightly their inheritance. We should encourage other believers that God will greatly reward faithfulness toward Him.

The Christian's Great Privileges (vv 18-24)

The author had said in the previous section that Christians should take their inheritance rights seriously. They should not be like Esau. In this closing section of chapter 12 we are told why. Because of what Christ has done, the Christian has tremendous privileges. Where there are great privileges there is great responsibility. To throw away these privileges would result in serious consequences.

> **[18] For you have not come to the mountain that may be touched and that burned with fire, and to blackness and darkness and tempest, [19] and the sound of a trumpet and the voice of words, so that those who heard it begged that the word should not be spoken to them anymore. [20] (For they could not endure what was commanded: *"And if so much as a beast touches the mountain, it shall be stoned or shot with an arrow."* [21] And so terrifying was the sight that Moses said, *"I am exceedingly afraid and trembling."*) [22] But you have come to Mount Zion and to the city of the living God, the heavenly Jerusalem, to an innumerable company of angels, [23] to the general assembly and church of the firstborn *who are* registered in heaven, to God the Judge of all, to the spirits of just men made perfect, [24] to Jesus the Mediator of the new covenant, and to the blood of sprinkling that speaks better things than *that of* Abel.**

In these verses the author compares the Old Covenant with the privileges of the believer in Christ today. It was at Mount Sinai that the Old Covenant was given to the people of God. The account is found in Exodus 19–20. The description of that place is given here in vv 18-21. The overall picture is that it was a fearful place. In addition, it was an earthly place.

It was a **mountain** that could be **touched**. This speaks of the fact that it belonged to this world. We are reminded that in chapter 11 the people of faith did not focus on worldly things but heavenly.

But the experience at Mount Sinai for the Jews was one that had **fire, blackness, darkness**, and a **tempest**. All these things in one way or another represent the power of the presence of God. His presence fell on Mount Sinai.

Exodus 20:18 tells us that when God spoke it was like thunder, which is probably what the author of Hebrews means by the **voice of words**. The people also heard the **sound of a trumpet**, which probably means that the angelic trumpeters announced the presence of God through these sounds.

Understandably, the people were afraid. They realized they were in the presence of a powerful and holy God. They knew they could not bear His presence or approach Him. So awesome was this presence, so holy was the One who had descended on Mount Sinai, that even if a **beast** were to touch the mountain it was to be killed.

As a result, the people **begged** that God **should not** speak **to them**. They asked Moses to speak to God for them (Exod 20:19). But even he experienced fear and **trembling** during this encounter.

The emphasis here is that under the Old Covenant, even from the beginning, the people could not approach God. Such a prospect was terrifying. The reader is reminded that the same thing applied in the tabernacle. A veil prevented the worshiper from entering into the presence of God (Heb 9:8).

But it is not that way with the NT believer. Unlike the earthly Mount Sinai, the Christian comes to **Mount Zion** (v 22). Mount Zion was the place where the temple was built in Jerusalem. It thus became synonymous with the dwelling place of God.

Clearly the author is referring to God's dwelling in heaven. This mountain is a heavenly one versus the earthly one of Sinai. The earthly mountain could not be touched (v 20). But the Christian can **come to** the greater Mount Zion. We can boldly approach His throne. This is unlike the experience of God's people at Sinai. There they were not able to come to God, but stayed back because of fear (vv 19-21).

This privilege for the believer also means he has come to the **heavenly Jerusalem**. This is the city Abraham looked for (11:10). It will be God's dwelling place forever (Rev 21:2-3). Just as the earthly

tabernacle pointed to the real thing in the heavens (Heb 9:23-24), so
the earthly city of Jerusalem and the mountain there on which the
temple was built point to the real dwelling place of God. Mount Sinai
was the place where God only temporarily displayed His presence. The
superiority of Christianity over Judaism is seen once again. Judaism
had elements that pointed to the real thing. In Christianity the real has
arrived. Who in their right mind would reject Christianity to worship
God under Judaism?

And in this heavenly city there are inhabitants. These include the
innumerable number of **angels** who did not sin when Satan fell. These
are the angels who are sent out to aid those who will rule with Christ
(1:14).

These angels are part of a **general assembly** (v 23). In the Greek
there is only one word. This is the only place where it occurs in the NT.
It refers to a joyful gathering. The angels are celebrating with the **church
of the firstborn**. While many think this is a reference to all Christians,
the context suggests something different.

There is a difference between being a child and being a firstborn
child. All Christians are children of God, but not all will be rewarded
with the rights of a firstborn son. Esau was a firstborn but gave up those
rights. The firstborn here refers to those who inherit these privileges. It
refers to those who have run the race well (vv 1-2) and those who will
rule with Christ in His kingdom. The men and women of chapter 11 are
examples. When all of these partners of Christ arrive in the kingdom,
there will be a joyful celebration for them.

If this is the correct understanding, then these firstborn believers are
those who are **registered in heaven**. This would indicate a special honor.
There will be a register of those who will reign with Christ because of
their faithfulness. An illustration of this is the Hall of Heroes in the
Pentagon. There is a list of names there. The list does not include the
names of every person who has served in the military. It registers the
names only of those who did heroic deeds on the battlefield.

In the heavenly Jerusalem **God** is also present. He is the **Judge of all**.
All men and women will be judged by God. In the case of Christians,
they will be judged at the Judgment Seat of Christ. This judgment has
nothing to do with whether a person goes to heaven or hell. Every
person at the Judgment Seat of Christ will be in the kingdom of God. At
that judgment, Christ will judge the works of each believer, and rewards

will be given out (1 Cor 3:10-15; 2 Cor 5:10). It will also determine those who will reign with Christ—those who will have firstborn rights.

The reference to **just men made perfect** could also refer to all Christians. All Christians are **just** before God because they have believed in Jesus Christ for eternal life. But once again, the context gives us a better choice. The word *perfect* could be used as it is in 11:40. Those who are perfect are those who have reached their goal. The goal of the Christian life is to reign with Christ. They will receive their inheritance rights as firstborn. They will arrive in the city they looked for, just as Abraham looked for it (11:10). These are the ones who ran the race well.

Perhaps the fact that the author refers to the **spirits** of these people suggests that he has in mind faithful believers who have died. Such faithful heroes are in heaven waiting for us. Their lives serve as an example of faithfulness (11:40; 12:1).

The **New Covenant** believer also comes to **Jesus** (v 24). This is a reference to the covenant the believer has with the Lord. He is our **mediator**. This means He gives grace and mercy and help to every believer who comes to Him. He is the One who enables us to run the race well, to reign with Him, and to obtain the rewards of our inheritance as believers (4:14-16).

It is the **blood** of Christ that makes all this possible. While the blood of **Abel** in the Book of Genesis called for vengeance against Cain, Christ's blood brings mercy.

We are reminded of what the author spoke of in chapter 8. There is a New Covenant coming with the nation of Israel in the kingdom of God. The Church is not under that Covenant, but we do have our own covenant with the Lord. The blood of Christ will be the basis for the New Covenant with Israel in the kingdom, but it is also the basis for the covenant Christians have with Christ as well.

This blood does more. It brings in **better things**. The NT believer has more than the promise of simply "going to heaven." There are many other privileges involved. The Christian can go directly into God's presence. We have a mediator we can go to in our times of difficulties. All Christians have the right of inheritance of being a firstborn ruler with Christ, the Firstborn Son par excellence (Heb 1:6).

With these privileges comes great responsibility. Great loss will be incurred by those believers who are like Esau and despise them. In the case of the original readers of Hebrews, to abandon Christianity and go

206 Hebrews: Partners with Christ

back to Judaism would result in such a loss. This causes the author to give one last warning to his readers.

The Final Warning (vv 25-29)

> ²⁵ See that you do not refuse Him who speaks. For if they did not escape who refused Him who spoke on earth, much more shall we not escape if we turn away from Him who speaks from heaven, ²⁶ whose voice then shook the earth; but now He has promised, saying, "Yet once more I shake not only the earth, but also heaven." ²⁷ Now this, "Yet once more," indicates the removal of those things that are being shaken, as of things that are made, that the things which cannot be shaken may remain. ²⁸ Therefore, since we are receiving a kingdom which cannot be shaken, let us have grace, by which we may serve God acceptably with reverence and godly fear. ²⁹ For our God is a consuming fire.

The first warning in the Book of Hebrews was found in 2:1-4. In that warning the author said that the readers needed to give heed to what they have heard. If they did not, they would not escape the consequences. The author now gives his last warning and repeats these themes. The first and last warnings are like two bookends that wrap up the message of the book.

When the people of God received the Old Covenant, they listened with fear and reverence (vv 18-21). New Testament believers have greater privileges than they did. We should listen and respond appropriately.

God spoke to the Jews at Sinai. He now **speaks** to the NT believer (v 25). He does so through Christ, the greatest Prophet of all time (Heb 1:2-3). At Sinai He spoke to His people from **earth**. In Christ, He speaks to us from the One who is in **heaven** at His right hand (1:13).

The Jews who disobeyed Him under the Old Covenant **did not escape** punishment. This is a reference to the second warning passage (Heb 3–4). Those Jews who rebelled at Kadesh died in the wilderness and did not inherit the land. How can a NT believer expect to **escape** punishment if he does not listen to the King who is seated in the heavens?

The One who spoke from earth at Sinai and speaks from heaven through His Son has a powerful **voice** (v 26). At Sinai that voice **shook the earth** (Exod 19:18). As impressive as that is, however, this voice will do something greater in the future.

This future event was prophesied by the OT prophet Haggai. God will one day **shake** both **the earth and heaven** (Hag 2:6). Revelation 20:11 and 21:1 speak of the day when God's word will create a new heavens and a new earth. The word *heaven* refers to what we call the atmosphere and space. In other words, God's voice will bring in a new creation. The author of Hebrews has already said this would occur (Heb 1:10-12).

Everything on this earth is temporary. On the day when God brings in His eternal kingdom there will be a **removal** of all **things** which are temporary, that is, that can be **shaken** (v 27). God will replace them with things that are permanent and **cannot be shaken**. In the end, these are the things that are important.

The point here is that the believer should focus on the things that are eternal. He should not live for the temporary things of this world. This was the whole point in chapter 11 of those faithful men and women of God. They lived for God's eternal kingdom. They laid up their treasure there. Esau was the kind of man who did the opposite.

Verse 28 gives us the purpose for the author's warning. His conclusion is signaled by the word **therefore**. There is only one proper response for the Christian. He should **serve God with reverence and godly fear**. The reason we should do so is because the Christian is in the process of **receiving a kingdom**.

This is the first time since Heb 1:8 that the word *kingdom* is used to describe the coming eternal kingdom of God. In 1:8 it referred to the fact that Christ was going to receive His kingdom and will rule over it. In 1:9 it says that He will have partners who will rule that kingdom with Him.

These faithful believers will also *receive the kingdom*. All believers will enter the kingdom. But only faithful believers will actually *receive* it. There is a difference between entering a place and owning a part of it. Faithful believers will receive an inheritance in it. It is an eternal inheritance that **cannot be shaken**.

In order to receive this reward, the believer needs God's **grace**. To faithfully run the race we must take advantage of the grace our

Great High Priest provides (Heb 4:14-16). This is the only way we can acceptably serve God. In the context of Hebrews this would mean receiving God's grace to continually worship Him in the community of believers (10:19-25), to endure during difficult times, and to encourage other believers in the same endeavors (12:12-15).

The people of God at Sinai knew that God should be taken seriously. They had a healthy awe of Him and His word. We should, too. We should seek God's grace to please Him with our lives.

In v 29 the author gives us another reason for seeking God's grace to obey Him. The reason is that God judges and punishes His disobedient people. This was also stated in the previous warning passage (10:27-31).

Here the author quotes from Deut 4:24. In this passage God tells His people that He is jealous about them. He will not allow them to forsake Him and go worship other gods. He warns them about forgetting the covenant He made with them. He is a **consuming fire** that will punish them. This is not a reference to hell, as Deuteronomy makes clear. But God would punish them with plagues, captivity, loss of crops, and defeat by their enemies.

If these things were true under the Old Covenant, surely they are true for the NT believer. If these readers rejected all the privileges they had and returned to worshiping under Judaism, not only would they lose their inheritance in the coming kingdom, they could expect the fire of God's judgment in their lives.

Concluding Remarks

IN THE BOOKS OF the NT, it is common for the authors to discuss doctrine first and then how the readers should live in light of that doctrine. The Book of Hebrews follows that pattern. The author has just said that the readers should serve God with a holy reverence (12:28). Now he gives commands that show how they can do just that. There are parallels between these commandments and the part of the Ten Commandments which deals with how God's people are to treat one another.

Five Important Virtues to Cultivate (vv 1-6)

¹ **Let brotherly love continue.** ² **Do not forget to entertain strangers, for by so** *doing* **some have unwittingly entertained angels.** ³ **Remember the prisoners as if chained with them— those who are mistreated—since you yourselves are in the body also.**

⁴ **Marriage** *is* **honorable among all, and the bed undefiled; but fornicators and adulterers God will judge.**

⁵ *Let your* **conduct** *be* **without covetousness;** *be* **content with such things as you have. For He Himself has said,** *"I will never leave you nor forsake you."* ⁶ **So we may boldly say:**

"The Lord is my helper;
I will not fear.
What can man do to me?"

In these verses the author gives us five commandments to follow if we are going to serve God.

The author's first command is to show **brotherly love** (v 1). This refers to loving other believers. In the Book of Hebrews that would mean to **continue** to meet with other Christians in worship and encourage them in the struggles they face. This was of particular concern for the author since some had already stopped doing this.

But this love is also demonstrated when they **entertain strangers** (v 2), which is his second admonition This is a concrete example of loving other believers. These two words are just one word in the Greek, and it means to show hospitality. The author probably has in mind the practice in the first century by which Christians, and especially Christian teachers, would travel. They would be dependent upon the hospitality of other Christians to provide lodging and food.

When Christians show hospitality to other believers, they may be showing it to **angels**. The word for *angel* means a messenger. We can think of Abraham who showed hospitality to angels in the Book of Genesis (Gen 18:1-3; 19:1-2). Even if a Christian does not take in an actual angel, we could say that whenever we show hospitality to a Christian worker, we are taking in a messenger of God.

The author's third exhortation is also related to loving other believers. The readers are to **remember the prisoners** (v 3). These readers were experiencing persecution for their faith. Some of their fellow believers were still in prison. The readers had ministered to such people in the past (10:33-34). But they were being tempted to fall away from the faith. With such a situation, it would be easy to decide to avoid association with believers in prison. That could only bring trouble in their own lives.

The author wants them to continue to show love to these persecuted believers because the readers themselves **are in the body also**. This probably means that they are in physical bodies as well. Those in prison are suffering physically, and part of loving other believers is putting ourselves in their shoes. How would they like to be treated by other believers if the roles were reversed and *they* were the ones in prison?

The author's fourth imperative deals with sexual immorality and finds a direct parallel with the Ten Commandments. The author had previously warned them about being immoral and that such conduct could lead to the loss of their reward of an inheritance in the kingdom (Heb 12:16). Just as in our own day, sexual immorality was rampant in the first century.

Sexual relations are only acceptable to God in the **marriage bed** (v 4). Those who engage in sex outside of marriage are **fornicators.** Those who are married and violate their vows with others are **adulterers.** Those who do these things find that **God will judge** them. Without a doubt this includes believers. Christians are susceptible and unfortunately often fail in this area. God's judgment will come either in their lives, at the Judgment Seat of Christ, or both.

The fifth appeal deals with **covetousness** and also is directly parallel to the Ten Commandments. Christians are to be **content** with what they **have** (v 5). They are not to covet material things.

This was very appropriate for the original readers. They had already suffered the loss of material things because of their faith (10:34). But the author had reminded them that all these things belong to this creation and are temporary (12:27).

To encourage them in this area, the author quotes from Josh 1:5 and Deut 31:6-7. In those verses God tells Joshua that as he faces his enemies in the land, God will not **leave nor forsake** him. God will be there in all the difficult times.

God is always with His people in their trials. What are material things in light of this reality? In v 6 the author once again turns to the OT and quotes from Ps 118:6 to make the same point. There is no need to worry about material things because God is the **helper** of His people. He will provide what His people need.

As a result, there is no need to **fear what man** can do to them. This was a message the original readers needed to hear. They were confronted with the enemies of God who threatened their safety and economic well-being. But they had nothing to fear. God had promised to be with them and help them.

The Importance of Leaders within the Church (vv 7-17)

⁷ Remember those who rule over you, who have spoken the word of God to you, whose faith follow, considering the outcome of their conduct. ⁸ Jesus Christ is the same yesterday, today, and forever. ⁹ Do not be carried about with various and strange doctrines. For it is good that the heart be established by grace, not with foods which have not profited those who have been occupied with them.

> ¹⁰ We have an altar from which those who serve the tabernacle have no right to eat. ¹¹ For the bodies of those animals, whose blood is brought into the sanctuary by the high priest for sin, are burned outside the camp. ¹² Therefore Jesus also, that He might sanctify the people with His own blood, suffered outside the gate. ¹³ Therefore let us go forth to Him, outside the camp, bearing His reproach. ¹⁴ For here we have no continuing city, but we seek the one to come. ¹⁵ Therefore by Him let us continually offer the sacrifice of praise to God, that is, the fruit of our lips, giving thanks to His name. ¹⁶ But do not forget to do good and to share, for with such sacrifices God is well pleased. ¹⁷ Obey those who rule over you, and be submissive, for they watch out for your souls, as those who must give account. Let them do so with joy and not with grief, for that would be unprofitable for you.

In this section the author begins and ends with the subject of teachers within the church. In v 7 he refers to their past teachers. In v 17 he refers to their present teachers. In between these verses he reminds the readers that they were taught that the NT was superior to the Old Covenant. This, of course, is a major subject of the Book of Hebrews. They would do well if they contemplated and did what these men had taught them.

Evidently the past leaders of these Christians were godly men who accurately taught **the word of God** to them (v 7). However, the readers were in danger of forgetting what these men taught (5:11-14).

But these men not only taught well, they also lived well. They served God in a pleasing way (12:28). The readers were to **follow** their **faith** and consider **their conduct**. These men, like the examples in chapter 11, lived lives of faith. Their actions matched their teachings.

We should imitate those who serve God faithfully. We will never see the men and women mentioned in chapter 11, but we can see faithful believers around us. We should also desire to be such examples to others.

Verse 8 is to be understood in light of v 7. Many people use it to argue that since **Jesus Christ is** always the **same**, all the spiritual gifts, such as tongues, are still for **today**. However, nowhere in the context of chapter 13 is the author dealing with spiritual gifts. Instead, it means that even when Christian leaders die, their teachings about Christ remain true. The content of their teachings are found in vv 9-16.

Since what their leaders had taught them is still true, they should avoid **various and strange doctrines** (v 9). The new teachings that were alluring them away from Christianity were not what their past teachers had taught them. While the context of Hebrews tells us it was Judaism that was attracting them, v 9 indicates that a particular sect of Judaism may have been the problem. Perhaps, like the Jews at Qumran, it was a particularly strict sect.

Part of the false teaching alluring them away involved **foods**. Judaism in general, and especially a strict interpretation of Judaism like at Qumran, placed a great deal of importance on what a person eats. They said that what we eat can make us closer to God. The author points out that growth in our spiritual lives does not occur with material things such as food. One grows by God's **grace** (Heb 4:16). False teaching, of whatever kind, does not teach the grace of God.

New Testament believers have a different kind of *food* to eat. Their leaders had taught them about the superiority of their privileges in Christ over Judaism. The Book of Hebrews does the same.

In Christ, we have a different **altar** than the one found in the OT. The word clearly refers to the death of Christ. In His sacrifice the Christian is able to find spiritual nourishment. We grow through contact with Him (John 15:4). We go to Him to find the grace and spiritual things we need (v 9; 4:16).

Those under the Old Mosaic Covenant had their own altar at the **tabernacle** and then later in the temple. With some sacrifices, the priests could eat the meat (Lev 6:22*ff*). But physical food does nothing for us spiritually (v 9). The Jews under the Old Covenant could not "feed" upon the spiritual nourishment Christ provides.

On the Day of Atonement, the priests in the OT could not even eat the physical meat of the animals. The **animals** killed on that day had their bodies **burned outside the camp** (v 11). With the word *camp*, the author refers to the time when the Jews under the leadership of Moses lived in the wilderness. The sacrificed animals were taken outside of where the Jews lived because their dead bodies were considered unclean; they had taken on, in a figurative sense, the sins of the people. By removing the bodies of these animals from their midst, the Jews were saying their sins were an unholy thing. They were symbolically removing everything associated with their sin.

The author wants to make a parallel with what happened on the Day of Atonement and Jesus. Just as those sacrificed animals were taken outside where the Jews lived, so **Jesus** died outside of the city of Jerusalem and its **gate** (v 12). This is a picture of Him being considered unholy and rejected by the Jews. He was **outside** of what Judaism considered good.

This would be very important for Christians who were thinking about returning to Judaism. They would be returning to a religion that had declared the King and High Priest unholy. They had rejected Him.

The irony of it all is that instead of being unholy, Jesus' **blood** had sanctified them. In Heb 10:10, 14, the word **sanctify** was used to describe how Christ's sacrifice had made believers holy forever. This sacrifice results in the gift of eternal life to all who believe in Him for it.

Clearly it would be a terrible mistake to return to Judaism. Instead, they should align themselves with Christ. They, too, are to go **outside the camp** (v 13). They, too, should leave Judaism completely behind. They needed to leave all the religious rituals, worship at the temple, and all the things associated with the Old Covenant. The Lord was rejected by the Jews. He died a shameful death. The readers are to stand with Him and share His **reproach**, including any persecution that went with it.

In Christ there has been a complete reversal. Under Judaism, the camp was the clean place. Outside the camp was considered unholy. In Christ, outside the "camp" of Judaism is now the place where one finds cleansing from sins.

And the Book of Hebrews has given us a very practical reason for sharing in Christ's shame, regardless of the cost. We do not **have** in this world a permanent inheritance. There is no permanent **city** (v 14). We serve the Lord as we look for a permanent **one to come** (11:10, 16; 12:22), that is, the New Jerusalem. The believer who remains faithful to Christ will share in that inheritance.

Being faithful to Christ involves worship to God that truly honors Him. The Jews had their system of worship which has been replaced. The **sacrifices** (v 15) that God now desires are not found in the Jewish system. Instead, they are found in the Christian "house" of worship (3:6), which is the community of Christian worshipers. We are to offer sacrifices as a group. These sacrifices no longer involve the blood of animals, since Christ's death has put an end to such sacrifices.

In this house of worship, we offer our sacrifices **by Him**, that is, Jesus Christ our High Priest. True worship is found only in Him. Our sacrifices include **praise to God** for who He is and all He has done.

But the Christian community, as a group, is also to offer to God the sacrifice of doing good and sharing (v 16). **God is pleased** when His people do good works and when they **share** in the needs of their fellow believers. Such sharing is a demonstration of brotherly love (v 1).

If the readers rejected the Christian community and returned to the sacrifices of Judaism, all of these pleasing sacrifices would cease. The readers would renounce the true worship of God and return to a system that offered worthless sacrifices and that had been replaced.

All of these things (vv 10-16), were taught by the past leaders of the recipients of Hebrews. The author had begun this section by mentioning these leaders (v 7). He now closes this section by returning to the subject of their Christian leaders. He tells the readers to **obey and be submissive** to them (v 17).

The author clearly had a positive view of their leaders. He wants the readers to listen to their teachings and follow the example of these leaders. These leaders were those who were responsible to **watch out** for them. This is a reference to their spiritual health. One day the leaders will **give** an **account** of how faithfully they performed their responsibilities.

They will give an account at the Judgment Seat of Christ. All believers will appear at that Judgment to determine their rewards in the kingdom. Leaders in the church will also give an account of how they performed as leaders (1 Pet 5:1-4).

Being a church leader is a difficult job. We see in the Book of Hebrews that some of those they were leading had become spiritually weak (5:11-14) amd were being led away by strange doctrines (13:9). Some had even quit worshiping with other believers (10:25). In addition, all of them were facing the prospect of persecution.

The author wants the readers to obey and submit to their leaders so that their leaders could perform their duties **with joy**. If they made their leaders' responsibilities ones of **grief**, it would **be unprofitable for** themselves.

The readers will also appear before the Judgment Seat of Christ. They will give an account of how they submitted to the teaching of their Christian leaders. If the readers refused the sound teaching of these leaders and therefore caused them grief, they would not benefit from the guidance of those leaders. In addition, they would suffer loss on the day they appear before Christ.

Personal Final Words (vv 18-25)

[18] **Pray for us; for we are confident that we have a good conscience, in all things desiring to live honorably. [19] But I especially urge you to do this, that I may be restored to you the sooner. [20] Now may the God of peace who brought up our Lord Jesus from the dead, that great Shepherd of the sheep, through the blood of the everlasting covenant, [21] make you complete in every good work to do His will, working in you what is well pleasing in His sight, through Jesus Christ, to whom *be* glory forever and ever. Amen. [22] And I appeal to you, brethren, bear with the word of exhortation, for I have written to you in few words. [23] Know that *our* brother Timothy has been set free, with whom I shall see you if he comes shortly. [24] Greet all those who rule over you, and all the saints. Those from Italy greet you. [25] Grace *be* with you all. Amen.**

As the author concludes this book, he asks that the readers **pray for us** (v 18). Whoever the author was, he had a least one partner with him in his ministry (*us*). Even though the readers of Hebrews had many spiritual problems, he covets their prayers. This is an indication of the humility of the author.

He points out that he has a **good conscience**. This probably means that he has the best interest of the readers in mind, even though he had to write a book that had such strong warnings. He wants to continue **to live** this way.

He also wants them to pray that he **may be** able to come to them even **sooner** than he had hoped (v 19). This is another indication that he is genuinely concerned for them.

After asking for their prayers, he prays for them. The One he prays to on their behalf is the **God of peace** (v 20). Because of Christ, these readers were at peace with God (Rom 5:1). In the midst of their difficult circumstances they should be at peace with one another.

In this prayer the **Lord Jesus** is called the **great Shepherd of the sheep**. In the OT the King was also called the shepherd of his people. Jesus Christ is *the* King of His people. This is an appropriate title for Him.

But as we have seen in Hebrews, Jesus is also His people's High Priest. The **blood** of His sacrifice makes possible all the benefits of the **everlasting Covenant**. It is an eternal covenant, unlike the Old Covenant that it replaced. Under this covenant, God raised Christ **from the dead** after His sacrifice and has seated Him at His right hand where He serves as our High Priest.

The author prays that God would **make** them **complete in every good work**. This means that God would strengthen them to do **what is pleasing** to Him. God is pleased with the good works of His people (v 16). These works can be done **through Jesus Christ**. It is in Christ that the believer finds the grace and mercy to serve the Lord and remain faithful to Him (4:14-16). It is only through the power He provides that one can obtain the reward of reigning with Christ, which is an overarching theme of the Book of Hebrews. Such a reward involves sharing in the **glory** of the One who will reign **forever and ever**.

The author has a final request of them. It is interesting that he calls them **brethren** (v 22; 3:12). Once again we see that he is writing to people he knows are Christians. Even though they contemplated renouncing their faith, he knows who they are. He wants these Christians to **bear** what he has **written to** them.

What he has written is an **exhortation**. The book has included perhaps the strongest warnings in the NT. However, the word here has the basic meaning of "encouragement." The author has not written to them because he doesn't think they are "truly saved." He knows they are his brethren. He knows they will be in the kingdom of God. But he wants to encourage them to remain faithful to the Lord, run the Christian race well, and obtain the reward of reigning with Christ in the world to come.

Verse 23 contains the only name mentioned by the author. He refers to **Timothy** being **set free**. The author and readers knew Timothy. This provides some clue as to the author's identity (Barnabas, Paul, Luke, Ananias, etc.), but it does not confirm his identity since many people would have known Timothy. This is also the only place in the NT that indicates that Timothy had been imprisoned.

In v 24 the author greets both the readers and their leaders. He includes in that greeting **those from Italy**. This also can give some clue to the identity of the author, but it provides nothing definitive. All that can be said is that he was acquainted with people from Italy.

Appropriately, the author ends the letter with the theme of **grace** (v 25). The readers, as beloved brethren, had experienced the grace of God when they obtained eternal life. But the Book of Hebrews exhorts them to continue to experience the grace of God through Christ so that they can finish their race well and be partners with Christ in His kingdom.

Conclusion

If we are going to properly understand the message of the Book of Hebrews, we must clearly understand two basic truths of Scripture. The first is that the believer in Jesus Christ has been eternally saved once and for all. The second is that the eternally saved believer can fail and fail miserably. Unfortunately, readers of the NT often do not understand these truths.

The Believer is Eternally Saved

As we have seen in this commentary, Hebrews 10 clearly teaches the wonderful assurance of eternal salvation for the believer in Jesus Christ. The Christian has been sanctified, or made holy *once for all*. These sanctified ones have become perfect *forever* (Heb 10:10, 14).

The author of Hebrews also knows that he is writing to such people. He calls them holy, or sanctified, brothers in Christ (Heb 3:1).

The readers, then, are those who are eternally secure. That is the audience of the book. They cannot lose their salvation

Of course, the rest of the NT teaches the same thing. Jesus tells the woman at the well that if she believed in Him and the gift He had to give, she would receive the gift of eternal life and could never thirst for that life again. It would be her possession forever (John 4:14). The believer in Jesus Christ will never stand before the Lord at the Great White Throne Judgment (John 5:24). The very fact that eternal life is eternal, by definition, means that it cannot be lost. Eternal life is the present possession of every believer. It is not something we receive when we die (John 3:16; 6:47).

Even though the original readers of Hebrews had this life, the author was also a realist. He knew that they could fail in their Christian walk. They could even deny the Christian faith. That is what the warning passages are about.

Failure Is an Option

As pointed out in the commentary, the author warns the readers of the possibility of spiritual failure. They could drift away from the faith (Heb 2:1). They could fail to enter into the "rest" that God provides His children (Heb 3-4). They could deny the faith (Heb 6:4-6). They could withdraw from the visible Christian community (Heb 10:22-25). They could choose to ignore what God has said to them through His Son (Heb 12:25-29). Each of these warnings carried with it the idea of God's discipline for such failure.

Indeed, these failures come with great consequences. The author does not spell out what these consequences are. He only tells the readers they will be severe. He uses the illustration of a field being burned. Using the OT, he says it will be just as when God disciplined His people in the OT with disease, famine, pestilence, and defeat at the hands of their enemies. For one generation of God's people, it resulted in the death of a whole generation of Jews after Kadesh Barnea (Heb 3-4).

Certainly, no wise thinking believer would want to experience these things during this life. Who would want to open himself up to such discipline? As the author says, it is terrifying indeed (Heb 10:30-31).

A believer should contemplate the loss such discipline could bring in his life. But there is more. The cost will go on in eternity. While the Christian cannot lose eternal life, he can lose eternal rewards.

Receiving Eternal Rewards

The teaching on eternal rewards is often neglected and misunderstood even in Christian circles. Part of the reason for this is believers think that as long as they are in the Kingdom of God rewards are not important. However, a careful study of the Book of Hebrews shows us why they are important.

The author knows that it is impossible for the "holy brethren" to whom he is writing to lose their eternal salvation. But they have a "heavenly calling" (Heb 3:1). It is to reign with Christ in the world to come, to be one of Christ's *metochoi* (Heb 1:9; 3:14). He wants them to have a "better resurrection" and at the Judgment Seat of Christ (Heb 10:35, 39) gain Christ's approval of how they lived their lives. While all believers will be *in* the kingdom, not all believers will receive these rewards.

To receive them, they will need to persevere. They are going through difficulties (Heb 10:32-34), and perseverance is not automatic. But God has given them all they need to live victorious Christian lives. They have a believing community in which they can find encouragement (Heb 10:24). They have the example of faithful believers of the past (Hebrews 11). Through the sacrifice of Christ, they can approach the throne of grace and find the help and mercy they need in their times of difficulties and temptation (Heb 4:16; 10:22). There they find a High Priest who is completely able to provide that help and understands what they are going through (Heb 2:17-18). That High Priest is one they can fix their eyes on because He is the ultimate example of being faithful to God under difficult circumstances (Heb 2:10; 12:2).

There is no need for any believer in any age to lose the rewards God will give to those who persevere in the faith. The Book of Hebrews is a letter of exhortation (Heb 13:22), calling its readers to clearly see the glory Christ will share with those who do. All Christians would do well to realize that the Book of Hebrews is telling us that there is much more to the Christian life than "going to heaven."

When I was younger, one of my favorite Christian songs was by an artist named Don Francisco. It was called, *Too Small a Price.* The song is told from the perspective of the believing thief who died on the cross next to Christ. The climax of the song is found after the Lord tells him that he will be with Him that day in Paradise (Luke 23:43). After hearing these words, the thief, in the song says:

"The shouts and curses did not stop
Even when the sunlight ceased,
But somehow in the midst of it
My soul had been released
Though the agony continued,
It's still too small a price

To be allowed to hear those words,
To die beside the Christ"

Certainly we can see the truth in the words of this song. The believing thief experienced almost unbearable pain on that wooden tree. But we can also see that he was given an unbelievable honor. He paid a heavy price for that honor, but at the same time he saw it as a small price. The honor? To die *with the Christ*!

Perseverance in the faith is also difficult. The original readers of Hebrews understood that very clearly. There is a price to pay. But what an honor awaits those who persevere. When compared to that honor, the price a believer has to pay is small indeed. Not only will they be in the eternal kingdom that is coming. They will be *partners with Christ!*

Commentaries on Hebrews: Annotated

F. F. Bruce, *The Epistle of the Hebrews,* NICNT (Grand Rapids, MI: Eerdmans, 1990). Written to Jewish Christians who were Hellenists outside of Jerusalem. They were reluctant to break ties with Judaism. Warning passages are addressed to unbelievers who can get to the point that they can no longer repent by repudiating what they have heard about Christ.

Paul Elllingworth, *The Epistle to the Hebrews,* NIGTC, (Grand Rapids, MI: Eerdmans, 1993). Written to a primarily Jewish-Christian group, but not the members of a local group. Some Gentiles were probably in the original recipients. The teachings at Qumran may have impacted some of the things said in Hebrews. Apostasy is a real danger and cannot be reversed. The book is an encouragement to persevere. Deals with final judgment in which apostates will be condemned. Heavy on Greek discussion and Second Temple literature.

Homer A. Kent, Jr., *The Epistle to the Hebrews* (Winona Lake, IN: BMH Books, 1972). Audience is Jewish Christians, living in Rome in the late 60s. Warnings are hypothetical since falling away is impossible for true believers. The better resurrection is not a reward but being a part of the kingdom of God, which is better than living on in this world.

Simon J. Kistemaker, *Exposition of the Epistle to the Hebrews* (Grand Rapids, MI: Baker, 1984). Based upon the political background of the first century, suggests a date in the early 80s. Written to Jewish Christians in Rome. The inheritance/reward is given to all believers. Takes the warning passages to refer to people who were not truly saved. Says the example of the Jews at Kadesh Barnea is a mystery. God led them out of Egypt but they were unbelievers. The true believer is sanctified once for all but this involves a life dedicated to God's service.

William L. Lane, *Hebrews*, Word Biblical Commentary, 2 vols (Dallas, TX: Word Books, 1991). Hebrews was written in the 60s to a small house of Hellenistic Jews. It was written as a sermon, to be read aloud. Commentary is technical and addresses the form/structure of each passage, with comments, and explanation. The readers were believers, but in danger of regression. They were a mature congregation, but deliberate apostasy would result in loss of salvation. Spiritual immaturity could lead to that. He has confidence they will go on, but the danger is real and not hypothetical.

G. H. Lang, *The Epistle to the Hebrews*, (London: The Paternoster Press, 1951). No need to discuss author. Not written to Jewish Christians since the New Testament does not make such distinctions in the church. Warnings addressed to true Christians, but punishment is not hell. It is exclusion from the millennial kingdom and the loss of reigning with Christ. Punishment could also include loss in this world and even death.

Thomas Lea, *Hebrews and James,* Holman New Testament Commentary (Nashville, TN: Holman Publishing, 1999). A semi-devotional commentary. The readers were Jewish Christians with a similar background to Qumran. Warning passages are addressed to professing believers who are not born again.

John MacArthur, *Hebrews*, The MacArthur New Testament Commentary (Chicago, IL: Moody, 1983). Three groups are addressed in Hebrews: believers; unbelievers who are intellectually convinced of the Gospel; unbelievers who are not convinced. We must determine who is being addressed in each passage. The book is primarily written to believers to encourage them to persevere but the warning passages are addressed to the two unbelieving groups. Does not see in Hebrews rewards for faithfulness. All true believers will be resurrected.

William R. Newell, *Hebrews: Verse-by-Verse*, reprint (Grand Rapids: Kregel, 1995). Written to a Jewish Christian audience, but some were not genuinely saved. The issue is not backsliding, but apostasy. God will not give repentance to professing Christians who have not been sealed by the Holy Spirit and then fall away. Maintains Paul was the author.

H. D. M. Spence, *Hebrews and James,* The Pulpit Commentary, reprint (Peabody, MA: Hendrickson Publishers, 1985). A homiletical commentary. Hebrews was written to Jewish Christians in Palestine, before AD 70 during a time of a close relationship between Christianity and Judaism. The warnings concern apostasy and the loss of eternal salvation. Takes particular exception with the view that non-genuine believers are being addressed.

J. Paul Tanner, "Hebrews," *The Grace New Testament Commentary,* vol 2 (Denton, TX: Grace Evangelical Society, 2010). Short commentary that takes the same position as this work. Holds that the book of Hebrews was written to a particular Jewish Christian group going through difficulties and were in danger of losing eternal rewards.

B. F. Westcott, *The Epistle to the Hebrews*, reprint (Grand Rapids, MI: Eerdmans, 1955). Heavy Greek emphasis. Written to Jews, no mixture of Gentiles. Not written by Paul, maybe Luke or Barnabas. Warnings deal with apostasy and loss of salvation. These warnings are partially hypothetical since none of the readers had committed apostasy.

Warren W. Wiersbe, *Hebrews: Be Confident* (Colorado Springs, CO: David C. Cook, 1982). Part of the *Be* series, written for the layman. Heavy on application, with questions for discussion. Warnings are addressed to true believers, but are hypothetical. True believers cannot lose salvation.

Discussion Questions

Chapter One

1. What two offices of Jesus Christ are discussed in Heb 1:1-4?
2. What are some ways the Lord revealed Himself in the OT? How is this different from the revelation of Jesus Christ?
3. What are some of the themes found in Psalm 2? What type of Psalm is it? Why is this important to the author of Hebrews?
4. In what way does chapter 1 argue for the deity of Christ?
5. What are the main points of the author in quoting Psalms 104 and 97?
6. Who are the *metochoi* in the Book of Hebrews?
7. In the Book of Hebrews, what does the word "salvation" mean?

Chapter Two

1. What type of danger are the readers in, according to 2:1? How might this be applicable to believers today?
2. What type of punishment does the author of Hebrews have in mind in chapter 2? What are some examples you can give of this type of punishment?
3. What does it mean to "neglect so great a salvation"? What does this look like in the believer's life?
4. In chapter 1, Jesus is presented as King. What new aspect of Jesus' identity does the author of Hebrews address in 2:5-18? What are the implications of this for believers?
5. What two themes can be found in the author's use of Psalm 8?

6. In chapter 2, why does the author refer to Jesus as our Captain? What imagery comes with this description? Why is this significant for the readers?
7. What does the word "sanctified" mean in the Book of Hebrews?
8. What is the history behind Isaiah 8? Why do you think the author of Hebrews quoted from this OT passage?
9. Give two reasons why the Lord had to become a man (vv 16-18).
10. What does it mean for Jesus to be our High Priest?

Chapters Three/Four

1. What is the "calling" in Hebrews 3?
2. What is the author of Hebrews most likely referring to when he says that Moses was over the "house" of God? What does the "house of Christ" refer to in this passage?
3. What is the consequence for the believer who visibly leaves the church?
4. What example in the OT does the author of Hebrews use to describe those who fall away? What price did they pay for their disobedience?
5. What does the term "rest" refer to in this passage?
6. Why do you think the author of Hebrews discusses Kadesh Barnea? What's the application for the readers? What are some applications for us today?
7. What sin is the author of Hebrews warning against in this chapter? What does it mean for us today?
8. What did the generation at Kadesh Barnea lose due to their sin? How does this apply to the church age believer?
9. What is the idea behind being "naked and open" in 4:13?

Chapter Five

1. What is the shift that takes place in chapter 5?
2. What are the requirements for being a high priest?
3. What OT character is mentioned in chapter 5, foreshadowing Christ as one who fulfills both offices of High Priest and King? What do we know about this man?

4. What is the significance behind the Lord holding both offices of High Priest and King?
5. What does it mean to be "dull" of hearing?
6. Give some examples of what the "first principles" might include?
7. What dangers are the readers of Hebrews facing due to their spiritual immaturity? How might this manifest in the church today?

Chapter Six

1. What does the word "perfection" mean in 6:1? What does it *not* mean? Why is this distinction important?
2. What are some examples which illustrate how Christianity is superior to Judaism? What examples did the author of Hebrews give?
3. To whom is the author referring in 6:4-8? What are some of their descriptions?
4. What is the punishment for those who fall away?
5. What does the phrase "tasted the heavenly gift" mean here in chap. 6? Where else is the term "tasted" used in Hebrews? Why is this important?
6. What does the author of Hebrews mean when he says it is "impossible to renew them again to repentance"?
7. What illustration does the author of Hebrews give to describe these believers? What does he mean by "fire" in his illustration?
8. In this context, what does it mean to be rejected?
9. What does the reference to "better things" mean (v 9)? What are some examples?
10. What was involved in the Lord's promise in Genesis 22? Why is this important in the context of Hebrews?

Chapter Seven

1. What are some of the comparisons between Jesus and Melchizedek?
2. Melchizedek is described as having "no beginning of days or end of life." What were the three options for what this could mean?

3. What aspects of Melchizedek's (and thus the Lord's) priesthood are better than the priests under the Old Covenant?
4. In what ways was the Levitical priesthood insufficient?
5. In the Book of Hebrews, what does the word "hope" refer to, and how do we obtain this hope?
6. Jesus surpasses the OT priesthood. In what three ways does the author of Hebrews describe His greatness as High Priest?

Chapter Eight

1. What is the significance of the Lord's being "seated" at the right hand of God?
2. In what way is the NT covenant "better" than that of the Old Covenant?
3. How is the tabernacle of the OT a copy or shadow of what was to come?
4. Why did the Old Covenant fail?
5. What is the difference between the New Covenant that Jeremiah speaks about and the New Covenant for the church?

Chapter Nine

1. What is the contrast between the tabernacle that Moses built and that made by Christ?
2. Why does the author of Hebrews spend so much time discussing the furniture in the tabernacle?
3. Describe some of the services that the high priest was responsible for doing in the tabernacle. How were these services inferior to the Lord's ministry?
4. What does the word "symbolic" mean in 9:9? Why is this significant for the author of Hebrews?
5. In what way is the Lord's sacrifice better than that which the OT priests offered? What are the benefits?
6. What two purposes did the OT sacrificial system serve?
7. What does the expression "dead works" refer to in v 14?
8. We are told in 8:6 that the New Covenant had greater promises (8:6). What promise is specifically mentioned in 9:15? What does this include?

9. Why was the Lord's death necessary?
10. How is the Lord's sacrifice "better"?
11. What is the context of the "salvation" found in chap. 9? Why is this important?

Chapter Ten

1. What was the Lord's intention in the sacrificial system? What was *not* the purpose/role of the sacrifices?
2. Verse 10 is a strong statement about the eternal security of believers in Jesus Christ. Why?
3. What two verses in chap. 10 are a good summary for the Book of Hebrews? Why?
4. The readers of Hebrews were instructed to draw near to God (v 22). How often can the church age believer draw near? How was this different in the OT?
5. In vv 22-24, what does the author of Hebrews instruct his readers to do? How might this be applied in the church today?
6. What is the "willful" sin that the author of Hebrews has in mind in v 26? How do we know this contextually?
7. What does the author of Hebrews mean when he says a "certain" expectation of judgment?
8. What can the believer expect if he commits apostasy?
9. What is the parallel with this warning passage and Deut 32:25-26?
10. The author of Hebrews ends this passage with a word of encouragement. What does this encouragement include? Why is this significant in light of the previous warning passage?

Chapter 11

1. What type of faith is the author of Hebrews addressing in chapter 11?
2. Why do you think the author of Hebrews first uses Abel as an example of one who lived by faith? What about the readership makes Abel a great example?
3. What does the idea of "rewarder" include in 11:6?
4. What does it mean to be "approved" in this passage (11:2, 39)?

5. What aspect of the patriarchs' faith is revealed in their deaths?
6. What does it mean to experience a "better resurrection" (11:35)?

Chapter 12

1. What does it mean that the believer has a "great cloud of witnesses" (12:1)?
2. How is the Christian life like a race, and how can it be run successfully?
3. How does Esau relate to the readers of Hebrews?
4. How can the phrase "just men made perfect" be understood in the context of eternal rewards (12:23)?
5. How does the final warning in Hebrews (12:25-29) motivate the believer to persevere in the faith?

Chapter 13

1. What is the connection between how chapter 12 ends and the commandments spelled out in 13:1-6?
2. What is the context of the statement that Jesus is the "same yesterday, today, and forever" (13:8)?
3. In what ways does the Christian have an altar (13:10)?
4. What does the author mean when he tells his readers to go "outside the camp" (13:13)?
5. What does Hebrews 13 say about the relationship of the leaders in a church and the believers in that church?

Scripture Index

Subject Index

239

More GES Books
www.faithalone.org

Anthony B. Badger
—*Confronting Calvinism*
—*Free Grace Theology on Trial*

Harlan Betz
—*Setting the Stage for Eternity*

Steve Elkins
—*The Roman Road Revisited: New Vistas on the Road to Resurrection Living*
—*Keys to Kingdom Greatness: An Exposition of the Sermon on the Mount*

Zane Hodges
—*Absolutely Free (2nd ed.)*
—*The Atonement and Other Writings*
—*The Epistle of James*
—*The Epistles of John*
—*Faith in His Name: Listening to the Gospel of John*
—*First Peter: The Salvation of the Soul*
—*A Free Grace Primer*
—*Grace in Eclipse*
—*The Gospel Under Siege*
—*Harmony with God*
—*Here Walks My Enemy: The Story of Luis*
—*The Hungry Inherit*
—*Jesus, God's Prophet*
—*The Journey of Faith: Sermons on Hebrews*
—*Luke (Vol 1)*
—*Luke (Vol 2)*
—*Power to Make War*
—*Power to Stand: An Exposition of Jude*
—*Romans: Deliverance from Wrath*
—*Second Peter: Shunning Error in Light of the Savior's Soon Return*
—*Six Secrets of the Christian Life (Second Edition)*
—*Spiritual Lessons from the Life of David*
—*Tough Texts: Did Jesus Teach Salvation by Works?*
—*Zane Hodges JOTGES Memorial Issue*
—*What Is the Outer Darkness?*

Lucas Kitchen
—*Eternal Rewards: It Will Pay to Obey*

Shawn Lazar
—*Beyond Doubt: How to Be Sure of Your Salvation*
—*Chosen to Serve: Why Divine Election Is to Service, Not to Eternal Life*

Bill Lee
—*Grace Recovered*

René López
—*Romans Unlocked*

C. Gordon Olson
—*Beyond Calvinism and Arminianism*

Lawrence Vance
—*The Other Side of Calvinism*

Bob Wilkin
—*Confident in Christ (2nd ed.)*
—*Four Views on the Role of Works at the Final Judgment*

—*A Gospel of Doubt: The Legacy of John MacArthur's The Gospel According to Jesus*
—*Inerrancy for Dummies*
—*Is Calvinism Biblical? Let the Scriptures Decide*
—*The Road to Reward (2nd ed.)*
—*Secure and Sure*
—*The Ten Most Misunderstood Words in the Bible*
—*Turn and Live: The Power of Repentance*

Various Authors
—*The Grace New Testament Commentary*

Kenneth W. Yates
—*Hebrews: Partners with Christ*

Made in the USA
Monee, IL
05 December 2021

83801265R00134